A THEORY FOR ALL MUSIC
Problems and Solutions in the Analysis of Non-Western Forms

Jay Rahn

Professor Rahn takes the approach to the analysis of Western art music developed recently by theorists such as Benjamin Boretz and extends it to address non-Western forms. In the process, he rejects recent ethnomusicological formulations based on mentalism, cultural determinism, and the psychology of perception as potentially fruitful bases for analysing music in general. Instead he stresses the desirability of formulating a theory to deal with all music, rather than merely Western forms, and emphasizes the need to evaluate an analysis and compare it with other interpretations, and demonstrates how this may be done.

The theoretical concepts which form the basis of Rahn's approach are discussed and applied: first to individual pieces of non-Western music which have enjoyed a fairly high profile in ethnomusicological literature, and second to repertoires or groups of pieces.

The author also discusses the fields of anthropology and psychology, showing how his approach serves as a starting point for studies of perception and the concepts, norms, and values found in specific music cultures. In conclusion, he lists what he considers to be musical universals and takes up the more controversial issues implicit in his discussion.

JAY RAHN has been a visiting assistant professor in the Department of Fine Arts at Atkinson College, York University, and in the Faculty of Music at the University of Toronto.

JAY RAHN

A Theory for All Music:

Problems and Solutions in the Analysis of Non-Western Forms

UNIVERSITY OF TORONTO PRESS
Toronto Buffalo London

© University of Toronto Press 1983
Toronto Buffalo London
Printed in Canada

ISBN 0-8020-5538-9

Canadian Cataloguing in Publication Data

Rahn, Jay, 1947–
A theory for all music

Includes index.
ISBN 0-8020-5538-9

1. Music – Theory.   2. Music – Philosophy and
aesthetics.   I. Title.

ML3845.R33   781   C82-094367-3

Contents

vi Contents

Part III Applications

Part IV Beyond music theory

Part V Review

Acknowledgments

During the years when I worked on this book, I relied heavily on many colleagues and friends inside and outside academe for support related to the present work. Their support took the form of friendly and informal discussion, counsel, and encouragement. I would especially like to thank in this regard Harvey Olnick, the late Mieczyslaw Kolinski, Joe Katz, Robert Austerlitz, Ben Boretz, Pat Carpenter, Gaynor Jones, Austin Clarkson, David Lidov, Jim Tenney, Duke Gray, Alex Knopf, and Sharon Harris. I am very grateful to them all. I am also indebted to Y & R Properties and the Toronto Transit Commission for providing environments congenial to much of the writing that went into this work.

The late Alan P. Merriam of the Anthropology Department, Indiana University, graciously allowed me to retranscribe his recording of the Flathead sweathouse song discussed in chapter 7. Bruno Nettl of the School of Music, University of Illinois, checked some points that I raised concerning the transcription of the *nai* piece against the original recording.

Both of these scholars, as well as John Blacking of the Social Anthropology Department, Queen's University, Belfast, Marcia Herndon of the Anthropology Department, University of Texas at Austin, Robert Kauffman of the Music Department, University of Washington at Seattle, and the late Mieczyslaw Kolinski of the Faculty of Music, University of Toronto, most obligingly clarified certain points that arose in certain of their writings that come under review here.

Copyright releases were kindly provided by Bruno Nettl, Kwabena Nketia, and Frederick Harris Music.

Charles Bogue and Dawn Morrissette helped considerably with the typing of the first drafts, Frank Nakashima copied the musical examples, and Zena Miller assisted in proofreading the galleys. Thanks should also go to the editors at the University of Toronto Press, particularly to Lorraine Ourom, who took such care in preparing the manuscript for publication.

This book has been published with the help of a grant from the Canadian Federation for the Humanities, using funds provided by the Social Sciences and Humanities Research Council of Canada, and a grant from the Publications Fund of University of Toronto Press.

PART I
PRELIMINARIES

1

The Question

How can one best interpret all music? The following pages contain an answer to this question.

For the purposes of this study, 'all music' includes not only twelve-tone and tonal music but also early modal music of the West, folk and popular idioms of Europe and America, and non-Western traditions of all types. Although I will not treat them in detail, this term could also include non-human music, such as the sounds of nature. My definition of *music* is thus quite broad: any observable scores (i.e., written music) or sounds. (In accord with this broad definition, I frequently use the general term *observables* rather than more specific designations, such as *sounds* or *the score*.)

A central preoccupation in this book is the interpretation of music. Musical interpretation has been called analysis, description, dissection, and hermeneutics, to list only a few epithets. In English, 'analysis' invites the phrase 'coldly analytical.' Similarly, descriptions are often denigrated as being 'merely descriptive.' Dissection connotes death and surgery. And hermeneutics is frequently used to describe sterile exercises in exegesis. Since I am convinced of the value of discussing music, I will generally forgo these potentially derogatory terms and phrases in favour of the more positive word *interpretation*.

The possibility that interpretation might be construed as a bad thing raises a number of highly emotional issues which should be dealt with at the outset. There is a feeling in some quarters that the interpretation of music is an arbitrary, uncalled-for, dull, or dehumanizing activity. Indeed, much that has hidden under the word *interpretation* (or its synonyms) has exhibited some of these characteristics. But much of what passes for science, philosophy, and other 'talk about things' could also be condemned on these grounds. There is no reason why an experiment, a theorem, an argument, or even a musical interpretation should be arbitrary, uncalled-for, dull, or dehumanizing. If C.P. Snow (1964), Jacob

Bronowski (1961), G.H. Hardy (1940), and others are right in their persuasive discussions, the human and physical sciences can be well-founded, compelling, inspiring, and ultimately humanizing. A scientific theory can consolidate or upset a person's world view as profoundly as a painting. A mathematical system can have all the grace, elegance, and mystery of a shadow play. Why, then, should musical interpretations not aspire to the excitement of the art itself?

One possible reason is that musical interpretations are frequently ugly. Accordingly, a central purpose of this study is to put some beauty into interpretations. This will not be accomplished by tricks of flowery language or irrational rhetoric, because one is inevitably disappointed whenever one tries to understand such fine phrases. The method I have adopted is to express beautiful relationships in a rigorous way, rather than to express banal or non-existent relationships in purple prose. A few unadorned facts about a piece of music are more interesting than all of the ecstatic reports that one might receive.

Another reason for lack of excitement about musical interpretation is the esoteric nature of the language used. The music of each of the world's cultures seems to have a special vocabulary developed all for itself. Yet how necessary is all this jargon? As will be seen in chapter 6, concepts needed to interpret music are quite few and so semantically basic that a child could understand them. It is hoped that apologies for the use of technical terms will become obsolete.

Throughout this study, I have tried to stick as closely as possible to the facts of music, to 'face the music,' as it were. There is a tendency today for musical scholars to discuss everything but music. Like religion, politics, and bodily functions, music seems to have become a topic that is taboo. Biographical, historical, and socio-cultural data; acoustics, physiology, perception, and behaviour: all are interesting subjects but they are ultimately para-musical. In accordance with this view, a development of the notion that musical interpretations require only musical observables as their data appears in chapter 2.

If one is to interpret music, any interpretation will not do. An interpretation of thunder and lightning in terms of Wotan rather than electricity is obviously inferior from the point of view of science. Similarly, some interpretations of music are inadequate in the face of the facts. Others are merely adequate, and still others are outstanding. Scientific fields of inquiry have developed methods for evaluating and comparing theories, but no accepted method has existed for aesthetic interpretations. Thus, in chapter 4, I develop a method for assessing musical analyses.

A theory without applications is of little use. Consequently, in chapters 7 and 8 individual pieces and repertoires are reinterpreted from the viewpoint of the theory developed here. The choice of pieces and repertoires has been made according to a number of criteria. Some of the music discussed has loomed large in the ethnomusicological literature. Other materials have been chosen because they are particularly well-documented. The sum, I think, represents a fair cross-section of recent studies in ethnic music.

In chapter 8, I deal with repertoires. At this point, some new notions are added. The concept of a repertoire, a unified set of pieces as opposed to an arbitrary collection of works, is investigated. And in the following chapters, special questions arising from studies in human perception and culture are discussed. This sets the stage for my final consideration: how a unified music theory might affect the future of musical studies.

Until very recently, serious scholars would have considered the question 'How can one best interpret all music?' preposterous. Particularistic studies were in vogue at the expense of universal perspectives. But times have changed. Music theory has entered a new era. In *Meta-Variations*, Benjamin Boretz (1969, 1970 a, b, c, 1971, 1972) has developed a truly radical approach to the analysis of music. One of the results of his study is a synthetic view in which tonal and twelve-tone music are seen to issue from a common basis as branches from the trunk of a tree. Boretz terms the systematic exposition of this common basis the 'all-musical system.'

In a sense, Boretz's term *all-musical* represents an unjustified claim: the empirical portion of his study deals almost exclusively with the European tradition. Pentatonic music, and the systems represented by *rags, maqamat, dastgahah*, and various kinds of *patet* are not confronted at all. In at least two other senses, however, one can justify the 'all' of Boretz's all-music theory. First, music theory that is creative – I exclude here historical and pedagogical music theory – has been of late almost exclusively preoccupied with tonal theory as developed by Heinrich Schenker and twelve-tone, or atonal, theory as expounded by Arnold Schoenberg and later writers. Thus, Boretz's contribution clarifies almost all of the recent literature on music theory. Second, though Boretz, like many other music theorists, pays little attention to phenomena other than Western art music of the last three centuries, his approach is so universal that one can apply it to other music as well. In other words the system of *Meta-Variations* contains the seeds of a theory for all music. Thus, the major task of the present study is to broaden the scope of musical theory, so that it might truly account for all music.

2

Choosing a Basis

In order to develop a theory, one must have a basis, a body of data that are going to be taken into account. In a study of music, one starts minimally with the sounds and scores themselves. However, it is plausible that additional aspects of music have to be taken into account. For example, psychological or cultural data might be necessary to achieve the best interpretation of some music. Since I will be considering music different from that treated in Boretz's all-musical system, and especially non-Western music, some consideration of the various bases that ethnomusicologists have proposed is in order.

Ethnomusicologists generally claim 'all music' as their subject matter. Recently, a number of prominent scholars in that field have expressed hopes that something resembling a theory for all music be developed. Bruno Nettl has written that 'it would seem to be the task of the ethnomusicologist to derive a method [of interpretation] which is equally applicable to all music' (1964: 135). Mieczyslaw Kolinski pleaded that 'what is urgently needed is the formulation of concepts and methods designed to bring about an objective, thorough, and meaningful analysis of [all] musical structure' (1967: 9). Earlier, the late Charles Seeger had written of the need for a 'rationale' in order to evaluate all music (1960: 224). Marcia Herndon has considered the 'need for a metalanguage' for all music (1974a: 250–1), and John Blacking has mentioned the necessity of 'a unitary method of musical analysis which can ... be applied to all music.' (1971: 93).

Clearly, ethnomusicologists, despite their differences of outlook, are unified in their desire for a theory for all music. One area where their differences of outlook clash is the choice of a potential basis of data. Their writings about music reveal a wide variety of data that might be incorporated into an interpretation, and each of these bases would lead to a different type of general music theory. In the following sections, these potential bases are roughly grouped according to whether they are mentalistic, cultural, or psychological in nature. But before considering these plausible bases, it is necessary to establish criteria by which they can be evaluated.

CRITERIA

The simplest criterion is range of applicability. Some bases cannot deal with all the types of observables that might be considered music. Accordingly, they restrict the definition of music, and are not likely to yield a theory for all music. A second criterion is the applicability of the assumptions. In other words, do they give rise to testable hypotheses? The final criterion is economy. In scholarly work, it is best to have the fewest possible undefined or primitive terms. If two theories explain the same range of observables and the first invokes fewer concepts than the second, the first is preferred as the basis because it takes less for granted.

Throughout the following discussion, these three criteria should be remembered as well as the essential problem to be solved: selecting a basis for interpreting all music. Along the way, a number of important approaches in ethnomusicology will be discarded. But they will be discarded not because they are totally without value – which they are not – but because they are inadequate to deal with the problem at hand: choosing a basis for a theory for all music.

MENTALISTIC BASES

One of the most tempting approaches to musical interpretation is mentalistic. By a mentalistic approach I mean one in which some or all of the following are components of, or justifications for, a proposed interpretation of music: what people think, conceive, consider, desire, hear, know, and feel; how they view or respond to music; and what their aesthetic experiences, ideals, fondnesses, mental processes, intents, motivations, or cognitive systems are, as well as whether they are aware, conscious, or unconscious of these.

To judge from the titles of recent television programs and books, such as *The Experience of Music* and *Music and Your Mind* (Bonny and Savary, 1973), the relationship between mental processes and music is a popular topic for the layperson. But the preoccupation with mind, experience, cognition, perception, and so forth has not been restricted to popular and pedagogical writers. Quite the contrary, a number of serious scholars have posited such mental entities as the basis for musical research. For example, Charles Seeger (1960: 257) considers what musicians think to be evidence that must be taken into account when one studies music. Alan P. Merriam (1964: 33; 1969: 226; personal communication:

1976) adopts what he terms 'concepts about music' as one of his three bases for musical investigation, stating that 'without concepts about music, behavior cannot occur, and without behavior, music sound cannot be produced.' And finally, Stephen Feld, apparently following Merriam's lead, proposes that mentalism be the theoretical basis of ethnomusicology (1974: 211).

These assertions involve at least two grave issues. Is it really possible to know what musicians think? And if so, is there a necessary, causal relationship between what musicians think and the sounds they produce? Both of these questions must be considered if one is to interpret all music, and, accordingly, both will be dealt with below.

If one must consider the 'experience of music' one must decide whose experience is relevant to the interpretation. For example, one could consider one's own experience to be of primary importance. The established method for doing so is that of introspection. Usually, however, ethnomusicologists have presumed that the experience of others is more important than that of the investigator. Thus, Marcia Herndon says that how they think about it is the primary consideration (1974a: 247); Alan Merriam states that the ethnomusicologist 'does not seek the aesthetic experience for himself as a primary goal ..., but rather he seeks to perceive the meaning of the aesthetic experience of others' (1964: 25); and during his discussion of the notion of octave equivalence, Bruno Nettl avers that 'all cultures may not consider tones an octave apart to be so close [sic] in identity as do Western musicians' (1964: 145). To judge from these statements, other people, and especially people from cultures other than our own, do not think about music in the same way as we do. Among ethnomusicologists, then, there is a mistrust of introspection as a method for interpreting music.

Though the assumption that others think about music differently than we do has often been merely asserted, there have been occasions when ethnomusicologists have gone so far as to describe in more positive terms just how other people think about their music. These range from Robert Kauffman's vague belief 'that the Shona people view their music ... as a process closely resembling the relationships found in the social structures of the society' (1972: 48–50) to McDermott and Sumarsan's precise assertion that 'Javanese ... are content to hear *nem* throughout lines one to three' of a given piece (1975: 242–3). Similarly, Penelope Sanger and Neil Sorrell ascribe a certain 'fondness for parallel whole tones' to the people of Umeda village in New Guinea (1975: 76), and George List considers important the question 'Would the Vedda know what a tonal center is?' (1971: 401).

Such assertions and questions imply that there is some method for proving or disproving the embodied hypotheses. Two important queries are, then: How did

Kauffman, McDermott, Sumarsam, Sanger, and Sorrell find out what the views, desires, perceptions, and fondnesses of their informants were; and how might List find out whether the Vedda know what a tonal centre is?

If one considers further the question of whose experience is relevant to an interpretation, one finds that composers, performers, and listeners have all been the subjects of mentalistic assertions. Thus, Bruno Nettl in discussing a certain piece, seriously considers the possibility that 'the repetition of rhythmic patterns and the basic identity of the four sections made the use of a strong tonal center (by the composer) unnecessary' (1964: 160). Vida Chenoweth states that 'composers have employed [a certain rhythmic device] to intentionally [*sic*] create suspense' (1974: 65). And John Blacking asserts that 'patterns are generated by processes that are in the mind of the composer' (1971: 91).

With regard to the experience of performers, Fremont Besmer says that it seems clear that the performer of a given Hausa piece 'had in mind a concept of form and variation' (1970: 431). Johanna Spector speculates on a given performer's 'intent' to produce a certain interval (1970: 248), and John Blacking has stated that 'we want to know what a musician sets out to do each time he plays a certain piece of music,' and his (Blacking's) 'transcriptions are intended to represent the musical patterns desired by any two Venda who set out to play [ocarina] duets' (1959: 15). Finally, Bruno Nettl, writing of a Persian performer under certain performance conditions, states that the performer 'may feel that it is desirable to develop one or two gushehs thoroughly and then to show his understanding of the total radif by bringing in another gusheh or two briefly' (1974: 408).

With regard to the audience, Nettl asserts that the listeners are 'constantly made aware of familiar signposts' in the music (1974: 411). Theodore and Theodore A. Stern state that 'to the listener [the leap of an ascending fourth] establishes the second tone as a sort of center' (1971: 192), and Vida Chenoweth says that 'some music systems interchange major and minor thirds indiscriminately; that is, no significant difference is heard between the two' (1974: 52). Finally, Judith Becker considers the experiences of composer, performer, and listener as relevant to one of her studies of Burmese music (1969: 268, 272, 277–8).

A mentalistic approach inevitably involves a consideration of musical consciousness. The thoughts, desires, and feelings that are ascribed to oneself or to members of one's own culture or other cultures – be they composers, performers, or listeners – can be located in the fully conscious mind, in the subconscious, or in the unconscious. As an example of location in the conscious mind, one can cite Habib Touma's statement that although 'the Near Eastern musician is certainly not acquainted with such terms as 'melody' and 'melodic line,' ... he is thoroughly aware of the difference between the two categories and assigns each of them an individual name' (1971: 39). By and large, however, ethnomusicologists have located the mental contents of musicians not in the fully conscious experience but rather in more remote levels of psychic activity. Accordingly, Marcia Herndon says that the 'rules for [compositional] choices ... may not be conscious and verbalized rules' (1974a: 248), and Vida Chenoweth states that 'those within a particular [musical] system respond to the principle [of tension-relaxation] subconsciously' (1974: 78). Finally, Charles Seeger goes so far as to assert that the formational (or creative) apparatus of music is 'unconscious to the creator' (1969: 231).

The possibility that musical cognition lies below the level of full consciousness would seem to pose a methodological problem. Must all interpreters of music be skilled at plumbing the depths of consciousness and thus be trained as musical psychoanalysts? Or should one, as Charles Seeger proposes, wait for the day when brain physiologists will be able to 'tap human motivation and purposiveness' with respect to music (1968: 35; cf. also 1969: 242)?

To be sure, all of the authors I have cited are not unyielding in their mentalistic assertions. Nettl's statements are riddled with *mays* and *mights*; Kauffman's statment is merely one of belief rather than an assertion of fact; and Blacking at one point confesses that he 'cannot be sure that [his] analysis is correct, in that it explains exactly what happened in the process of [a given group of] songs' creation' (1971: 105). Nevertheless, the mentalistic approach is a major one in ethnomusicology, and its implications are potentially so serious for anyone interested in interpreting all music that it deserves further scrutiny.

First, one can consider some of the consequences of a mentalistic approach on the range of phenomena that might be analysed. If mental experience of both composer and performer were considered primary, no music resulting from inanimate things could be interpreted. If knowledge of the composer's thoughts were considered a necessary factor for an interpretation, no mechanically created music (e.g., that produced by aleatoric means, such as the casting of dice) could be interpreted, nor could one interpret anonymous works. If the performers' thoughts were considered necessary information, one could provide only the most trivial accounts of machine-made music (e.g., the music of calliopes, music boxes, and computers). And if the listeners' thoughts were deemed necessary data for an interpretation, what analysis could one offer for historical works for which no appropriate criticism survives? For these reasons a mentalistic approach would severely restrict the types of music that might be interpreted, and would lead to 'a theory of some music.'

If one were to follow a mentalistic approach, there might also be a danger that people's thoughts about music would take methodological precedence over the usual observables of music. For example, John Blacking continues his comments about his desire 'to know what a musician sets out to do each time he plays a certain piece of music' with the observation that he (Blacking) does not want to know 'exactly what [the performer] did on one particular occasion' (1959: 15). Thus the accepted observables of music (i.e., sounds or notes) would take a back seat to, and ultimately might be replaced by, a new set of observables: thoughts.

Just how these thoughts are to be observed raises another question: What is the appropriate methodology for dealing with musical thoughts? If our study of such thoughts is to be determinate, there must be some observables. Despite Seeger's injunctions which recommend the study of brain physiology, no one has yet observed (i.e., felt, seen, smelled, tasted, or heard) a thought, be it musical or otherwise. What one does observe are the presumed effects of thoughts. These consist chiefly of what people say they are thinking and what they do. With regard to verbal reports, it takes little imagination and even less scepticism to recognize that what people say they think and what they actually do think need not be the same. Indeed, one should note that in English usage 'I think' means 'I am not sure.' One shrinks, then, from the idea of a scholarly pursuit founded on untestable verbal reports, that is, rumours. In the end, what people say they think is merely indirect evidence of what they do think, just as, according to genetic theory, one's height is only indirect evidence for the height of one's father. Similarly, what people do is also merely indirect evidence of what they think. One can get around this problem by taking an extremely behaviouristic position and observing only what people do (or say) without speculating about what they think. This approach, however, would result in a complete withdrawal from the mentalistic stance.

It is difficult, then, to understand why Marcia Herndon insists that one can isolate a 'type of cognitive system, based on and capable of being reduced to empirical knowledge' (1974a: 246), and that there are 'methods of description' of cognitions that 'are public and replicable' (1974a: 249). Her statements can make sense only if 'cognitive system' means a dual system of behaviour and thought. Since the system of behaviour (including verbal behaviour) is the only portion of this construct on which determinate observations can be made, it seems superfluous to erect a hypothetical 'thought system' beside it. Hence, John Blacking's promise that 'an accurate and comprehensive description of a composer's cognitive system will provide the most fundamental and powerful explanation of the patterns that his music takes' will, barring some unprecedented breakthrough in neurological research, remain ever unfulfilled and, as we shall see, unnecessary in any case.

CULTURAL BASES

Related to mentalism, and overlapping it to a certain extent, is the cultural approach. According to this approach, music is presumed to be a product of culture. Accordingly, the cultural background of the music must be studied before the music can be adequately interpreted. Thus, Marcia Herndon writes that ethnomusicologists 'must direct [their] attention ... to the musical performance in its cultural context' (1974a: 246); Ashenafi Kebede states that 'any musical investigation which confines itself only to analysis and description cannot give a comprehensive presentation of any music' and that one must 'understand music in terms of its own cultural context' (1970: 502–3). Equally emphatic is Philip Peek when he asserts that 'a study of music without thorough consideration of the people who make that music is only a study of sound' (1970: 507). Whether a truly comprehensive study of music is possible or even desirable, and whether a mere 'study of sound' is undesirable are questions that will occupy us later in this chapter. Suffice it to remark for the present that there is a preoccupation on the part of all these authors with music as a human phenomenon.

These writers are not alone in this preoccupation. Alan Merriam defines music specifically as a 'cultural activity' (1969: passim, esp. 217), and a 'uniquely human phenomenon which exists only in terms of social interaction; that is, it is made by people for other people and it is learned behavior' (1964: 27). For Merriam, the justification for such a humanistic or anthropocentric approach seems to be that 'the ultimate interest of man is man himself' (1964: 16). Merriam's definition, of course, would exclude from the category of music mechanical and natural phenomena as well as antisocial or, rather, asocial forms of music. In the latter class are all instances of 'self-delectative' music, such as much *mbira* and bow music of Africa and much of the music sung in showers, hummed, or whistled in our own culture (cf. List 1971: 401–2). Attempts to force such phenomena into a social framework – such as Kauffman's insistence that there is in the case of self-delectative music a 'social group' consisting of the performer and his instrument (1972: 49) – have been far from convincing: asocial music remains an anomalous phenomenon for socially oriented scholars.

The cultural approach also results in a number of special problems for those who would like to interpret music. Questions of social acceptability, communication, and folk evaluation, as well as the possibility that music might be determined by non-musical phenomena, all arise from this approach. Accordingly, I will deal with each of these issues in turn.

Social Acceptability
Farnsworth defines music as that which 'is composed of patterns of sound acceptable to the people of some subculture' (1969: 17). Merriam observes that

'each culture decides what it will and will not call music; and sound patterns as well as behavior which fall outside these norms are either unacceptable or are simply defined as something other than music' (1964: 27). Marcia Herndon defines the 'boundaries of a musical system' in part as 'that range of sound-configurations which is accepted by a particular group or ingroup as music' (1974a: 246). And Charles Seeger bases his rationale for evaluating music on 'acceptable' sounds and ways of using sounds (1969: 237).

If one follows these writers, a problem arises when dealing with so-called avant-garde music, music that is often not accepted until long after its first appearance. Is this music to be interpreted or evaluated only after it has been accepted? Often, it would seem that interpretation of seemingly intractable works is the first step in their acceptance: the analyses that appear in contemporary music publications are a means of inducing acceptance of arcane pieces. Accordingly, interpretation can precede acceptance.

When these writers speak of music and non-music, it is evident that they do so relativistically. The distinction is, for example, between music and non-music for Navahos, or for a given moiety, or for Lions Club members. The consequence of defining music and non-music in this way is far-reaching: all of the music – as opposed to the non-music – could be considered a repertoire, a unit of study, the empirical basis for a given interpretation of music. For such a body of music, it would be true that every member of the cultural group accepted every unit of the set of musical observables. Following this methodology, the cultural group would be defined first and the set of musical observables would follow from this definition. However, this methodology could also be reversed: a given set of pieces could be fitted to a given group of people. Epistemologically, there is no preference for one or the other approach since they are logically equivalent and would yield the same results. If one is eventually going to interpret music and not people, there would be a decided advantage in defining the set of people in terms of whether or not they accept a given repertoire. Thus one would define a repertoire musically rather than culturally. Following this reasoning, the basis for a true sociology of music might be social groups that were defined by the types of music they accepted, rather than of social groups defined by non-musical criteria.

Communication

A second consequence of the cultural approach is the assertion that music is a form of communication. Charles Seeger, for example, deals with music as communication (1960: passim), though his later definition of communication as mere transmission in the sense that pipes communicate heat (1971: 391) trivializes the term to imply no more than that observable sound waves move from one place to another.

What is communicated by music (other than sound) or how it is communicated has not been determined by ethnomusicologists (cf. Merriam 1964: 10–13). However, George List has opined that 'music communicates what cannot be expressed in speech' (1971: 400). But it is not clear whether List's negative statement means that music communicates all or part of the non-semantic, non-grammatical things not communicated by speech.

List (and following him, Herndon 1974a: 246) goes on to state that 'whatever it communicates is communicated to the members of the in-group only' (1971: 399). This leads one to the cliché that music 'consists of a number of dialects, some of them as mutually unintelligible [*sic*] as are found in language' (Herzog 1946: 11), or that 'many of [the music communities of the world] are mutually unintelligible' (Seeger 1941: 122). If this means that 'each group has learned to pay attention to certain differences and to ignore others' (Pantaleoni 1972: 159), it is merely a comment on some people's laxness as interpreters of music, or at best their victimization by their musical surroundings. If it were to mean, how-ever, that people of different cultural groups cannot – rather than do not – understand the music of other groups, it would be a grave assertion indeed. For the entire discipline of ethnomusicology would be in jeopardy, reduced to the point where each of several small isolated groups of scholars would study the music of its own culture and be unable to communicate with other groups. There is little fear for the truth of this assertion since it is faulty to begin with, resting as it does on a conceit. This conceit – that music is like language – gives rise to unfalsifiable hypotheses, for either music communicates referential meanings or it does not. Extensive referential meanings have only been discerned in a few musical contexts, for example, the thought songs of the Tepehua (Boilès: 1967) and drum languages. When music does not communicate referential meanings, what does it communicate? To this nobody has provided an answer that can be tested. Accordingly, if handled improperly, the otherwise harmless conceit that music communicates something can deteriorate into a misleading fallacy which has no place in serious discourse.

Folk Evaluation

Alan Merriam makes a distinction between analytical and folk evaluations of music. Analytical evaluations are interpretations made by a scholar, and folk evaluations are interpretations made by members of the culture that produced the music. Merriam states that analytical evaluations should follow and be based upon folk evaluations and presents the view that 'only if we know the folk evaluation, can we be sure we are analyzing what is actually present in the data' (1964: 32, after Bohannan). Since Merriam's pronouncement, several scholars have interpreted music in terms of folk evaluations. For example, throughout her account of *chīz*, Bonnie Wade avoids Western terms in favour of Indian words, such as *sthāī, aṅtarā, ālāp, tān, mukhrā,* and *tāl* (1973). And Bruno Nettl defends his interpretation of one aspect of Iranian music with the remark that it 'seems to correspond more or less to the Persian musician's appraisal of his [own] music' (1974: 405).

Is the folk evaluation, then, an adequate basis for interpreting all music? On the one hand, Merriam claims that the folk evaluation distinguishes between 'what is actually present in the data' (1964: 32) and what is not. Such a claim evokes the image of rhythms and tonal structures disappearing from the music as soon as one waves the magic wand of folk evaluation over the observables. Nevertheless, the observables themselves defy such a transformation: stubbornly they stay right where they have been all along and will surrender none of their detail even to the most persuasive magician. 'What is actually present in the data' cannot be evicted by either a folk or analytical evaluation, because what is present in the data are the data themselves: everything else is read into, or out of, the data.

Nevertheless, folk evaluations do have a methodological place. First, since they are usually offered by people who have much more first-hand contact with a given body of music than the scholar, they can provide the initial clues for how to go about interpreting the observables. Second, one can consider such evaluations to be a special type of para-musical data in addition to the music itself. Accordingly, one might wish to interpret both the music and the evaluation simultaneously. In this sense, folk evaluations and circumstantial evidence function in much the same way: they are things to be explained rather than things that explain.

Related to folk evaluations are native categories and conceptualizations, and aesthetics. Marcia Herndon advocates the isolation of native categories and conceptualizations as a 'primary goal' of ethnomusicology (1974a: 250), and Adrienne Kaeppler declares that 'if we are to understand (rather than just appreciate) an aesthetic, or even an art style, it is essential to grasp the principles on which it is based, as perceived by the people of the culture which holds them' (1971: 176). Insofar as Herndon and Kaeppler are considering verbalized categories, conceptualizations, and aesthetics, their remarks have to do with folk evaluations. However, where their terms designate concepts inferred from non-verbal behaviour, they are advocating a mentalistic basis for interpreting music.

Cultural Determinism
A number of authors express the view that music is a product of culture. Most notably, Alan Merriam asserts that 'music sound is the result of human behavioral processes that are shaped by the values, attitudes, and beliefs of the people who

comprise a particular culture' (1964: 6). Moses Asch states that 'the research to date tends to argue against those musicologists who claim that the social context of a composition is external to its music sound structure,' concluding that 'the study of music sound structure must be integrated with social contextual factors' (1975: 255). Whether and to what extent cultural phenomena cause musical phenomena, and the degree to which 'the research to date' supports this view are issues that deserve critical attention.

That musical and cultural observables should be studied together seems to be a most convincing directive when one considers the symbolic function of music. Often the members of a given culture attribute a special ethos or affective connotation to a specific set of tonal relationships, such as sadness to minor tonality and the mood of 'delighted adoration in a gentle, loving sentiment' to *raga Todi* (Merriam 1964: 265; Kaufmann 1968: 551).

As Alan Merriam points out, there are few studies of such symbolic conventions 'quite possibly [because of] the difficulty of knowing the culture well enough to learn symbolic meanings' (1964: 247). I would also submit that there is another reason, namely, that such phenomena depend on knowing the music itself well enough to explain symbolic meanings.

Nevertheless, where they are found, such symbolic meanings pose a problem to an interpreter of music. At first, it would seem that affective states, such as sadness and extraordinary passion, deserve a place in an interpretation. However, there are three good reasons for excluding these states. First, since symbols are notoriously multivalent, (i.e., plural in their referents), symbolic conventions are usually ill-defined even within one culture. Second, symbolic conventions are easily detachable from the interpretation: the ascription of 'sadness' follows from the ascription of 'minor' not vice versa, and is thus superfluous to the data required for an interpretation. Finally, the musical relationships involved in such correlations are quite gross: they do little justice to the fine-textured structure of the music per se, as where a complex piece might be reduced to the description 'sad.' It follows that an interpretation that consists of affective and structural terms can always be sliced into two parts: a musical interpretation and a correlative affective interpretation. Collapsing the two into a single musico-affective interpretation is an uneconomical duplication of information already contained in the purely musical part.

Despite the frequent claims that music and its cultural context must be studied together, there is little evidence to support such an injunction. When it comes down to presenting such evidence, suddenly the tone of prescriptive writers seems to become meeker. Thus, for example, Blacking says merely that musical 'patterns are related to the social and cognitive processes of a particular society and culture' (1971: 92); Sanger and Sorrell only conclude that 'the music of Umeda does reflect the characteristics and priorities of the society at large'

(1975: 79); and Blacking, again, simply asserts that the dance and music of the *domba* initiation rite 'symbolize' sexual intercourse (1971: 107).

What is the status of the verbs *relate, reflect,* and *symbolize*? Trivially, anything can be related to anything else, since a relationship of resemblance, identity, or difference holds between any two things. Things that reflect other things are called mirrors, and there is no evidence that a mirror is determined by what it reflects. Finally, there can be several symbols for a given thing, and vice versa, so that the thing symbolized does not specifically determine its symbol.

Occasionally, such writers become bolder in their statements. Merriam interprets some comments by Colin McPhee to mean that Balinese 'music structure is such as to emphasize group rather than individual activity and excellence' (1964: 153). Moreover, there is the famous experiment conducted by Paul Farnsworth (1969: 60–1) in which it was shown that the tempos preferred by young Americans for the performance of waltzes and foxtrots increased substantially over a six-year period.

Do these studies then mean that music is caused by non-musical variables such as 'groupiness' or the passage of time? If this were true, the effect on interpreting music would be profound simply because of the nature of causality. If a given value (e.g., a cultural value) causes another value (e.g., a musical value), the two are said to be independent and dependent respectively, and one needs to study only the independent variable in order to predict the value of the dependent variable. Tremendous economies could thus be introduced into the study of music. If culture caused music, one could dispense with studying music and devote all of one's attention to studying culture, since the music would follow inevitably from the culture. The potential results of such a causal approach are obviously enormous. If the causes were known, the music would be a foregone conclusion.

What then is the evidence for the cultural determination of music? Merriam and Farnsworth present their evidence quite cogently. Here, however, there is no assertion that all or even several details of the musical observables are caused by extramusical factors. In one example, certain aspects of texture seem to be determined by Balinese 'groupiness' and in the other, tempo is influenced by a variable no more specifically defined than the passage of time or the definition of a genre of dance. The apparent effects of Balinese groupiness on the musical observables are duplication of instrumental lines as in the practice of playing in pairs and the distribution of tones among the players. These slightly affect the timbre or dynamics and the spatial organization. Alteration of tempo affects only one variable in a piece, the absolute size of the durational unit. But certainly one cannot predict the enormous richness of a piece by knowing its demonstrated causes.

The demonstrated effects of culture on musical observables are quite slight.

These effects are limited to purely qualitative or absolute values, such as timbre, loudness, and tempo. Indeed, in the theory that I will describe, such qualitative and absolute values, because of their structural superficiality, are transcended in favour of quantitative relationships which yield much richer interpretations.

Finally, one must consider the position that, though music might not be caused by culture, both music and culture are caused by even deeper variables. Merriam, using the language of mirrors, says that 'it is clear that music is an integral part of culture and, like all other aspects of it, is bound to reflect the general and underlying principles and values which animate the culture as a whole' (1964: 250). Blacking states that it is 'more satisfactory to find structural explanations of both sociological [sic] and musical forms' (1971: 104). He says further that 'music and its associated social and cultural situations are understood as expressions of cognitive processes which are contained in the physiology of the body and the central nervous system, but developed and modified in an infinite variety of ways in the course of shared experiences in society' (1971: 103), a statement reminiscent of Kolinski's opinions (1967: 3). Blacking adds that 'musical relationships may reflect social relationships, and both may be generated by cognitive processes which are used in other fields of human behavior' (1971: 108), and considers it an ultimate purpose of ethnomusicology to 'describe *both* the music *and* its cultural background as interrelated parts of a total system' (1971: 93).

One of the few examples of the allegedly pre-social and pre-musical causes of music is found in Robert Armstrong's interpretation of Javanese culture. He finds throughout Javanese culture a general avoidance of three-dimensionality and states that the 'same flatness is to be found in the music of the gamelan, which, predominantly eurhythmic, fails to display any concern with dynamic melodic development' (1963: 8, quoted in Merriam 1964: 251). However, the equation of spatial flatness with commetric rhythmic organization and the lack of an (undefinedly) 'dynamic melodic development' can at best be a conceit. The flatness of a music might be expressed in terms of the absence of changes in dynamics or pitch (neither of which is peculiar to gamelan music), but the relationship between dynamic melodic development and commetricity on the one hand and flatness on the other is far from clear.

Perhaps because the physical sciences enjoy great prestige throughout our society, scholars try to find the causes of everything under the sun, including musical observables. Whatever the reason, the undertaking is a perilous one when phenomena as complex as music are involved. For, as the philosopher of science, Henri Poincaré, has pointed out, all observables might be the result of causes but only some can be interpreted – and probabilistically at that – by a deterministic framework (1946: 340–2). The pedestrian killed on the way to work by a brick that 'accidentally' fell from a construction site overhead serves as a good illustration. What were the causes of the accident? The pedestrian's routine of going to work at a certain time? His decision to tie a shoelace on the way? His rush to catch a bus? His pause to look into a shop window? The bricklayer's hangover? His decision to work on that portion of the wall? The distraction of a bird flying past his head? Usually the situation with musical observables is as complex as that of the unfortunate pedestrian: there are simply too many causes to be taken into account. As an exercise, consider the possible causes of the half-note e♭ that opens the fourth measure of Beethoven's *Eroica*. What were its possible causes? How could one verify whether these possible causes were also the true ones? Finally, consider the plausibility of answering the question 'Why?' before the question 'What?' has been considered.

Not surprisingly, cultural values have been introduced only rarely into interpretations of musical observables. In one such undertaking, Fremont Besmer reports that he decided to look at the chorus part of a responsorial African song because 'the individual initiative of any member would have resulted in heterophony' and therefore it was 'theoretically possible to assume that [the chorus] melody was governed by some system of linguistic-melodic correspondences' (1970: 423). This decision, however, is not necessary to the interpretation; rather it was an heuristic device, one of the discovery procedures often used in analysis. Such hunches, along with folk evaluations, qualify as clues or circumstantial evidence rather than as necessary parts of the interpretation or its basis.

In sum, cultural data often provide clues for interpreting music. They might also constitute added observables that could be interpreted along with the music. But they cannot be considered necessary for an interpretation, because cultural values have been demonstrated to determine only a small, and relatively superficial portion of the musical observables in any given instance.

PSYCHOLOGICAL BASES

Like the cultural approach, the psychological approach to the interpretation of music is widespread. Its basis is closely related to, and indeed overlaps, that of the mentalists. According to users of psychological bases, the percepts and affective states evoked by musical observables ought to be taken into consideration in an interpretation.

The main sources of the psychological knowledge that ethnomusicologists have exploited are closely connected with writings of scholars belonging to the Gestalt school: Wolfgang Köhler (1947), one of the founders of the movement; Leonard Meyer (1956), a neo-Gestalt music critic; and Victor Zuckerkandl (1956), a contributor to the phenomenology of music. Characteristic of the psychological approaches taken by ethnomusicologists is a general avoidance of the findings of behaviourism. This, however, might merely be a symptom of the experimental psychologists' almost total refusal to deal with musical stimuli more complex than three-tone melodies (see, for example, Divenyi 1971).

Problems of perception have been more seriously broached in recent ethnomusicological writings than have affective matters, a trend due largely to Mieczyslaw Kolinski's persistent attention to perceptual topics. Kolinski's writings concern both the limits and tendencies of musical perception. Thus, with regard to possible limits of perceptibility Kolinski asserts that one is 'absolutely unable to perceive [a given polyrhythmic piece] at the same time in 6–8 or 3–4' (1973: 502). With reference to perceptual tendencies, he has written that the 'trend towards periodic or irregular organization of a pulsation [i.e., a series of periodic attacks] is a psychologically rooted universal' (1970: 88).

Ethnomusicologists have also used less formal perceptual terms, such as 'link' and 'grasp.' Thus, Kolinski states that certain 'tone reiterations link motives a + b + c + d and f + a' (1972: 419), and that 'pendulum 2 links motives a + b' (1972: 419). Similarly, the late Norman Cazden wrote about 'our direct auditory grasp of the underlying [tonal] genus' of a song (1971a: 64). In the psychology of perception, these activities of linking and grasping correspond to the processes of grouping surface structures and identifying substructures. Accordingly, one would expect such assertions to be accompanied by verified statements from the psychology of perception concerning necessary relationships between stimuli on the one hand and perceived groups or identities on the other. Yet this is not done. The reason for this lack of theoretical underpinning lies not so much in ethnomusicology as in the discipline of psychology itself. Although the Gestaltists completed several experiments on the perception of visual stimuli, they presented only the most modest findings with regard to auditory-temporal stimuli. Thus, even when justifications do appear (as in Kolinski 1967), they are based on untested analogies between visual and auditory perception.

Overlapping perceptual comments are accounts that involve such phrases as 'sense of completion.' The following passage by Nazir Jairazbhoy is an example: 'A note which falls on the penultimate beat of a North Indian time-cycle (tāl) will necessarily have imposed on it a sense of incompletion and anticipation, while a note occurring at the main beat will have a feeling of completion associated with it; ... if, however, such a note is sustained, the memory of the function imposed by the completion of the time-cycle will gradually fade and its inherent dynamic function will return; then the note may need to be resolved again' (1972: 68). The term *completion* is an important one in the theory of pattern perception. However, the vague usage of it here, the reference to Zuckerkandl's metaphysics (e.g., the phrase 'inherent dynamic function'), and the affective terms *sense* and *feeling* all serve to render the entire account difficult to comprehend.

More clearly affective in connotation are Charles Seeger's terms *tension*, *detension*, *tonicity*, and *mood*, which form a part of his theory for all music (1968: 36; 1960: 260). Similarly, Vida Chenoweth considers 'the principle of tension/relaxation' a universal in music (1974: 65, 78), and Bruno Nettl says that 'there is an increase in dramatic tension' (1974: 408) during a certain passage of a Persian piece. These tension entities are, however, a mere fiction. They correspond to no necessary response that has been experimentally established. At best these tension entities constitute compact ways of referring to the distinction between consonant and dissonant values in the broadest sense (see chapters 4 to 8). They thus provide unnecessary commentaries on specifically musical – i.e., not affective – phenomena. To use tension entities so is equivalent to describing a geometric progression as exciting or suspenseful: they provide a vivid rhetorical adjunct to determinate discourse, but nothing more.

Despite the fact that few musical phenomena have been accounted for by psychologists, ethnomusicologists persist in speculatively asserting what perceptual mechanisms are at work determining psychological responses. Thus, Kolinski avers that what he calls 'tint' is 'psycho-physiologically rooted and constitutes, therefore, an intrinsic facet of man's auditory perception' (1967: 21), and postulates 'biologically rooted and, therefore, universally valid laws of tint relations' as 'the source of [certain] types of tonal construction' (1967: 22; cf. also pp. 2–3).

How such assertions might arise is a reasonable question. Kolinski offers no biological verification of his tint principle. With regard to certain of his rhythmic theories, he reports that his findings are based on the composer's notation – not available for all music – and an (unidentified) 'normal listener's response' (1973: 495). Who is this normal listener? The only identified population Kolinski appears to have considered is himself. He writes introspectively that, in the absence of psychological data, he 'came to realize that a performer or listener is not capable of a truly polymetric perception' (1973: 501), and that 'when intervals are simultaneously sounded and compared according to their placement in the cycle of fifths, one observes a gradual modification of their character' (1967: 17).

Despite the shortcomings of the psychological approach, it has been widely applied in ethnomusicological research. Generally it has served as a rhetorical dressing-up of statements about non-affective, purely musical relationships. Only a few authors, such as Kolinski, have made the psychological approach the primary basis for interpreting music. Nevertheless, perceptual questions do seem to enter into the act of transcribing musical observables by ear, since the limits of auditory discrimination enter into any transcription. George List has pointed out that disagreement among transcribers concerning exact durations of phrase finals or inter-phrase rests is probably a result of perceptual difficulties since 'attention or concentration seems to dminish at the interstices of phrases' (1974: 374). Nevertheless, as will be seen, such perceptually indeterminate spots in a piece would not be the source of important relationships in the best interpretation of the work.

SUMMARY

The bases used by ethnomusicologists that have been discussed here turn out to be defective for a theory for all music. Some would be too narrow: they would exclude music involving inanimate or at least non-human producers or receivers of music, works by unknown composers, historical pieces lacking a body of criticism, unaccepted forms, such as incompetently produced works or music of the avant-garde, self-delectative music, or music lacking symbolic meaning. Some bases would give rise to untested or untestable hypotheses, such as the alleged causal relationship between certain cultural values, perceptual values, or neural mechanisms on the one hand and musical observables on the other. And finally, a number of bases would be uneconomical, involving the redundant addition of cognitive systems, symbolic meanings, and affective values to structures inferrable from the musical observables alone. At the same time, some approaches provide circumstantial evidence or clues for what is happening in the music. One is left therefore with the original data base, the observables of music (sounds and scores), as well as a few clues gathered from observations of the context surrounding the music. For the rest of this study I will adhere very closely to the observables of music and will avoid the introduction of types of data that cannot be inferred from them. The challenge will be to extract the maximum of meaning from this parsimoniously restricted array. The first step towards achieving this aim will be the choice of a method for interpreting all music.

3

Choosing a Method of Interpretation

Interpretation is an activity that unites scholars of the sciences and the humanities. Plasmas and portraits, planets and poems, plants and palimpsests: all of these are subject to scholarly interpretation. Just as one can interpret microbes or musty books, so too can one interpret music.

Always there is an interplay between that which is in the phenomenon under study and that which can be got out of it. A judicious handling of this interplay can result in adequate interpretations, and an outstanding treatment can give rise to even better interpretations. What, then, are the important types of relationship that can exist between a set of observables and an adequate, or even a better-than-adequate, interpretation?

CRITERIA FOR ADEQUACY

The most obvious relationship is one of transcendence: the interpretation must transcend or go beyond the observables in some way. For example, suppose the observables of a musical study consisted of the score in example 3.1 and the music was described as follows: there is a dotted-eighth *b*, then a sixteenth *a*, then four eighths on *g*, *a*, *b*, and *b*, and then a quarter *b*. Such a description would not be an adequate interpretation of the observables because it would only be a restatement or translation of them. Such translations do not qualify as interpretations because they add nothing new to what one already knows. Apart from this deficiency, the above description does resemble an adequate interpretation in at least three respects. First, the translation is consistent with the observables; that is, it never contradicts them. Secondly, it is complete: none of the observables is suppressed or swept under a rug. And finally, it is self-contained: no other observables or interpretations are invoked to justify its conclusions.

3.1

The importance of consistency, the first of these criteria, is immediately clear. If there were no provision for a direct relationship between the observables and the values in an interpretation, any statement about any piece would be an equally valid statement about any other piece. The importance of the second and third criteria is, however, not so obvious and is thus subject to misunderstanding. For example, the requirement that interpretations account for all of the observables often seems to be confused with the impossible requirement that a 'complete,' or 'exhaustive,' interpretation be offered. Marcia Herndon, for instance, writes of 'a complete ethnomusicological study' (1971: 340) as though this were a desirable thing. In a similar vein, Bruno Nettl states that an 'exhaustive analysis' would be possible with computer technology (1964: 136). But as Nettl himself says earlier, 'an infinite number of things could be said about a piece of music' (1964: 132). What is desirable, then, is not the final word, the last testament, on a piece of music or even a repertoire. Rather it is a type of interpretation which does not lead into analytical dead ends but sets one on the right track for extracting the most possible from the music.

The third criterion, self-sufficiency, is also open to misunderstanding. In other disciplines, it is usually clear that one, and not another, phenomenon is being studied. Thus, if rock formations in the Andes are being discussed, references to the emotional make-up of the prime minister of Canada would be considered beside the point or even an affront to the reader in the absence of demonstrated causal relationships between the two. Similarly, it would make little sense to have the interpretation of one piece depend on that of another (or others), as Leonard Meyer does under the guise of stylistic analysis (1956: passim). One must, as Marcia Herndon says, approach each piece or repertoire with a 'clear mind,' as though the observables were 'raw sound' (1974a: 251).

The four adjectives that describe what an interpretation should be – transcendent, consistent, complete, and self-sufficient – can be amplified by three that describe what it should not be: arbitrary, subjective, and indeterminate. Examples of arbitrary interpretations abound in ethnomusicology, but only one need be cited here: Habib Touma's use of the concept 'nucleus' with regard to Arabic music. Touma says 'the nucleus consists of all axial tones which appear three or more times' (1971: 43). In the absence of any stated reason why numbers larger than two should be considered special, one can only conclude that integers of three and higher have some mystical, a priori, or numerological property.

Otherwise, the nucleus could be defined just as arbitrarily in terms of two, four, five or more axial tones.

More difficult to deal with than arbitrary interpretations and much more prevalent are those involving indeterminate concepts. In contrast to arbitrary concepts, which are usually well-defined but always meaningless, indeterminate concepts are often ill-defined but potentially valuable.

Because of its prevalence, indeterminacy can be represented here by only a few examples. Mieczyslaw Kolinski writes that motive '*g* is a free imitation of [motive] *a* in the lower fourth' (1972: 419). Unfortunately, any motive can be described as a free imitation of any other motive. Thus, this interpretation can be rendered determinate only when the reader consults the passages pointed at by the letters *a* and *g* and defines the nature of the resemblance for himself. Similarly, when Bruno Nettl writes that 'there seems to be good reason for considering [a certain pitch] simply a variant of the tone *g* rather than an independent tone' (1964: 156), one is burning with curiosity to know what is the seemingly good reason. Alas, again one must discover this for oneself.

The entire issue of subjectivity is a thorny one and is open to all sorts of confusion. First, subjectivity should not be equated with insight. Certainly a great deal of inspiration goes into such a creative act as the interpretation of a piece of music. But in a fully creative analysis, the apparently private experience is translated into public terms. In a subjective interpretation on the other hand, there is no way of publicly verifying or falsifying the statements made about the observables. An instance of this is Alan Merriam's use of the term 'subjective tonic', a term that is undefined but seems to mean a pitch that a Western listener feels as the tonal centre (1967). Here the lack of a public definition precludes any possibility of falsifying the statement that a certain pitch is indeed the subjective tonic of a given piece. One can only take such a statement on blind faith.

The ethnomusicologist's usual response to indeterminacy and subjectivity is to prescribe their apparent opposites, determinacy and objectivity, as an antidote. Unfortunately, these notions are also subject to considerable confusion. For example, objective and determinate methods can easily be misconstrued as the equivalents of certain methods specially employed in the physical sciences, methods that may or may not be appropriate to the aesthetic domain of music. Accordingly, both deserve more extensive treatment here.

OBJECTIVITY

One of the most tempting means of achieving objectivity is a transcription of the observables of music that is made mechanically rather than by ear. However, every transcription – whether mechanical or aural – represents only an approximation to the observables. This is because every measurement is but an approximation of the quantities measured. Thus, one must choose a basis on which approximation will be made.

Such a basis might be arbitrary. For example, one might measure pitches to the nearest ten cents, or one cent, or 0.1 cent; and durations to the nearest 0.1 second, 0.01 second , or 0.001 second. The problem with such arbitrary bases is twofold. Their meaning is far from clear: what is so special about pitch differences of one cent or time differences of 0.01 second? And there is no apparent connection with the remainder of the interpretation: are pitch differences of one cent related to the conclusion that the piece is in C major?

Another solution is the consideration of pitches and times that differ by more than a perceptually discriminable amount discrete. However, pitch discrimination varies considerably among individuals, and again there would be no apparent connection with other aspects of the interpretation.

A preferable course is a theoretical, rather than an arbitrary or perceptual, interpretation of the observables. Thus, in a piece to be interpreted in terms of twelve semitones to the octave, pitches falling within a band of a given width (where the bands are located 100 cents apart) might be considered the same. Here there would be a determinate relationship between the basis for approximation and the remainder of the interpretation. Consequently, the magnitude of 100 cents would have meaning.

It follows that Marcia Herndon's remark that 'we cannot reach precision in transcription' (1974a: 244) is at best an observation that every transcription is an approximation, and a warning that even the most precise transcription is a mere shadow of the observables. Stephen Erdeley's call (following Charles Seeger) for 'an objective analysis of sound waves' (1972: 119) is valid only if one adds the proviso that a theoretical basis for approximation be specified in each analysis. Accordingly, it seems that when List (1974: 374–5) 'corrects' aural transcriptions on the basis of mechanical transcriptions without specifying the theoretical basis for his 'corrections,' he is advocating pseudo-objectivity. For a transcription (i.e., a type of interpretation) with unexplained precision only begs unanswered questions.

A second issue that arises from the use of 'objective' transcription devices is that of detail. A number of features of musical observables – for example, slight vibrato and portamento, events that happen 'between the notes' (Seeger 1958: 186) – are picked up by a melograph but often missed by the human ear. Should such observables be included in a transcription? Some might object that since these slight nuances cannot be experienced consciously, they do not represent true observables of the piece. However, the critical word here is *observables*, which does not imply such a specific method of observation as aural perception but includes any method that is public and subject to falsification. To insist on aural perception alone would be to submit to the psychological approach and all of its dangers. Indeed, since we know more about electric circuitry than we do about our own perceptual mechanisms, the melograph or similar devices ought to be, for the time being, the final arbiters in such disputed matters of fact.

Nevertheless, there are some scholars who seem to deny the importance of exact values in transcription (e.g., Blacking 1971: 93). If by exact values these scholars mean values that are precisely measured but unexplained, one can only agree with their denial. But if they mean that there need be no ultimate judgment of the relationship between the observables and the interpretation based on them, one cannot agree in the least.

With regard to mechanical transcriptions, then, distinctions must be made between the observables (i.e., the reality) and an approximation to them (i.e., a transcription), and between unexplained precision (pseudo-objectivity) and explained precision (interpretive objectivity). Those observables that are open to public scrutiny should correspond to the symbols in the transcription, and all other observables should be neglected. And finally, even imperceptible observables can be allowed a place in transcriptions if their presence is verifiable in a public manner.

Even after a preliminary interpretation of the observables has been made in the form of a transcription, objectivity continues to rear its head. A special instance of objectivity in ethnomusicology is the assignment of single absolute values to entire sets of observables as pieces. For example, Bruno Nettl records the total duration of a single song as being 'slightly over 15 seconds' (1964: 157). Such a value can be meaningful only if compared with values from other pieces. Thus, Nettl's observation raises the question of repertoires as opposed to pieces, an issue that will be discussed later. With respect to a given piece, Nettl's observation begs the question of what is the significance of 15 seconds. Unless one were referring to the experience or perception of time per se (as distinct from what happens in time), such an entity has no musical meaning even of a psychological sort (cf. Ornstein 1969).

One absolute value that refers to both temporal duration and what happens in time is the so-called tempo figure of a piece (cf. Nettl 1964: 157, 159, after Kolinski 1959). This measure of the average number of notes per minute in a piece raises the question of the definability of *notes*. Notes are generally distinguished by attacks or changes in pitch. But the distinction between a sustained tone and a tone with an attack is not always clear. String tremolos in Western music, and pulsations in native North American music are but two illustrations of ambiguity in this regard. And pitch changes cannot be defined without recourse to interpretive criteria. For example, there is no objective, measurable difference between a wide vibrato and a narrow trill exclusive of other features of the musical structure. Ultimately, one wants to know how attacks and changes of pitch function in piece before assigning absolute values, since these absolute values depend on the meaning of attack and pitch change in the piece itself.

These difficulties do not mean, however, that such absolute values could not form a meaningful part of an interpretation. There is evidence that they are not always random but sometimes recur regularly. As long ago as 1918, Frances Densmore (1918: 60–1) reported that Mandan and Chippewa singers rendered songs in the same absolute pitch and tempo over periods of from six months to three years. Absolute pitch might have an effect on the timbral structure of a piece, and absolute tempo could be related to such micro-temporal aspects of music as the relationship between the duration of an attack and the duration of a tone as a whole. However, the critical word here is 'might': these relationships have not been demonstrated and, until they are, the status of single absolute values that are assigned to individual pieces is very low: they are just another instance of unexplained or meaningless values which had best be left out of interpretations.

Related to such single absolute values are techniques of counting. Thus, Olsen counts the number of tones used in a certain piece and thereupon describes it as 'tritonic,' that is, a piece made up of three distinct pitches (1972: 35). Similarly, Nettl distinguishes among tetrachordal, pentachordal, and hexachordal pieces, that is, pieces that have respectively, four, five, and six tones separated by seconds (1964: 145). One wonders, however, what is so special about the number of tones in a piece. Is the fact that a piece has three, four, five, or six tones related to other features of its structure, or is it just another instance of counting 'the number of ladybugs on the planet' (cf. Poincaré 1946: 362) simply because they are there to be counted? Furthermore, Nettl's definition of intervals in terms of 'seconds' can, in the absence of a functional definition of the second, only be considered an arbitrary criterion which would equate such tetrachordal pitch collections as ($b\sharp$ $c\sharp$ d $e\flat$) and ($a\flat\flat$ $b\flat$ $c\sharp$ $d^\times$). Olsen's definition of *tritonic*, lacking as it does any criterion for pitch identity, is even more problematic.

A practice connected with counting is 'objectively' locating the beginnings and endings of phrases by observing where the performers breathe (cf. Chenoweth 1974: 65; Herndon 1971: 347). Physiological behaviour can, of course, reinforce musical values or be co-ordinated with them: dance and baton-twirling are obvious examples where critical points in the music are emphasized by coterminous critical events in the pattern of gestural or physiological behaviour. But the relationships in music generally form a much deeper and more substantial hierarchy of non-referential relationships than have been demonstrated for accompanying behavioural events, such as breathing. Behavioural events that run parallel to the music can be considered part of a piece if the definition of observables is stretched somewhat. But their musical function will remain one of reinforcement or emphasis of relationships already found in the music. Thus, to make a musical decision of interpretation on the basis of behavioural observables would be to put the cart before the horse.

One approach that has the aura of objective science about it consists of analysis couched in terms of the so-called elements of music. Geometry, algebra, physics, and chemistry all have their well-defined, simple entities called *elements*, which form the basis for investigating more complex phenomena. But there have been other scientific elements too: the famous earth, air, fire, and water of early physics. Between these two extremes of validity, where do the elements of music lie – elements such as melody, harmony, rhythm, metre, form, and texture?

First, it is evident that these terms are ill-defined. Few musicologists would agree on definitions for melody, rhythm, or form, because there are no demonstrated and necessary relationships between these elements and other phenomena, as there are for example, between platinum and a given atomic weight. And second, these elements cannot exist independently of one another. For example, melodies imply rhythmic, metrical, harmonic, and formal values. Each rhythm is the rhythm *of* given tonal values, and each form is the form of some rhythmic, harmonic, or melodic content (cf. Rahn 1982a). As a result, the elements of music lie closer to the alchemist's domain than to the chemist's.This, however, does not mean that the elements are entirely without value. On a pragmatic level, they constitute intuitively obvious categories in terms of which interpretations can be discussed. And each element has acquired certain determinate connotations that can be systematically investigated. For example, 'form' minimally implies relationships among contents that occur at different times; harmony implies relationships among simultaneous pitch events.

Yet another apparently objective approach is the listing of traits. Chenoweth advocates this method of interpretation when she states that 'a melody may be described ... in terms of external features such as its compass, range and placement ... movement ... characteristic dynamics and embellishments,... rhythmic structure,... [and] contour' (1974: 93–4). Merriam writes that 'the analysis of a musical style depends upon breaking down a structure into its component parts and understanding how these parts fit together to form a coherent whole,' and later adds that 'some thirty to forty different parts can be isolated' (1964: 300).

Can these parts be fitted together 'to form a coherent whole'? And is the number of parts that can be isolated only 'some thirty to forty'? According to the way in which trait lists have usually been compiled, there is no immediate connection discernible among the various features. For example, it is difficult to find relationships among isometric structure, level dynamics, and descending contour that might give rise to an holistic view of a style. Each such trait represents an independent interpretation of the piece; when these various interpretations are fitted together they must be piled one on top of another, like so many slices of beef, rather than integrated as are the organs of a living steer (cf. however, chapters 7 and 8, and Rahn 1978a).

Since no body of theory provides an explanation of how the *definientes* of such traits are related to other aspects of individual pieces, traits of this sort must have been arbitrarily conceived in the first place. Therefore, because the number of arbitrarily defined variables is potentially infinite, Merriam's encouraging determinate estimate of thirty to forty seems somewhat conservative.

DETERMINACY

An apparently determinate way of interpreting observables is in terms of boundaries, or limits. Kolinski, for example, states that the 'startling variety of musical idioms is contained within the boundaries of certain basic principles of sound construction ... which, evidently, are deeply rooted in the structure of the central nervous system of *homo sapiens*' (1967: 1). In a similarly psychological vein, Chenoweth declares that 'there is a limit to how long a phrase can be and still be absorbed mentally' (1974: 65). And Merriam speaks of the 'normal range of variation in a trait' (1967: 318). Despite the evident biases towards psychological or trait-listing approaches, these statements do contain a general notion that might bear fruit, namely, that musical observables stay within certain limits. If this were so, one could profitably attempt to determine the boundaries surrounding musical variables when one interpreted pieces.

Is this so, however? Is there, for example, anything that cannot happen in a tonal piece, or a pentatonic piece, or a twelve-tone piece? Is there anything that cannot happen in 2–4 or 3–4 or 7–8? The answer to each question is 'no,' because to describe a piece according to a certain tonal or metrical system is generally not a truth-statement that can be falsified by the presence of a piece of contradictory evidence in the observables. Rather it is merely a statement that the observables are best interpreted according to the given system.

The notion that analysis should discover the boundaries of musical observables also has the disadvantage that it does not allow one to predict what might happen in a piece one has not already encountered. Each previously unobserved piece in a repertoire that one is studying threatens to make a mockery of one's earlier generalizations about what does *not* happen in the repertoire.

Related to but somewhat more imaginative than this idea of limits or boundaries is the notion of distribution borrowed from structural linguistics. In some languages, it is true that the phoneme *P* corresponds to *p* when followed by *t* (as in the word 'ap*t*itude') and to *b* when followed by *d* (as in the word 'ab*d*icate'). In these circumstances one says that the phones *p* and *b* are in complementary distribution when followed by *t* or *d*. Following this analogy, Bruno Nettl points out that in the Western melodic-minor scale, the major seventh and minor seventh are in complementary distribution (1964: 144–5). The major seventh is followed by the tonic, whereas the minor seventh is followed by the minor sixth (e.g., in C minor: *b c*, and *b♭ a♭*, respectively). Similarly, Chenoweth observes that in some songs of New Guinea minor seconds are found only directly below the tonal centre, and major seconds are found elsewhere (1974: 57).

The problem with such statements is that they do not go far enough. On the basis of linguistic theory, one can often say that *p* precedes *t* and *b* precedes *d* because a voiced stop tends to be followed by its own kind and, similarly, an unvoiced stop tends to be followed by an unvoiced stop. But in the musicological usage of this concept of complementary distribution, no reason is given for the choice of a given type of interval in a certain circumstance. In order to provide a reason, more interpretation is necessary. And even if a reason were given, such an approach could not handle situations where overlapping rather than complementary distribution prevailed. Such approaches are also like those that posit boundaries to musical observables: they begin with the observables and never transcend or point beyond them.

TERMINOLOGY

A discussion of determinacy in interpretations eventually leads to a reconsideration of questions of terminology and discourse in general. Though the discussion of a lexicon or metalanguage in which interpretations might be couched could soon deteriorate into matters of taste and pedantry, I will try to avoid such considerations in favour of issues involving the relative determinacy of various terms. Despite Herndon's complaint that 'we cannot ... agree as to the meanings of the terms we use' (1974a: 244), I prefer to think that one can extract from even the most recalcitrant and empty terms some vestige of determinate meaning. In order to achieve such an end, it is useful to consider how musical terms have been used by ethnomusicologists. And in this regard, one sees that scholars of non-Western music have resorted to several sources for their terms, the most prevalent of which – probably because it involves following the line of least resistance – is Western music theory. If one is judicious, this tactic need not lead one into error. For example, much of the music interpreted by ethnomusicologists corresponds to Western notions of scale and metre and thus such terms as *major* and *duple* are applicable. But much music does not conform so conveniently to Western ideas.

Relatively harmless examples of dissonance between non-Western musics and the Western terms used to describe them occur with respect to the names given to intervals and degrees. A number of authors, such as Nettl (1964: 159), and Stern and Stern (1971: 198) use terms such as *minor third* and *perfect fourth* in descriptions of pentatonic music. This practice conflicts with the fact that these terms have a determinate meaning only when used in the context of heptatonic music. To rectify this situation, Herndon has suggested that the physical sizes of intervals (expressed in cents) be employed, (1974: note 1,259). However, the use of cents in such a context would be pseudo-objective: an arbitrary amount of detail would be introduced into the interpretation. A compromise would be to describe such intervals in terms of either the gamut from which they are drawn or the degrees of the scale from which they are derived. Thus, the interval $e–g$ in the pentatonic scale with the pitch classes $c, d, e, g,$ and a could be described either as three semitones (or $3/12$, or simply 3, as is now the practice in descriptions of twelve-tone music) or as one pentatonic degree (or $1/5$, or simply 1). The two nomenclatures could be combined by describing, for example, $d–e$ as a minor version of the interval of one pentatonic degree, $e–g$ as the major version of the same interval, $c–e$ as a diminished interval of two degrees, and $d–g$ as a perfect interval of two degrees.

A similar problem arises when Western degree names are misapplied. Thus, Bonnie Wade (1975: 139), following Willem Adriaansz (1973: passim), writes of 'degrees IV and V' when, in the context of the five-tone modes she is dealing with, degrees III and IV (or, as I will explain later, II and III) would be more appropriate designations. All in all, these imprecise usages with regard to intervals and degrees are easily translated into more appropriate language. Accordingly, they are not nearly as dangerous as the indeterminate use of Western terms that I will discuss presently.

Habib Touma discusses at great length several Western definitions of *melody* in order to show that the Arabian notion of *maqam* is not equivalent to the Western notion of 'melody' (1971: 40–1). In a similarly detailed fashion, Bruno Nettl discusses the problem of how to isolate ornaments in non-Western music (1964: 154). The problem with both authors' use of Western terms is that the meanings of these words are far from clear even to a Western musicologist. Thus, Touma's demonstration of a basic dissimilarity between Oriental and Occidental notions is ultimately invalid because the Western word, which serves as his point of departure, is defined insufficiently precisely in the first place. And Nettl's apparently objective solution to the ornament dilemma does not do justice to the original Western notion – the source of his speculation – because it fails to account for acknowledged Western ornaments, such as appoggiaturas, where the ornaments need *not* be 'made up of shorter notes than the non-ornaments.' Such indeterminate Western terms can, of course, be used as a

♫ ♩ First eighth bisected

♪ ♫̄ Second eighth bisected

3.2

rhetorical short cut, but it would be dangerous to assume that they have a specific meaning in the West. A more fruitful approach in both situations would have been to redefine ambiguous Western terms in such a way that the definitions could be applied to all music. This is done to a certain extent in Parts II and III of this work.

Another possible approach is to abstain from the use of established Western terms in favour of non-Western terms. This, however, is useful only when one is dealing with cultures possessing a highly developed body of music theory. And ultimately, the native terms must be translated into a widely understandable metalanguage.

A third approach is to avoid established terminology whether it be Western or non-Western in origin, and to create new terms. This approach, however, can also lead to difficulties.

An illustration of these problems is Kolinski's coining of the term *semi-split* (1972: 419) to describe rhythmic patterns where one of two durations in a periodic succession is divided into two halves (example 3.2). Though the term is adequately defined, one wonders what important distinction it embodies. Its only purpose appears to be as a shorthand for pointing to a given configuration, and in this it resembles such other pointing terms as *dotted figure, Scotch snap* (see, however, Rahn 1978d), or Kolinski's own 'monorhythmic row' (an apparently numerological term for a succession of four or more tones of equal duration, (1972: 419).

The same author also writes about the four 'main' tones of a given Iroquois piece (Kolinski 1972: 417), just as Herndon discusses the four tones that 'predominate' in one of the Cherokee songs she analyses (1971: 342). And Jairazbhoy devotes an entire article to 'important notes' in North-Indian music (1972). Unfortunately, the first two authors do not reveal the sense in which these tones deserve such terms as 'main' and 'predominate.' Jairazbhoy's assertion that *sa* is important because it serves 'as a frame of reference and as the perfect resolution' (1972: 68) for the pitches of the *rāgs* makes sense from the structural point of view and justifies his equating *sa* with the Western tonic. However, his other criteria (derived from Indian music theory itself) for determining the 'importance' of various other tones is somewhat backwards in approach. For example, the appearances of a pitch at the beginning or end of a piece or section and the frequency of a pitch's appearance do not explain why the pitch is an important tone: they are phenomena that might be explained by assigning special functions – such as tonic, dominant, or mediant – to certain pitches and then observing how these functions are projected in individual pieces. It is not surprising that Jairazbhoy finds that, in Indian theory, there is no consensus about which tone is the most prominent of a *rāg* (1972: 66–7), because pseudo-objective criteria can lead only to ambiguous interpretations.

In some instances, Western terms and neologisms collide. One instance is the clash between the venerable Western term *tonic* and such a relative upstart as *duration tone*. Unfortunately, this confusion is not restricted to the West; as McDermott and Sumarsam report (1975: 236), the Javanese have appropriated the Western *tonik* in order to interpret their own music. Added to this is the so-called subjective tonic invoked by Merriam (see chapter 2 and Cooke (1971: 86, 88). The latter term, since it does not represent a publicly verifiable value, and is dependent on how the music 'feels,' need not be considered here. But the conflict between the music theorist's tonic and the ethnomusicologist's tonal centre deserves to be explored.

Peter Crossley-Holland defines the 'primary tonal centre' of a piece as the pitch that has the greatest duration count (calculated by summing the durations of each tone where the pitch occurs) (1971: 30). Chenoweth gives two 'rules of thumb' for determining the tonal centre of a piece: the tonal centre 'occurs most frequently and with freer distribution syntactically than other tones.' To this, she adds the observations that the tonal centre 'carries the heaviest rhythmic weight, and would be expected as the cadential tone, ... may be the initial tone as well, or the strongest initial tone, [and] throughout a song ... will likely appear as accented or in long note values' (1974: 75). Similar criteria are proposed by Nettl (1964: 147).

Among the problems with such definitions is the possibility that two or more pitches would tie for the honour of being the tonal centre. Apparently to accommodate such situations, Chenoweth (1974: 76) posits the possibility of more than one tonal centre, though by this she might mean merely that tonal centres are simply important tones. A second problem consists in the multiplicity of criteria that might be invoked in order to justify one's decision that a given pitch is the tonal centre. How are these criteria to be weighted? Is terminal position more decisive than frequency, and if so, by how much does it exceed frequency? In the absence of non-arbitrary measures for the relative importance of various criteria, one can proceed only in an arbitrary way. This brings us to the third problem. Ostensibly an objectively determined value, the tonal centre is ultimately an arbitrarily defined entity. Once one has established which tone is the tonal centre, of what use is the information? Does it clarify other relationships among the observables, or is it an analytical dead end? All of the studies published to date indicate the futility of the tonal centre approach.

By contrast, the Western tonic leads to an evaluation of, for instance, modulations, modal changes, cadences, and non-harmonic tones. It is intimately connected with every other value in the piece, and the decision that a given pitch class is the tonic is the most critical choice in an interpretation of tonal music: all of this, in spite of the lack of 'objective criteria' for its determination. Furthermore, there is no question of an arbitrary weighting of criteria or the possibility that two or more tones will tie for the honour: the tonic is simply chosen. By definition there can only be one tonic in a piece or part thereof (though there can be situations in which there is no advantage to choosing any of the pitches as tonic). Finally, as will be seen in later chapters, the choice of a tonic need not be arbitrary.

Questions of objectivity, determinacy, and terminology thus seem hopelessly intermixed. However, if objectivity means simply a correlation between the statements of an interpretation and the observables on which these statements are based, and if determinacy means that such correlations should be unambiguous, confusion need not arise. If this is remembered, objectivity and determinacy can be added to transcendence, consistency, completeness, and self-sufficiency as interpretive criteria.

The requirement for determinate discourse is related to issues of intersubjectivity and definition. With regard to intersubjectivity, Bruno Nettl, for instance, insists that a 'description of the music ... must, above all, be communicative, and ... must make some concessions to the reader's frame of reference' (1964: 132). However, there is no guarantee that a person other than the interpreter will be able to understand a given interpretation. To insist that one's interpretation is intersubjective would be to insist that one knew what was in the minds of others, which in turn, would be obviously mentalistic. What does one do with a person who maintains that the existence of pitches or the validity of tautologies is not obvious? Ultimately, the situation is hopeless, and any solutions are pragmatic rather than absolute: the simplest, most logical definition of terms, the establishment of a conventional usage based on these definitions, and the consistent employment of the terms.

A source of the problem of intersubjectivity is the ultimacy of many concepts. For example, such terms as *pitch* and *duration* must usually be taken as primitive, or undefined. In some circumstances, an operational definition can be offered but such a definition will ultimately depend on even more primitive notions. For example, if one person describes two durations as the same and another person refuses to understand the concepts of identity, or sameness, there is little one can do. Notions such as identity and diversity are ultimate and when discourse arrives at these it has reached a dead end: either one understands or one does not. Fortunately, it would seem that most people could readily understand the ideas on which the present theory is based.

The pragmatic solution to the problems of intersubjectivity and definition is to invoke the fewest possible primitive, undefined concepts and define other values and relationships in terms of the primitive ideas.

A final requirement for interpretive adequacy is that the interpretation should identify the observables. For example, an analysis of Beethoven's Fifth Symphony that would be equally applicable to Beethoven's Third would be inadequate. It would be more appropriate to qualify such an interpretation as being a description of the musical type represented by Beethoven's Fifth and Third, rather than as an interpretation of the Fifth itself. Accordingly, identification can be added to the other requirements of an adequate interpretation.

QUALITY OF INTERPRETATIONS

At the outset of this chapter I indicated that some interpretations might be better than others. Thus some consideration of aesthetic matters that eventually involve questions of value is in order.

Considerable attention has been paid to aesthetic matters in recent ethnomusicological writings. For example, Chenoweth writes of such apparently aesthetic concepts as unity, variety, rhythm, and climax (1974: 97), and Bruno Nettl posits a tension between unity and variety in some Persian pieces (1974: 41). By and large, ethnomusicologists have located aesthetic values in the observables themselves. Thus, Kolinski says of some Iroquois songs that 'the music is extremely well organized' (1972: 417); Petrović speaks of the 'seeming simplicity of the music' of Yugoslavian folk songs (1970: 65–6): Blacking writes about 'the logic of the melodic pattern' with regard to some Venda songs (1971: 92); Merriam asserts that 'music ... has structure' (1964: 7; cf. 32); in a similar vein, Herndon insists that 'music is patterned' (1974: 245).

If one considers the possible meanings of such statements, however, one is forced to conclude that the observables of music need not have any aesthetic properties at all. What these writers' remarks boil down to is that one interpretation of Iroquois song has good organization, one interpretation of Yugoslavian folk song is marked by simplicity, one interpretation of Venda songs is logical, and indeed that some alleged interpretations of all music are structured and patterned. In other words, there is no necessary beauty in the observables, only a potential for beauty in the interpretation of them. As the old saw has it, 'Beauty is in the eye of the beholder,' – not in the object that is beheld. If one wants to do so, one can usually derive organization, structure, pattern, logic, simplicity, unity, or variety from the observables.

All the same, George List denies that an objective approach is compatible with an aesthetic approach (1971: 402), and Robert Kauffman objects to the application of a universal aesthetic to works from cultures where certain aesthetic values are not revered (1972: 47). Both contentions have a certain validity, but they can be perverted too easily into a form that would forbid some very fruitful approaches to interpretation. With regard to List's objection, one can observe that objective science, as it is generally understood, has to do with causes of phenomena whereas a causal approach to musical intrepretation has been shown to be sterile, because of the complexity of the observables and, more importantly, the overwhelming multiplicity of possible causes. Thus, ethnomusicologists need not feel compelled to toe the causal and objective scientific line.

However, the issue of whether music should be interpreted objectively runs even more deeply than this. First, one must deal with the apparent dichotomy between fact and value, which Charles Seeger has emphasized (1960: 257–9; 1968: 35–6; 1969: 233, 243). In positivist philosophy, statements of value or goodness (such as, 'It ought ...') have been banished from discourse in favour of statements of fact or truth (such as, 'It is ...'), largely because there is no method for testing the validity of value statements without introducing blanket and arbitrary decrees on matters of morality or taste. In music, this problem might arise in analysis if one were to say that a certain half-note $b\flat$ ought not to be there or, conversely, that it makes the piece a good or better thing. However, the aesthetic values and their application which I consider useful for interpretation do not imply universal canons of good taste or beauty. For example, when one can state that certain aspects of the observables – rather than all of the observables – can be interpreted in a way that produces unity and variety in the interpretation, one is not asserting that the observables themselves are good. When one shows that a given interpretation reveals more relationships of unity and variety among the observables than another does, or that one interpretation reveals such relationships among more observables than another, one has not demonstrated that the observables have become better, but that the interpretation has become better. And this improvement is precisely equivalent to the sense in which one scientific interpretation (or theory) is better than another: it is not better in terms of morality or taste, but in terms of falsifiable knowledge.

Having asserted that aesthetic and scientific interpretations can be evaluated in a similar way, some explanation is in order. Consider, for example, the following interpretations of natural phenomena: (a) an object when placed in water causes the level of the water to rise; (b) an object when placed in water

3.3

causes the level of water to rise the same amount each time; (c) if the object sinks, the amount of water displaced is equal to the volume of the object; if the object floats, it can be observed that objects of the same material displace amounts of water proportional to their volumes; (d) the amount of liquid displaced by a solid put into it is a function of the masses of the liquid and the solid. Each of these is an adequate interpretation of the observed phenomena. But obviously (d) is better than (c), which is better than (b), which in turn is better than (a). Statement (a) is plainly a simplistic reduction of the phenomenon to a regular but trivial explanation. Statement (b) is more general but expresses only a uniformity, a recurrent regularity. In statement (c), more complexity is introduced by the valid distinction between floating and sinking objects. Finally, statement (d) is at the same time the most general and the most specific, and reveals a certain richness of relationships between mass and space. Each of the terms used to describe these statements, viz., simplistic, uniform, complex, and rich, embodies an aesthetic concept.

A similar account can be given of musical interpretations of the same observables. Consider the following statements about example 3.3: (a) successive pitches are in the same direction; (b) successive pitches are higher by the same (pitch) interval; (c) the attacks of successive pitches are separated by the same duration; (d) following from (b) and (c), pitch and time relationships are isomorphic. Again, more precision and more generality are added with each statement. The first reveals a simple regularity; the second and third introduce complexity into the accounts of tonal and rhythmic structure; the fourth reveals a richness of relationship between the pitch and time orderings in the example, and is at once more specific and general.

These examples of increasingly better scientific and aesthetic interpretations are typical of situations encountered over and over again in theory construction. One can observe a number of special features of such situations, taking the examples as a point of departure. First, a number of observations that might have been made were not included in the interpretations. The colours and shapes of the objects, and the tempos and timbres of the melodic succession were not taken into account because they add nothing to the interpretation. The scientific interpretation applies to objects of any shape or colour, and the music interpretation applies to any melodies of a given type regardless of the tempo or instrumentation. In such instances, there is a residue of observables which are not accounted for. In musical interpretations, these residues generally consist of such absolute values as tempo or such purely qualitative values as tone colour. It would seem that these residual aspects are most likely to be influenced by para-musical phenomena, such as the social, cultural, or psychological conditions surrounding the observables.

Such residual aspects tend not to be included in an interpretation because they refuse to take part in the rich relationships to which pitch and duration give rise. It is difficult to specify what relationships other than mere identity or diversity obtain among the timbres produced by, for example, a sitar, a *shenai*, and a tabla pair playing together. Similarly, it is not evident what special relationships exist between tempos of M.M. ♩ = 119 and ♩ = 81 per se – that is, apart from their closeness to 120 and 80, which stand in a ratio of 3 : 2. It would seem that timbres and tempos simply 'are' rather than 'are related to something else.' Accordingly, a distinction must be made between the values and the relationships inferred from music.

The distinction between a value and a relationship brings to the fore a basic distinction to be observed in the use of the term 'beauty.' A colour, shape, tone colour, or rate of progression can be considered beautiful in the sense that it is 'just so.' A relationship between two or more numbers, quantities, pitches, or durations can be considered beautiful in the sense that it has 'just proportion.' In an interpretation, such relationships can be considered beautiful because they are 'just right.' It is usual to reserve the term *beauty* for aesthetic objects. No generally accepted word exists to express the beauty of a theory, a theorem, an argument, or an analysis. The best candidate is *elegance*, which is frequently used to describe the aesthetically positive features of mathematical deductions. Accordingly, the beauty of an interpretation will be referred to as its elegance.

The first stages in an interpretation involve the use of such basic and apparently undefinable concepts as identity and diversity, and the end result is evaluated by such weighty and seemingly paradoxical notions as unity-in-variety, and specificity-in-generality. If an interpretation is to be maximally determinate, these outer limits of discourse should be examined in as definite and rational a way as is possible. One wants to know what is the minimum number of undefined, primitive terms required to produce a satisfactory interpretation. And one wants to know how to compare the relative merits of interpretations. Accordingly, the next chapter is devoted to questions surrounding such basic concepts and ultimate values.

PART II
A THEORY FOR ALL MUSIC

4

Basic Concepts and Ultimate Values

Although the subject matter of ethnomusicology is artifical, ethnomusicologists have long striven to be scientific. They currently trace their lineage back to scholars such as Alexander Ellis, Carl Stumpf, and Erich von Hornbostel, all of whom were scientists in the narrow sense of the word. Consistent with this ancestry is the current preoccupation of ethnomusicologists with scientific equipment – such as the melograph – the widespread use of statistics, and the vocabulary in which ethnomusicological publications are couched. Thus, one reads of 'hypotheses,' 'theories,' 'data,' 'causality,' and other concepts that have traditionally been the domain of the natural sciences. But one also reads of 'unity,' 'variety,' and other aesthetic values. One might well wonder whether these two approaches to a single subject matter are compatible, that is, whether one can discuss music in aesthetic and scientific terms without contradiction.

Almost two decades ago, C.P. Snow (1964) provoked a hot debate among English-speaking intellectuals that has considerable relevance for the present question. Snow's thesis was that contemporary intellectual life is split between the scientist on the one hand and the humanist on the other. However, there is no necessary break between the activities of those engaged in the sciences and those in the humanities. For example, both fields can be founded on logic, both respect the observables, and both involve evaluations of findings. Since there is considerable basic agreement between the two, it seems odd that conflict should arise between them. Nevertheless, it has.

In ethnomusicology, one of the foremost advocates of a scientific approach was Alan P. Merriam. For Merriam, the humanities and the sciences would treat the same subject matter in different ways, and the better way is that of the scientist. In order to illustrate his claim, Merriam established a set of dichotomies between the two approaches which includes the following pairs of opposites (1969: 218; after Harold Gomes Cassidy 1962: 72–103):

Sciences	Humanities
Objective	Subjective
Quantitative	Qualitative
Presentational	Discursive
General	Particular
Repeatable and general	Unique and individual
Theoretical	Aesthetic

At stake here is whether the attributes on the scientific side are better than those on the aesthetic side, and whether this classification is appropriate to distinguish the sciences from the humanities as they have been practised. As it turns out, Merriam's dualities represent crude caricatures of both the sciences and the humanities, and neither type of attribute can be said to be better than the other. Furthermore, similar sets of values are implicit in both types of scholarship.

These points can be demonstrated if one goes down Merriam's list item by item. The first dichotomy is inapplicable simply because every theory or interpretation, be it in the sciences or the humanities, involves purely subjective phenomena as embodied in its undefined concepts, and every discipline worthy of the name respects the observables being studied and does not try to bend them to fit into some scheme. Thus all scholarly endeavours are at the same time subjective and objective: they depend on notions internalized in some fashion by the individual scholar and they are faithful to the object of their inquiry.

A more salient criterion is that of the publicness of the means to gaining knowledge. In this respect, all but the most esoteric realms of theology and metaphysics insist that the means to knowledge be publicly accessible. This is often provided by making operational the definitions on which the observations rest, so that another observer can follow a given 'recipe' and arrive at the same interpretation.

Merriam's distinction between quantitative and qualitative descriptions of the observables is quite surprising since he was a student of cultural anthropology, which, with its established techniques of interviews and participant observation, is among the most qualitative of the social sciences. Until the advent of spectral analysis, most of linguistics, another social science, was qualitative. Since Emil Durkheim, descriptions of sociological data have been both qualitative and quantitative. And one need only mention psycho-analysis, humanistic psychology, chemistry, organic biology, or geology, to see that scholars in the sciences have maintained a dependence on both quantitative and qualitative accounts. In the traditional humanities, one finds that historians – social, political, and economic – have come to rely heavily on quantitative methods, as have writers of literary studies. In music, one need only point to the works of Jeppesen, Chappell,

Picken, Bartók, and Brailoiu to find major instances where quantitative methods were employed long before Merriam's dichotomies were drawn up. Indeed, music theory itself has been numerate in nature from at least the time of the Greeks to that of recent studies by information theorists.

The claim that the sciences are presentational and the humanities are discursive is largely unfair and in any case beside the point. The huge volume of work and the fast turnover of theories in the sciences precludes discursive treatment if only for economic reasons. All the same, the social sciences, with their case histories and ethnographic studies, are often far from concise in style, while the humanities, with the apparatuses in their editions, which frequently represent the principle accomplishments of a generation of scholarship, can be quite laconic.

With regard to the distinction between general and particularistic studies, one has only to note an important tendency of historical musicologists during the last three decades towards style analysis and away from focusing on individual works or creators, and to observe the cultural anthropologist's reliance on the case study of a single small group of people to recognize that there is little truth in this general statement. And unless one posits fictitious classes of things, the study of a group of phenomena logically depends on the study of individual units.

With regard to repeatability, Merriam's comments seem astounding since the social sciences pre-eminently involve observables that are constantly changing, while the humanities take as their subject matter texts that will never change, frozen as they are in history. In this sense, a recent study of a contemporary society soon will not be replicable, whereas a study of historical documents will, barring loss or mutilation of the sources, always be repeatable.

Merriam's last dichotomy which involves an opposition of theoretical and aesthetic approaches will be dealt with presently. In the meantime, it will suffice to observe that given the recent spread of scientific methods into fields that have long been considered to belong to the humanities, the role that scientific approaches can play in the liberal arts need not be demonstrated further. However, the role that aesthetic approaches have played in the sciences seems not to be as widely recognized, and thus a brief exposition appears warranted.

AESTHETIC CRITERIA IN THE SCIENCES

One need not look far to find statements about the salutary effects of beauty or elegance on the search for knowledge. The essential purpose of science has often been described as the imposition of order on chaos, and one proceeds from dilemmas of contradictory theses and antitheses to resolutions in syntheses of a higher order, that is, from diversity, contradiction, and paradox to unity, consistency, and agreement. As one writer has put it, the advance of science is the 'discovery at each step of a new order which gives unity to what had long seemed unlike' (Bronowski 1962: 27). In at least one instance, a positivist (Max Born) has even conceded praise to a colleague with whom he otherwise disagreed on these very grounds, stating that the colleague's conception produced a view of creation that was 'more beautiful and grander' than any of its predecessors (cf. Koestler 1964: 275). Indeed, some scholars have gone so far as to place beauty above accuracy. An outstanding example of this is Paul Dirac's assertion that 'it is more important to have beauty in one's equations than to have them fit experiment.' The eminent physicist goes on to remark:

It seems that if one is working from the point of view of getting beauty in one's equations, and if one has really a sound insight, one is on a sure line of progress. If there is not complete agreement between the results of one's work and experiment, one should not allow oneself to be too discouraged, because the discrepancy may well be due to minor features that are not properly taken into account and that will get cleared up with further developments of the theory. (1963: 47)

The contrary view is that of the empiricist, who in his extreme form slavishly follows the injunction to gather facts dispassionately and to avoid theorizing. Despite the current prestige of empiricism, a number of objections must be raised to its more extreme forms. A distinction should be made between exactitude and explanation. The beautiful theories that are advanced to explain phenomena will never match the observables precisely. On the other hand, successive theories do provide closer approximations to the data, as is suggested by Arthur Koestler's image of a curve (such as a hyperbola) that increasingly approaches its asymptotes (1964: 249). However, Koestler's model also predicts that a perfect fit will be attained only 'at infinity,' that is, indefinitely in the future. This arises in part from the inherent inaccuracies involved in measurement and description. Such empirical exigencies simply preclude the possibility that a strict match between the 'reality' of the data and the 'pure forms' of a theory will ever be achieved. This dilemma has two consequences: (a) a theory is never true but is at best more true than competing theories, and (b) experimental evidence can confirm expectations based on theory but not the theory itself. Finally, one can object to the extreme empiricist position on the grounds that its practitioners are neither objective nor wholly disinterested, for a prior selection of means of interpretation is always involved. Thus, one must ultimately confront the values that underlie the biases and preferences inherent in the initial choice of interpretants.

If one reads what scientists have to say about their 'epistemological tastes,' one will find only vague references to notions of order, synthesis, unity, beauty, and grandeur, such as I have already cited. If one considers the scientists' achievements, however, one is impressed with three values above all others: unity, richness, and economy. A number of examples can be offered to illustrate scientific achievements that have embodied these values: the linking of astronomy and physics by Kepler, the uniting of algebra and geometry in analytic geometry by Descartes, the collapsing of the walls between space and time and between energy and matter by Einstein, and the century-long endeavour that culminated in explanations of heat, light, colour, electricity, friction, and magnetism all in terms of energy. Superficial distinctions seem consistently to give ground to deep-seated unities rather than vice versa.

In a sense, the successful scientific theorist ends with both less and more than he started with: fewer undefined terms and relationships account for more phenomena. In other words, the less that is assumed, the more one explains.

In music theory – which is about as old as physics, astronomy, and mathematics, from which I have drawn the preceding examples – quite the reverse of the normal progression of science seems to have taken place. Today there is a plethora of recently added concepts, especially in the theory used to describe non-Western musics. Examples include tonal centre, additive and divisive metre, tonal nucleus, tension and relaxation or detension, intervallic neutrality, disphony, subtonic juncture, chain of thirds, and timbral hardness. Such concepts result in a theory that can only be termed diverse and spendthrift, rather than unified and economical. What seems needed is restraint in the introduction of new notions and a reconciliation of old concepts, rather than a continuing proliferation of diverse and divisive ideas.

This is not to say that controversy and debate would end overnight should a relatively economical and unified theory be introduced, for it is in the nature of interpretation that differences of opinion arise. One has only to turn to the hard or causal sciences again to find several examples of long-standing conflict. Most famous are the incompatibilities between Newton's corpuscular theory of light and Huyghens's wave-theory; Bohr's notion of statistical probability as the basis for interpreting subatomic phenomena and Einstein's idea of strict physical causality; the big-bang and steady-state theories of cosmologists; and the neo-Darwinian and neo-Lamarckian approaches in biology (however, cf. Piaget 1978). It is in the nature of the conflict between reality and its interpretation that more than one theory will fit the observables and, more importantly, that two theories might tie for first place as the 'best' current theory. (In chapter 6, an apparent instance of this will be described with regard to a simple piece of music.) That two theories are best need not be discouraging, for all theories are mere approximations to reality.

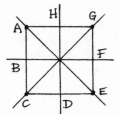

FIGURE 4.1 A square

The interconnection of unity, richness, and economy can be easily demonstrated with regard to two positive attributes which are frequently invoked in
aesthetic discussions and are implicit in the regular figures of geometry and the
classifications of biology and arithmetic: symmetry and hierarchy. Why do we
value these attributes? In both cases it would seem that we value them because
a great wealth of information is compressed into a minimum number of types
of values and relationships. For example, the geometric figure of a square (figure
4.1) is special because it reveals so many symmetries. If this figure is spun
around through 90 degrees on any of its four axes (AE, BF, CG, and DH), its
basic features will be preserved, and yet all that is required to define this superb
figure is a line segment in Euclidean space (such as AC) and a right angle (such
as ACE). Two bits of information, a pair of points and an angle, give rise to a
figure that embodies much information: four axes of symmetry, four equal sides,
and four equal angles.

Similarly, the hierarchical structures by which biological types (e.g., kingdom,
division, class, order, family, tribe, genus, section, series, species, variety, and
form) are classified compress much into little (cf. Charles Jeffrey 1973: 2–3).
Another example is found in the standard counting systems for natural numbers
(e.g., binary, octal, and decimal), which provide a highly economical method
for using a few characters (e.g., two, eight, or ten digits) to specify an infinite
number of values. The means to accomplish this is quite simple: every level of
the hierarchy (e.g., in the decimal system, each of the columns for units, tens,
hundreds, and thousands) is related to its adjacent unit according to a single
geometric relation, as in the following series for the decimal numbers: 10^0,
$10^1, 10^2, 10^3, \ldots 10^{n-1}, \ldots$ In this way, a minimum basis (two, eight, or ten
digits, and a single geometric relationship) gives rise to a system for dealing
with infinite diversity. One need only compare these systems with the unwieldy
Roman numerals to recognize the advantages of economy. Ultimately, one can
do no better than to quote Nelson Goodman: 'To economize and to systematize
are the same' (1966: 67).

All the same, it could be argued that the search for theoretical elegance, that is, for unity and economy, could produce results that would be as sterile as those of the extreme empiricists, since the quest for beauty might blind one to the observables. However, it should be pointed out that if one of two equally elegant theories explains more of the observables, it is in all respects the better theory. Precision and elegance need not be incompatible. Another form of blindness might result from ignoring phenomena which do not fit into an elegant paradigm but which are related to the observables. For example, the behaviourists have frequently been condemned for the artificiality of their experimental situations. It has been contended that the great amounts of information that they have published on rats running in mazes do little to explain the psychological make-up of humanity. Nevertheless, one can maintain that a great deal is known about behaviour in mazes, so that at least some progress has been made. Also, one can point out that a scholar's reach frequently exceeds his grasp: knowledge is often paralysed; the time is not ripe for certain studies. Familiar examples of this phenomenon include the Pythagoreans' inability to deal with irrational numbers, the so-called unspeakable numbers, and the long-standing failure of early music theorists to describe a truly cyclic circle of fifths because of their apparent unfamiliarity with cube roots. That all of the things one would like to know cannot yet be known is no justification for despair: quite the contrary, that certain topics cannot be studied seems good for the soul in that it encourages humility instead of hubris and gives prior focus to inquiry.

Although it seems hopelessly idealistic, the quest for elegance does, in fact, have practical consequences. In an economical system that posits few terms, the chances that communication between scholars will break down is minimized. Also, the primitive, or undefined, terms are held in the spotlight, so that if by some breakthrough they become defineable or can be reduced in number or complexity, the resulting economies will be immediately discernible. Finally, an economical and unified system has coherence: one always knows where one is in the system and what steps might take one to another part of it. This is especially helpful since all areas of a system are not necessarily uniformly investigated at any given time, so that the more esoteric realms – which often lead to profound discoveries and redefinitions in the theory – can be isolated easily for future study.

THEORETICAL ELEGANCE

The elegance of a theory can be described in terms of aesthetic values. Among these are unity and richness, which I have already mentioned, and other values related to these: variety, wholeness, simplicity, and complexity. Aesthetic terms like these are often described as 'glow-words.' Many people are familiar with a certain type of orator whose speeches boil down to a series of such words with connectives interspersed: 'Peace ... Love ... Charity ... the Good of All ... Justice ... Freedom ... Grace ... Unity.' These fine terms are called glow-words because they seem to produce a positive narcotic or hypnotic effect on the listener. The rational mind seems unable to handle such words because they represent transcendent, undefined ideals. Such ideals cannot really be described in words, for, as the ancient *Tao Te Ching* points out, 'The way that can be spoken of is not the Way.' In desperation, one is forced to reach for these overworked terms, if one is to communicate even a small hint of the vague but powerful associations for which they stand. Nevertheless, such words are not without value in rational discourse provided determinate meanings can be wrested from their private, unutterable connotations.

It might seem blasphemous to apply such terms in rational discourse, but two factors encourage such a tactic. First, there are just no other words to express even the relatively mundane and definable concepts that they embody, and, second, the words themselves are not sacred, only the aura of metaphysical values that surrounds them. Also one can distinguish the two types of meaning that might be associated with these potent terms – the *sacred* and the *secular* – by observing an orthographic distinction between capitalized and lower-case forms, respectively. Since the present discussion is decidedly secular, I will make statements about, for example, 'unity' rather than 'Unity.'

In its secular sense, unity implies similarity among distinguishable things. This is conveyed by the relationship of resemblance. Two things that resemble one another are in some respects one thing and in other respects two. This relation is (a) reflexive (a thing, A, resembles itself); (b) symmetric (if A resembles B, then B resembles A); and (c) non-transitive (if A resembles B and B resembles C, A does not necessarily resemble C). (An example of non-transitivity is that of a green apple which resembles a green pear in colour, but not a yellow pear with regard to either shape or colour.) Whereas unity can be asserted of values or rather groups of values (such as colour and shape), the term *simplicity* can be reserved for relationships. An example of this is the following succession of letters: ABACA, where B and C resemble one another in that they are adjacent to, and between, As.

The apparent opposites of unity and simplicity are variety and complexity. Both of these have to do with diversity or differences. Though apparently opposites, unity and variety go hand in hand with one another as a complementary pair. For example, resemblance requires not only similarity between two values but also dissimilarity. In much the same way, simplicity and complexity form a pair with respect to relationships. Thus, when one speaks of similarities among different values or relationships, one can use the terms unity and simplicity,

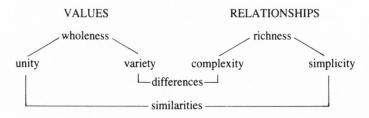

FIGURE 4.2

whereas when discussing the differences among similar values and relationships, one can refer to variety and complexity. However, should one allude to both the similarities and differences in a given set of values or relationships, the terms *wholeness* and *richness* can serve. Accordingly, the pair of triads in figure 4.2 can serve to denote the aesthetic properties of a theory or an interpretation. Using these terms one can offer the following outline of how elegance might be sought in an interpretation:

1 Establish the greatest number of similarities among the values and relationships by which the observables are interpreted.
2 Invoke the smallest number of types of values and relationships in the interpretation.

Both points must be followed. If directive 1 is followed without following directive 2, the result will be an interpretation that is complicated rather than complex and that features diversity rather than variety. If the second is followed at the expense of the first, the resulting interpretation will be merely simplistic rather than simple, or it will be marked by uniformity rather than unity.

One can add two more aesthetic prescriptions: one that is formal in significance and ensures economy, and another that is empirical in import and ensures fidelity to the observables. Once again there is a tension, this time between the few (economy) and the many (empirical fidelity):

3 Employ the smallest number of primitive concepts.
4 Achieve the closest approximation to the observables.

Since prescriptions 2 and 3 are essentially the same in that each prevents a proliferation of undefined concepts, whether these be in the form of types of values and relationships or of primitives, the four points listed above can be reduced to three (i.e., numbers 1, 3, and 4).

Although the directives for ensuring wholeness, richness, and fidelity can be carried out only in an actual interpretation, questions of economy can and must be dealt with at the outset. This leads to a consideration of undefined terms, what they are, and how – in the absence of definitions – they can be understood.

An example from high school geometry can serve to illustrate the distinction between defined and undefined concepts. Since a parallelogram can be defined in terms of vectors, it is a defined notion. A vector in turn is an entity that has both a given length and a given direction. As such, it too is defined. But length and direction themselves are not defined. For a plane surface they can be illustrated by concretely drawing various lines of, for example, ten centimetres, and by drawing what seem to be parallel lines on a flat surface. But these are only approximate illustrations of the concepts of length and direction: they do not define these primitive concepts. Ultimately, one is always left with terms such as these which can only be demonstrated. The demonstrations help by providing an intuitive feel for the meaning of the concepts, but the concepts themselves cannot be defined. The theory developed here is like any other theory in that it has such undefined concepts. Accordingly, some attempt at providing an intuitive feel for them is in order.

UNDEFINED CONCEPTS

The most basic terms of the theory presented here are also found in many other theories. These are the undefined terms of formal logic (such as *and, or,* and *not*) and the relations of set theory (such as $=$, ϵ, and $\subset$ which represent the relationships of identity, membership in a set, and inclusion of one set in another). The relationship of identity can be described as one of equivalence or sameness. In the theory presented here, the term *identity* is used not only pre-systematically but also to describe the similarity of otherwise different things. For example, two tones that occur at different times might be identical with respect to pitch, or two tones that are different in pitch might be identical with respect to time. The relation between a set and its members can be exemplified by a scale degree that is a member of the set of pitches in the scale, or of a moment in time that is a member of the set of moments in a measure. A familiar example of a set that is included in another set is that of the pitches in a pentatonic scale that all belong to the set of pitches in a heptatonic scale.

The remaining terms are quite specifically of musical significance. Four of these refer to properties of tones. For example, the notation in example 4.1 represents a tone consisting of a single pitch (b), a series of 'moments' including the first (attack) and last (release), and a number of 'loudnesses' ranging from *mf* to *p*. Since all the relevant features of a tone are covered by these three undefined qualities (pitch, moment, and loudness), the term *tone* itself can be dispensed with in a strict development of music theory, in favour of statements dealing with the three primitives (cf., however, Seeger 1960: 237). To these

4.1

4.2

4.3

basic qualities of tone, one can add *interval* and *duration*, which imply two pitches and two moments, respectively. An interval (such as a perfect fifth) can be identified as such, and so also can a duration (such as that between attacks a and b of example 4.2). Since intervals and durations can be identified, a relationship of identity can be asserted between two such entities. For instance, in example 4.3, the intervals and durations marked a–b can be considered identical with those marked b–c.

A number of other primitive relationships can be posited between musical features. The relationship of 'precedence' specifies that one moment precedes another. If moment A does not precede moment B, and the two are not identical, then A succeeds B. An analogous relationship for pitches is 'altitude.' Pitch A can be higher than pitch B, identical to it, or lower than it. The corresponding relationship for loudness is 'intensity': A can be louder than B, identical to B in loudness, or softer than B.

Relationships of precedence, altitude, and intensity are all irreflexive (a moment, A, cannot be before or after itself), antisymmetric (if A is higher than B, B cannot be higher than A), and transitive (if A is louder than B, and B is louder than C, then A is louder than C). In this respect, they constitute analogous relationships among three different categories of sound. It should be noted that pitch and time have three primitive concepts associated with them, whereas loudness has only two. This is because the notion of identical intervals of loudness seems to be inapplicable. This is not to say that such a notion cannot be developed. It is only to observe that no means for applying it, or pieces to which it might fruitfully be applied, have been found.

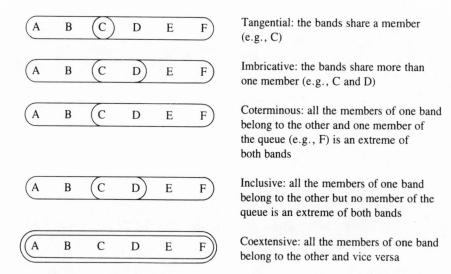

Tangential: the bands share a member (e.g., C)

Imbricative: the bands share more than one member (e.g., C and D)

Coterminous: all the members of one band belong to the other and one member of the queue (e.g., F) is an extreme of both bands

Inclusive: all the members of one band belong to the other but no member of the queue is an extreme of both bands

Coextensive: all the members of one band belong to the other and vice versa

FIGURE 4.3

The final concept to be invoked is *adjacency*. Since this notion has had little treatment in the literature, and since it is very important for the theory developed here, considerable space will be devoted to both adjacency and certain relationships and values that can be derived from it.

A concrete image for adjacency is provided by a queue, a set of people standing in a line. The people need not touch one another, though they might, and they do not have to be a given distance apart, though again they might. Generally speaking, in a queue every person is adjacent to two others: if one is adjacent to more than two others, the queue has deteriorated into a crowd. In a queue, two people are exceptional in that they are not adjacent to two other people in the group, but only to one other person. These people represent the ends, or 'extremes,' of the queue. Every other person is adjacent to and between two others.

Members of a queue can be grouped in different ways. For example, a six-member queue might be partitioned into two or three 'bands,' as in the following arrangements:

A B C/ D E F
A B/ C D/ E F
A B/ C D E F
A B C D/ E F

Such bands can be formed of any number of members in any arrangement provided that members of each band are adjacent members of the original queue. Thus, the arrangements in figure 4.3 are also possible (where a line surrounds members of the same band). If the people in the analogy are considered to correspond to pitches, moments, or loudnesses, the notion of adjacency can be applied in a specifically musical way. If adjacency is coupled with precedence, altitude, or identity, an absolute orientation or direction can be given to the queue: one member is considered the first, highest, or loudest, and the other extreme the last, lowest, or softest. If the notion of adjacency is joined with the notions of interval and duration, the concepts of bisection and cycle can be developed, as will be done in chapter 5. In this way, adjacency is central to the theory developed here.

CONCLUSIONS

The cliché that scientific and aesthetic approaches to a given set of observables are incompatible is far from the actual situation in the sciences or the humanities. Both types of discipline employ undefined concepts and evaluate their theories in aesthetic as well as empirical terms. In the traditional sciences, the aesthetic component is usually less visible because syntheses of findings into grand theoretical complexes seem to occur so seldom; when such a synthesis does occur, however, the occasion is auspicious and is often termed a scientific revolution. In the humanities, such syntheses seem to be more frequent; indeed, they occur every time that a work of art has been successfully interpreted. Both the sciences and the humanities rely on evaluative criteria and primitive notions. The former can be summarized in four prescriptive rules, and in the case of music, at least, nine concepts (in addition to those of logic and set theory) can be considered basic. (It should be noted that further reduction of the basis is possible by adopting the approach of Goodman's *The Structure of Appearance* (1966).)

In the following chapter, each of these concepts will be developed in a musical context and applied to individual examples. And two of these interpretations will be compared according to the aesthetic criteria for evaluation.

5

The Isomorphism of Pitch and Time

The few concepts illustrated in the last chapter provide a more-than-adequate basis for the interpretation of any piece. In order to demonstrate this point, a detailed exposition of these concepts and some corollary notions is presented in this and the following chapter. Applications of these ideas to individual pieces and repertoires are found in chapters 7 and 8.

One of the by-products of this formulation of a theory for all music is that almost no numbers need be invoked in an interpretation. One can understand the essence of the discussion in the next two chapters without being able to count beyond two: where higher integers do appear, their only purpose is to save space and avoid unnecessary circumlocutions.

Throughout my exposition, I have adopted to a great extent the approach first fully outlined in Benjamin Boretz's *Meta-Variations* (1969, 1970a, b, c, 1971, 1972). Though the formulation presented here differs somewhat from Bortez's scheme, I hope to have retained the spirit of his study.

In order to render a highly abstract development as comprehensible as possible, musical examples are offered as illustrative material. One in particular, the children's tune 'Merrily We Roll Along' (sometimes the setting for the words 'Mary Had a Little Lamb'), serves as an example throughout the next two chapters. This tune was chosen for two reasons: it is widely known by English-speaking readers, and since it does not have an aura of 'art,' the elegance of the interpretation ought not to be confused with any alleged beauty in the observables. To those who find this choice of an omnibus example surprising, I hold out the prospect of more 'serious' examples in the rest of the study.

Another strategy to ensure comprehensibility is the division of the discussion into two parts. Since analogous relationships of extent (i.e., interval and duration) and adjacency are necessary for the interpretation of individual pieces, parallel developments of notions for pitch and time are offered in this chapter. Treatment

5.1

5.2

of notions of sequence (i.e., altitude, precedence, and intensity), which are typically invoked in interpretations of repertoires rather than single pieces, is reserved for chapter 6.

PITCHES AND MOMENTS

A position in pitch-space and a temporal moment can be considered irreducible atoms (or quanta) because they cannot be analysed further: they have no proper parts. In this way, analysis can begin with a multiplicity of discrete pitches and moments. One purpose of interpretation is to organize this chaotically diverse array of different values.

A first step is provided by recognizing that two pitches or two times are equivalent to each other. In example 5.1 the pitches of the first and second tones (*b* and *a*) are identical with the pitches of the fifth, sixth, and seventh tones, and the fourth tone, respectively. At this point, there is no question of the first being higher than the second, or higher by a given interval: the three classes of pitches are simply different and they might be represented by arbitrary letters, such as x, y, and z.

Each of the seven tones is composed of various times or moments, irreducible temporal positions. Thus, example 5.1 might have been notated as in example 5.2 to indicate moments that occur during each tone.

SPANS AND BANDS

Two moments might be adjacent or non-adjacent. A set of moments in which each moment is adjacent to two others except two that are adjacent to only one other forms a *span*. This might be roughly indicated by the notation in example 5.3 where sixteenth notes stand for moments and ties join adjacent times. Thus, from the notions of moment, adjacency, and set is derived the notion of span.

Every span has two moments which are exceptional in that they are adjacent

5.3

b is between a and c
a b c   a and c are on opposite sides of b

5.4

a b c d e f g h

5.5

to only one other moment of the set: these are the 'extremes' that mark the boundaries of a span. There is no question here of one extreme being considered the first or last moment of the span: at this point in the development, extremes are simply exceptional moments.

If three moments are related in such a way that one is adjacent to the other two, but these in turn are not adjacent to each other, the first is said to be 'between' and adjacent to the other two, and the other two are said to be on 'opposite' sides of the first (example 5.4). A fourth moment adjacent to c but not to b is on the opposite side of c from a and b, and on the same side of b as c. There are, then, two 'directions' in a span depending on whether a moment is on the same side or opposite sides of the two extremes with respect to a third moment. In example 5.5, b and c are on the same side of e as the extreme a, and on the opposite side of e from f and h: An analogous set of relationships can be posited for pitches. A string of adjacent pitches can form a band with pitches that are (a) extreme, (b) between two other pitches, (c) on the same side of a given pitch as other pitches, (d) on opposite sides with respect to a given pitch, and (e) beyond or outside two pitches. All of these notions depend on the concepts of pitch, adjacency, and set.

It is ultimately assumed, then, that pitch and time orderings are essentially linear rather than cyclic. If they were cyclic, there would be no extremes, that is, points that are adjacent to only one member of the span or band.

The specification of spans and bands serves to solve three problems. First, a set of observables can be delimited by its extreme moments, thus rendering determinate interpretation possible: one can say that the observables to be interpreted occur within a given span. Second, the overall duration of the observables can be sliced into subspans so that one can concentrate on individual parts at various stages of the analysis. Thus, one might isolate, for example, measures five to eight of a given piece and inspect only these, ignoring the rest of the observables for the time being. Third, pitches can be grouped into bands so that varying intonations of what is functionally the same pitch can be treated as instances of a single pitch band.

Both bands and spans can be compared. To demonstrate such comparisons, I will resort to the general term *extent* to refer to a band or a span, and the term *point* to refer to a pitch or a moment. Seven situations emerge:

1 If no points of two extents are adjacent or coincide, the extents are discrete:
   . . . .

          . . . .
2 If an extreme of one extent is adjacent to that of another, but none of their remaining points coincide, the extents are contiguous:
   . . . .

          . . . .
3 If two extents coincide only with respect to one point, they are tangential:
   . . . .

          . . . .
4 If one extreme of one extent is between the extremes of the other extent, and the other extreme of the first extent does not coincide with any of the points of the second extent, they are imbricative:
   . . . .

       . . . .
5 If both the extremes of one extent are between the extremes of the other extent, they are inclusive:
   . . . .

          . . . .
6 If an extreme of one extent coincides with an extreme of the other, and the other extreme of one extent is between the extremes of the other extent, they are co-extreme:
   . . . .

          . . . .
7 If the extremes of two extents coincide, they are coextensive:
   . . . .

   . . . .

These distinctions are frequently applied in analysis. The difference between

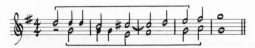

5.6 Point of imitation

5.7 Strummed chord

5.8 Strict chordal homophony

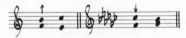

5.9 Overlapping pitch bands

5.10 Discretely organized polyphony

5.11 Two instances of mode I, imperfect in ascent, perfect in descent: rises to c^1, falls to c

staccato and legato is that between discrete and contiguous spans, respectively. In points of imitation, the spans of the imitating parts are related imbricatively (example 5.6).

In the hierarchical analysis of much music, the spans accounted for by one level often include the spans accounted for by the next higher (or 'more foregound') level. The span of the tones in a strummed chord are coextreme, as are the spans of parts in a fugue (example 5.7). And in strict chordal homophony, each tone of each part is coextensive with the tones of the other parts (example 5.8).

With regard to tonal relationships, a distinction can be made between performance practices in which pitches are produced distinctly and those where they are produced tangentially or imbricatively. For example, fixed-pitch instruments, such as fretted lutes and the piano, generally produce discrete pitches, whereas groups of unfretted lutes or voices often produce pitch bands that overlap. A special case occurs in tonal music where a b in the context of C major is performed on a violin higher than a $c\flat$ in the context of G$\flat$ major (example 5.9). Another instance is the frequent phenomenon of flattening or sharpening of pitch throughout a performance, so that, for example, a c at the beginning of a rendition might be the end correspond to a b or a $d\flat$.

Frequently, the various parts in polyphony are rendered discretely in terms of pitch, one part always being the highest, another the second-highest, yet another the third-highest, and so forth. A distinction is also frequently made between the inner and outer (i.e., extreme) parts of a polyphonic piece. Often the outer parts (such as soprano and bass) include the inner during each moment of the piece and are singled out for special treatment by composers and performers (example 5.10). Finally, a repetition of the pitch content of a given passage always results in two sections that are coextensive with respect to pitch. This accounts for the identity of a mode in the sense of a given ambitus (example 5.11).

The notion of extent, be it temporal or tonal, is one of the most useful in music theory, for it is not restricted to the special cases of grouping pitches and moments but has applications in higher spheres as well. Ultimately, all of the relationships and values that involve bands or spans depend only on the notions of an atomic unit, identity, and adjacency. To these basic concepts, one can add another, that of interval.

INTERVALS

A pair of pitches or moments gives rise to an interval. Since *interval* is usually reserved for pitches, I will follow this usage and adopt the word *duration* to designate a pair of moments. Just as pitches and moments can be identified, so too can intervals and durations. For example, the durations between adjacent attacks of the tones in example 5.12 can be grouped into three sets corresponding to a dotted eighth, a sixteenth, and an eighth. In such a monophonic piece, the three sets can be simply labelled w, x, and y, without any implication that w is larger than y, which is larger than x (or in notation, w > y > x). In a polyphonic

5.12

5.13

5.14

version, such as example 5.13, the conclusion is unavoidable that $z > w > y > x$. This can be inferred directly from the relationships among simultaneous spans. The span of w is coterminous with the bass's first g. Since one of its extremes lies beyond the extremes of the g, it is conventionally defined as longer than g. Thus, it follows that $w > y$. Similarly, when the simultaneous a's are compared, it follows that $y > x$. And if the bass's b is compared to the coterminous g and a in the top part, then $z > y$. Thus, in summary, $w > y > x$ and $z > y$. The relationships between z on the one hand and both x and y on the other are, however, still in doubt. Accordingly, another convention for relative length can be introduced: if two contiguous durations, such as w and x, are both coterminous with a third duration – such as the quarter-note duration between the first and third attacks in the lower voice, then the third duration is longer than either of the first two. It follows from this that $z > w$, and, therefore, $z > w > y > x$. The ratios of z to w, w to x, etc., and the number of metrical units in w, x, y, or z are still unknown, however, because no proper system of quantification has been introduced. Before doing so, an evaluation of the pitch intervals of the example is in order.

In the example, there are two sets of intervals, corresponding to $b–a$ and $a–g$ on the one hand, and $b–g$ on the other. Since the intervals of the first set are coterminous with the second and contiguous with each other, it follows that $b–g > b–a$ and $b–g > a–g$. Note that the pair (b, g) is derived from non-successive tones: b and g never succeed each other immediately. The same approach might have been used in evaluating the durations of this example. If this were done, the durations marked by braces in example 5.14 would have been found to be identical and their corresponding spans could have been considered coterminous, revealing an underlying chordal homophony.

INTERVAL BANDS AND DURATIONAL SPANS

Just as a pitch or moment can be 'widened' into a band or span by means of the concept of adjacency, so too can an interval or duration. Pitch bands give rise to interval bands, so that, for example, a perfect fifth might vary in size between 680 and 720 cents. Intervals might be discrete (e.g., 180 to 220 cents, 280 to 320 cents), imbricatively related (e.g., 140 to 260 cents, 240 to 360 cents), or related in some other way. Similarly, a span or cluster of moments can give rise to a range of durations, a durational span. Special cases include rubato, accelerando, and ritardando passages where the sizes of intervals are compressed or expanded. Such instances are parallel to changes of pitch level in the course of a piece.

The potential consequences of the notion of extent with the resultant concepts of band and span could be quite disconcerting for Western musicians, especially those who are conservatory-trained. Is there not just one correct way to perform: in tune and in time? However, if one inspects automatic transcriptions, it would seem that there are great differences from culture to culture in the widths of bands and spans which are treated as though they were individual pitches or moments, and, indeed, the West – with its frequently wide vibratos and extreme rubatos – would seem to be among the cultures that tolerate the greatest ranges of variation.

From the viewpoint of determinate analysis, the introduction of an idea like extent might seem to encourage arbitrariness and incompleteness in interpretation. However, it should be remembered that the original precise pitches and moments are not thrown out in an interpretation in favour of grosser spans and bands: whenever their inclusion would be of value, they are always available to be incorporated into the analysis. And, of course, the ultimate justification for grouping adjacent pitches, moments, intervals, and durations into extents is to achieve the best possible interpretation of the observables.

QUANTIFICATION

One cannot get very far in musical analysis without introducing the notion of quantity. Some pitches are higher than others, and some intervals are of two semitones, others of three or more. A possible way to introduce such notions would be to take quantitative concepts, such as 'greater than' or 'integer,' as primitive. However, this is not necessary, and would be uneconomical, involving as it would the addition of undefined concepts that are not required. As it turns out, all of the apparently quantitative notions needed to achieve a good interpretation can be defined in terms of purely qualitative concepts. Chief among these is pulsation.

Two moments define both a duration and the extremes of a span. Identical spans that are tangentially related define a pulsation, a class of moments that are spaced equidistantly in time (example 5.15). Pulsations of which the spans are not coextensive define a resultant pulsation (example 5.16). The shortest span in a pulsation is the unit span, which, in the case of resultant pulsations, can be called the resultant unit span.

In order to ensure that interpretation is fully empirical, the extremes of at least one of the spans in a pulsation must correspond to events in the observables. If this were not required, one could infer from or, more precisely, impose upon the musical observables pulsations that had no correlates in the facts of music.

In example 5.17, the attacks of tones in the pulsations of (a) give rise to a resultant pulsation (c), which might not have been immediately anticipated from the bare observables. Example 5.18 illustrates the imposition of pulsations that have no correlates in the music.

It should not, however, be assumed that every moment in a pulsation need be represented by an event in the observables. Pulsations are implied by, not determined by, the observables. In other words, they are constructs. Thus, the pulsations in example 5.19 can be inferred from the observables.

In the first group the unit interval ($\flat$) is presented only once; in the second group, it is never presented but only implied by the other intervals.

The unit interval of a pulsation forms the basis upon which durations can be compared. Thus, one can state that the first tone in example 5.20 is three times as long as the second, which is half as long as the third, which is equal in length to the following tones, and so on. The use of such phrases as 'half as long' implies a rational scale of measurement (i.e., one that allows ratios such as one half). To the best of my knowledge, such a scale need never be invoked in a musical interpretation (cf. Rahn 1978d). In keeping with one aim of this section, which is to develop quantitative values and relationships without assuming such concepts as rational numbers, a way around this type of presumptuous quanti-

5.15

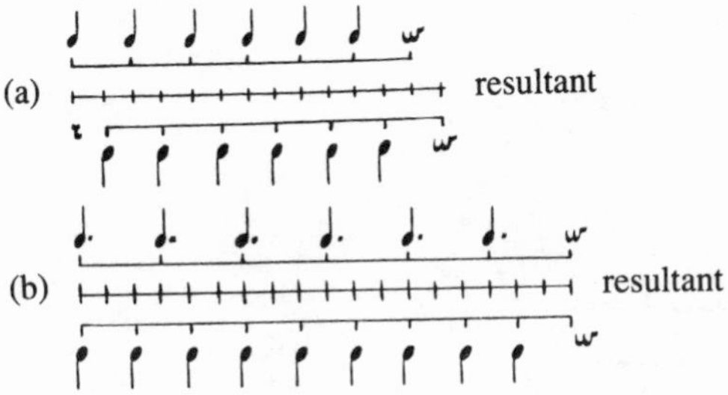

(a)   resultant

(b)   resultant

5.16

(a)

(b)

(c)

5.17

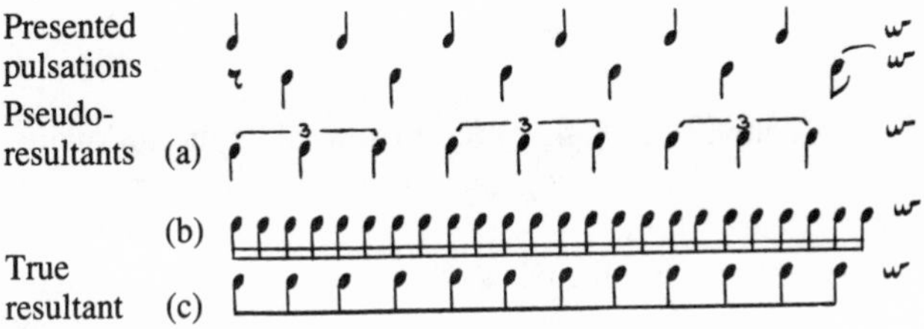

Presented
pulsations
Pseudo-
resultants   (a)

              (b)
True
resultant   (c)

5.18

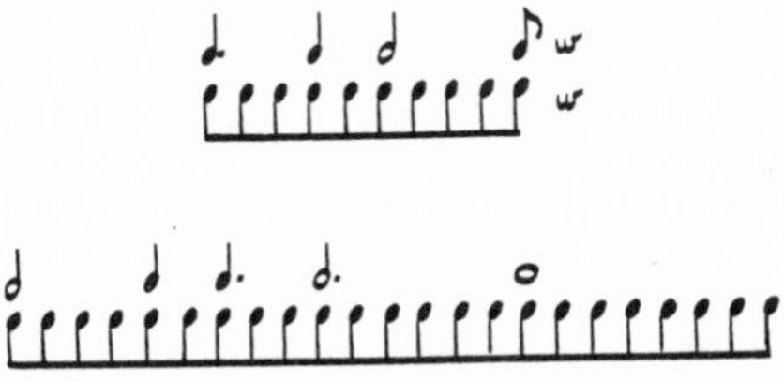

5.19

5.20

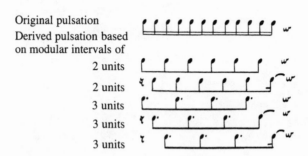

Original pulsation
Derived pulsation based
on modular intervals of
       2 units
       2 units
       3 units
       3 units
       3 units

5.21

5.22

fication must be found. The conclusion of this section and all of the following sections in this chapter are devoted to solving this problem. A first step is to define modular intervals.

Any span larger than the unit can form the basis of a modular pulsation. Thus, in example 5.21, modular units corresponding to two or three sixteenths might be inferred from the given pulsation. The choice of a modular pulsation depends on what makes the best sense of the observables. In example 5.22, the indicated modular pulsations appear to make good intuitive sense and might be exploited at later stages of the interpretation. Those pulsations indicated in example 5.23, on the other hand, seem to be of less potential value.

(Just as a pulsation defines a class of moments, so too does a resultant or a modular pulsation. In the former, the moments can be described as belonging to a pulsation class; in the latter, to a resultant or a modular moment class.)

Similar relationships can be inferred from the pitches of a piece. From example

5.23

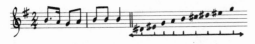

5.24

5.25 Pitches that occur in the piece and imply the gamuts are circled.

5.24, one can infer a 'pulsation' of pitches. To prevent confusion, such tonal pulsations will be referred to as *gamuts*. The continuation of this excerpt implies even more gamuts and a resultant which corresponds to the gamut of twelve semitones to the octave (example 5.25).

Two regularities that continually recur in interpretations of pitch structure should be pointed out here. First, bands and intervals are usually considered identical if they correspond to pairs of frequencies having equivalent ratios. For example, an interval that corresponds to a frequency ratio of $2^{1/12} : 1$ is considered equal to any other interval whose pitches correspond to frequencies in the same ratio ($2^{1/12} : 1$). Thus, gamuts are generally associated with geometric progressions of frequencies, such as the following: $2^{0/12}$ ($= 1$), $2^{1/12}$, $2^{1/6}$, $2^{1/4}$, $2^{1/3}$, $2^{5/12}$, $2^{1/2}$, etc. (e.g., c, $c\sharp$, d, $d\sharp$, e, f, $f\sharp$, ...). Another convention might have been chosen. For example, in the ethnomusicological literature, there is frequent reference to pitches whose corresponding frequencies form an arithmetic progression of natural numbers: 1, 2, 3, 4, etc. This is, of course, the renowned overtone series. The choice of a particular convention is not prescribed by the theory presented here: any convention that gives rise to the best interpretation is eligible (see, however, Rahn 1978b, 69–71).

Second, in most music, it would seem that an interval corresponding to an octave provides the basis for an important modular periodicity. This is expressible in terms of the following geometric progression: 2^0 ($= 1$), 2^1, 2^2, 2^3, 2^4, etc. (e.g., c, c^1, c^2, c^3, c^4, ...). Again, the present theory does not prescribe octave equivalence, allowing as it does any non-unit intervals to be considered modular, but neither does it forbid or discourage octave equivalence. The octave is but one of many intervals that might be considered modular. The theory provides only that some intervals might be considered modular; it does not specify which ones (see, however, chapter 11).

All that has been said about intervals and durations could have referred equally well to interval bands or duration spans. The essential relationship in terms of which gamuts and pulsations are defined is that of identity. If intervals or durations belong to the same band, they can be considered to be identical to each other; from this, gamuts and pulsations and the full complement of resultant, unit, and modular bands can be inferred. Such bands lack nothing in precision and often give rise to a gain in interpretive flexibility: they are just as important as 'pure' intervals or durations.

BISECTION

The relationship between bands and quantification is not restricted to pulsations. On the contrary, it gives rise to one of the more important corollary notions in the theory, namely, 'bisection' (cf. Rahn 1976a; 1977a; 1977b; 1978a, chaps. 4–7; 1978c; 1978d; 1981a).

If something is bisected, we usually mean that it is cut into two equal parts. For example, an interval of twelve semitones can be cut into two equal intervals of six semitones each. Similarly, an interval of ten can be cut into two of five; one of eight into two of four, and so forth. The case with even-numbered quantities is obviously straightforward. But how does one divide a span or band that consists of an odd number of units? For example, a span of three quarter notes or a band of seven semitones. To infer a pulsation of eighth notes or a gamut of quarter tones where there were no eighths or quarter tones inferable from the observables would be to open a Pandora's box of entities which have no empirical justification. A solution to the problem of bisection when the inferable units are too large is, in fact, not difficult to achieve. It merely involves redefining bisection.

Though it might not be clear what one half is, it is clear that one half is less than the whole and greater than one third. It is also clear that two halves make a whole. These two points help to clarify the problem of cutting an interval of, for example, seven semitones into two parts. The candidates include the complementary pairs (0, 7), (1, 6), (2, 5), and (3, 4). Of these, (0, 7) can be discarded immediately: a half is less than the whole (7). Similarly, (1, 6) and (2, 5) can be withdrawn because 1 and 2 are less than a third of 7: one half is larger than one third. This leaves the pair (3, 4). Bands of three and four semitones are both less than the whole and greater than a third, and together their sum is the whole.

In order to avoid the use of integers, a half can also be defined in terms of extents. The following convention is applicable. If two extents, x and y, are tangential and together they are coextensive with another extent, z, they are complements of the third extent (figure 5.1). If two units in the 'grid' (i.e., pulsation or gamut) of one of the two extents (e.g., y) are as long as or longer than the third extent, and if three units in the grid of the other of the two extents (e.g., x) are as long as or longer than the third extent, then the two extents are halves of the other extent (figure 5.2). The use of the numbers two and three in defining this convention can also be done away with. 'Two units' can be replaced by 'a set of tangential spans such that no span is between other spans of the set,' and 'three units' can be replaced by 'a set of spans such that one and only one span is between other spans.' In this way, bisection can be defined without recourse to numbers higher than 2.

It follows from this that spans of 3 can be bisected, for example, into 1 and 2; 5 into 2 and 3; and 7 into 3 and 4. It also follows that many even-numbered spans can be bisected in more than one way. For example, 12 can be bisected into 6 and 6, 5 and 7, or 4 and 8.

In a sense, all of this is an extension of the principle of extents. Ranges of extents from one to two units of 3, from two to three units of 5, from three to four units of 7, from three to six units of 9, and so forth are held to be equivalent. Indeed, the notion of extent is made even more specific here by introducing a convention in terms of which extent sizes can be defined as halves.

The notion of bisection is useful in expressing the common theoretical basis of so-called additive and divisive metres. From the examples in figure 5.3, one can see that repeated bisection might give rise to a hierarchy of durations: the units on the lower levels are included in the upper levels. A notated instance of this hierarchical structure can be observed in the familiar tune of example 5.26. Here, every attack coincides with one or more levels of the pulsations, which are in a hierarchical relationship of bisection.

Relationships of bisection are not restricted to temporal values: intervals and

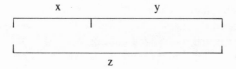

FIGURE 5.1

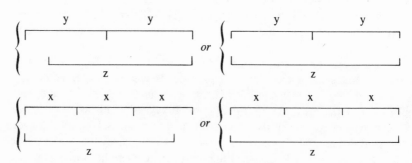

FIGURE 5.2

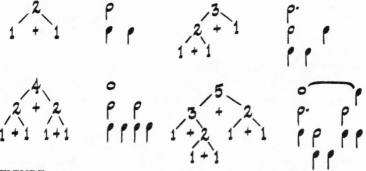

FIGURE 5.3

pitch bands can also be bisected. In example 5.27 *g–b* is bisected by *g–a* and *a–b*, and *g–b*, in turn, bisects *g–d*. Once again, repeated bisection gives rise to a hierarchy.

One cannot overestimate the aesthetic value of such hierarchical arrangements. They introduce into an interpretation maximum richness by means of maximum economy. In $4 = 2 + 2 = (1 + 1) + (1 + 1)$, one can see that a single relationship, 'is a half of', unites three types of durations (4, 2, and 1). The durations of the first level are to those of the second level as those of the second

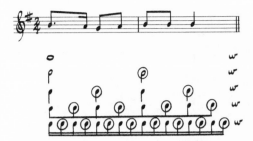

5.26 Circled notes mark the points of bisection of longer durations in the next higher levels.

5.27

level are to those of the third. In the case of $5 = 3 + 2 = (1 + 2) + (1 + 1) = (1 + (1 + 1)) + (1 + 1)$ one can observe a similar type of economical richness with an added feature: determinate ambiguity. Durations of one unit appear on two different levels. In this way, the 'same' thing has two types of significance. In order to maximize these aesthetic properties, two more notions will be developed presently: selection and cycle.

CYCLES AND SELECTION

In major-minor tonality, one frequently makes a distinction between pitches that belong to the scale of a piece and those that do not: those that belong are called diatonic and the remainder are termed chromatic. One way of stating this dichotomy is to say that the seven pitch classes that belong to the scale form a subset of the twelve pitch classes that form the chromatic gamut. Similarly, pitches of the pentatonic scale can be regarded as a subset of the twelve-semitone gamut or as a subset of the diatonic scale of seven pitch classes. Yet another way of discussing these relationships is in terms of selection: seven are chosen from twelve, and five are chosen from twelve or seven. The possible types of selection are many, but only one will be dealt with here, namely, cyclic bisection (cf. Rahn 1977a, 1978c).

In music based on the chromatic scale, the modular interval that defines pitch classes corresponds to an interval of twelve semitones. Intervals that bisect this modular interval correspond to a range of from four to eight semitones. Of these, the interval of seven semitones and its complement of five semitones are prime

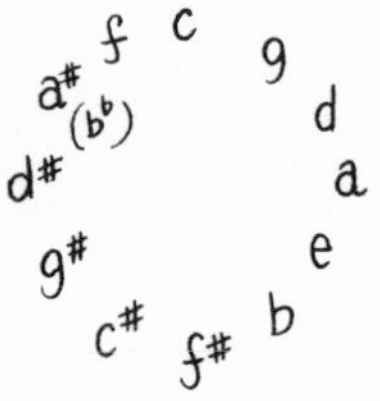

FIGURE 5.4

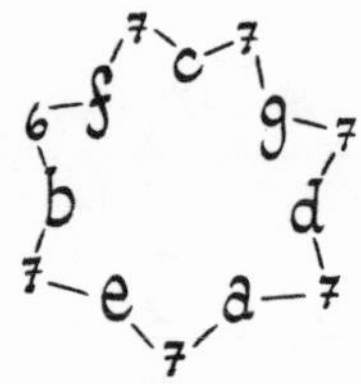

FIGURE 5.5

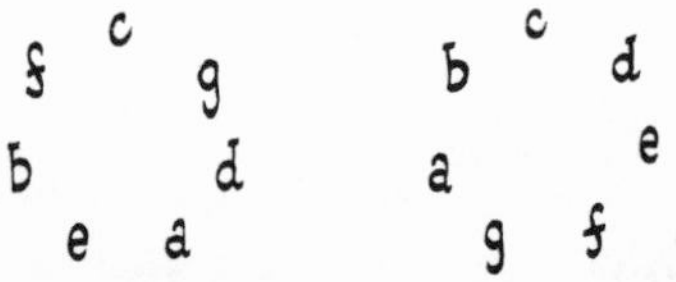

FIGURE 5.6

to the modular interval: 12 and 7 (or 5) share no common factors. This is not true of 4 (or 8) and 6, which share the common factors 2 and 4, and 3 and 6, respectively, with 12. Since 7 is prime to 12, a cycle of pitches can be defined such that each pitch is seven semitones from adjacent members of the cycle, and all twelve pitch classes belong to the cycle (figure 5.4). This cycle, famous from its early appearance in Chinese music theory, has two special features: it is uniform, because every pitch is separated from adjacent members of the cycle by the same interval (7), and it is improper since all pitch classes of the twelve are chosen and none is rejected. In such a 'selection,' there is no distinction between diatonic and chromatic tones. The only change to the original set of twelve pitch classes is the addition of a new basis for arranging them. Prior to the inference of this uniform and improper cycle, the only basis for arrangement was in terms of the relationships of adjacency and simple bisection.

By contrast, the cycle according to which the diatonic scale is selected is marked by intervallic diversity and propriety of selection: intervals of seven and six semitones are involved, and the resulting cycle forms a collection of pitch classes that constitute a true, or 'proper,' subset of the original twelve (figure 5.5).

Although the intervals used are diverse, they are united by both being bisectors of the modular interval 12, and the exceptional interval occurs only once. All of the scales considered in this study share properties of the diatonic collection just described: they are cyclic selections from a gamut; they are based on intervals that bisect the modular interval; they form proper subsets of a gamut; and they involve diverse intervals between adjacent members of the cycle. Another prop-

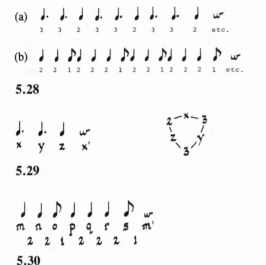

5.28

5.29

5.30

erty that these scales share is that there is a correlation between the cyclical ordering and the original ordering based on adjacency.

This correlation can be demonstrated by comparing the 'cycle of fifths' outlined in figure 5.5 with the 'cycle of seconds' which results when the pitches selected by cycling are compared in terms of adjacency (figure 5.6). As can be seen, intervals (such as *f–g, g–a, a–b, b–c*) that are two steps apart in the cycle of fifths are always one step apart in the cycle of seconds.

A final property shared by all of the scales I will be dealing with is that every interval in a cycle has a bisector within the cycle. For example, *f–a* (4) is bisected by *g* into 2 + 2, *e–g* (3) is bisected by *f* into 1 + 2, and *f–c* (7) is bisected by *a* into 4 + 3. The same holds true for seconds, fourths, sixths, and sevenths. The significance of this property is great. If the pitches of the diatonic collection are arranged by adjacency, every pitch is midway between the adjacent pitches, i.e., every pitch bisects the adjacent ones. In the original gamut (*c, c♯, d, d♯, e, ... b*) this is also true. Thus, cyclic bisection transfers the features of equidistance, by which gamuts are ultimately defined, to a subset: in this way, the scale represents a new 'gamut' in which the principle of approximate bisection is transferred from interval bands to bands of intervals (cf. Rahn 1977a, where similar features are found in scales around the world).

All that has been said about pitch cycles could be said about rhythmic cycles. The notion that time can move in circles might seem rather odd at first. However, one has only to consider calendars and clock faces to find concrete images of time swallowing its own tail. Since rhythmic cycles parallel pitch cycles, only two examples need be cited (example 5.28). The first, so-called Habanera rhythm (a), is familiar from many African or African-derived pieces. A cycle based on the bisection of eight eighths by 3 + 5 eighths and five eighths by 3 + 2 eighths provides the basis (example 5.29). (A superscript denotes a moment belonging to the same modular class as a moment bearing the same letter: cf. x and x'.) Example (b) corresponds to a percussion pattern that is widespread in Africa. It is based on a sevenfold cycle of a seven eighth-note duration mixed with one instance of a six eighth-note duration within the context of a modular interval of twelve eighth notes (example 5.30). The parallel with the cycle for the seven-tone diatonic scale which was described above is striking. Indeed, this pattern can be considered a translation into moments of the pitches of the diatonic scale.

SUMMARY

Throughout the discussion thus far the same concepts have been applied to the descriptions of both pitch and time relationships. From this arises an important problem in analysis. On the one hand, the description of a piece ideally contains only relationships inferred from the observables. Thus, a piece consisting of the events in example 5.31 might be described as having three moments of attack such that one could infer two pulsations, one of which bisects the other (example 5.32). As far interpretation goes, this is a two-pulsations piece in which one pulsation bisects the other. By the same token, example 5.33 is a two-gamut piece in which one gamut bisects the other. Were it not for the difference between moments and pitches, the two pieces would be indistinguishable. One can translate the rhythmic relationships of any piece into pitch relationships, and vice versa. The two aspects are interchangeable and one can often 'reverse' a piece, as shown in example 5.34. Here, the succession of two and one semitones in (a) becomes a succession of two and one eighth-notes in (b), and the periodic succession of dotted eighth notes in (a) becomes the gamut succession of whole tones in (b). If one wanted to 'save a primitive', one could dispense with the distinction between pitches and moments and refer to them jointly as merely *points* (as was done above to save space). This, however, seems to be one place where a phenomenal distinction is necessary: pitches and moments are different things, though their interpretations might be similar. In certain pieces of the 'totally serial' variety, the two types of events can be reversed, but not in the music I will be dealing with. Also, the two types of events are not strictly interchangeable. An interval is always bisected by a pitch, and a duration by a moment, not vice versa. Accordingly, the desire for systematic economy yields in this case to common sense and pragmatism. Nevertheless, the basic parallelism of pitch and time relationships should not go unnoticed.

Even at this point in the development of the theory, one can observe a bifurcation between twelve-tone music and the systems I will be describing later. In twelve-tone music – or, more properly, in its theory – each interval has only one value and two different intervals are never equated. Thus, in twelve-tone music theory one simply describes for instance, c–g as seven semitones, c–$f\sharp$ as six semitones, or c–$a\flat$ as eight semitones. But the systems I will be dealing with are all based on approximate bisection, so that intervals of six, seven, or eight semitones might also be considered to be identical with one another in their function of being halves of twelve semitones. In twelve-tone theory, no such similarity is posited among such 'different' intervals.

This determinate ambiguity in systems based on bisection is only one facet of their deep-seated richness. Some of this richness can be summarized here. First, all of the relationships described thus far can be economically defined in terms of the concepts of set, identity, adjacency, and pitch or moment (as well as the truth-functional predicates 'and,' 'or,' 'not,' which are presumed in any formal system). Second, all relationships that are based on pitches have parallels based on moments (and vice versa). Third, the relationship of identity is equally applicable to pitches and moments, and intervals and durations, just as the notion of adjacency is applicable to pitches and moments, bands and spans, intervals and durations, and interval bands and duration spans. Furthermore, pulsations and gamuts are ultimately defined in terms of identity and adjacency as are relationships of bisection, and modular intervals give rise to classes of pitches and moments. Finally, linear and cyclic organizations of pitch and time, though they appear contradictory, are in fact derivable from the same primitive concepts and can be linked to one another as can be done where features of gamuts are transferred to scales.

All of this has been accomplished without recourse to quantitative notions such as 'higher than' and 'before.' Whether such concepts need to be introduced and if so, when, are issues of great importance. For example, if there were no notion of 'higher than,' rather only a notion of 'in a different direction from,' the two pieces in example 5.35 would have to be considered identical. In some instances, such pairs of pieces might be considered identical, and in other instances they might not. In the music I will be discussing, distinctions between higher and lower, and before and after, often turn out to be important, not necessarily for the interpretation of an individual piece, but for the description of a repertory. Accordingly, they will be introduced in chapter 6.

6

Orientation and Reference

The type of rhythm and pitch constructs that I have described thus far might be conveyed by the image of an anchorless ship: pulsations, gamuts, and scales seem to float on a linear or cyclic sea without reference to a stable point. In order to describe a specific interval, such as g–b, or a given time-interval, such as that between the attacks of the third and fourth tones of example 6.1, one can, so far, only describe it as belonging to a given gamut, scale, or pulsation and then point to it. In this sense, such constructs are merely 'referential' for the tones. Greater economy can be imparted to a description by anchoring it in some way, that is, by providing points of focus or orientation.

♩ ♩ ♩ ♫ ♩

6.1

A spatial analogy can serve to convey the effect of orientation. Suppose, for example, that one is dropped in the middle of a desert with a map. If one does not know which direction corresponds to the map's north, one is lost. However, if one waits until sunset or sunrise a way out is possible. Such natural phenomena provide good indications of west and east respectively. Once west or east is known, the other directions can be inferred. The specific direction that is the basis for such inferences is irrelevant: any direction will do. Phenomena such as sunsets and sunrises provide an economical means of orientation because only one piece of information need be given and many other pieces fall into place: south, northwest, east-by-southeast, and so forth.

RELATIVE ORIENTATION

Similarly, if one pitch class of a cycle is labelled, the other pitch classes will fall into place. For example, if one member of the cycle is labelled 'o', the other

FIGURE 6.1

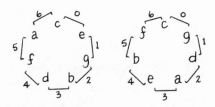

FIGURE 6.2

c d e f g a b $[c^1]$

0 1 2 3 4 5 6 $[7(=0)]$

FIGURE 6.3

members – depending on the intervals that they form with it – can be labelled 1, 2, 3, etc. (figure 6.1). In a cycle with seven members, there will be seven labels: 0, 1, 2, 3, 4, 5, 6.

Such cycles can be rewritten as cycles of thirds or fifths as well, and an interval, rather than a pitch, can be chosen as the basis for orientation, so that schemes like those in figure 6.2 might result. Since these cyclic schemes are fully symmetrical, the numbering can be reversed: 1 becoming 6, 2 becoming 5, 3 becoming 4, and vice versa. In summary, if a pitch class or interval class is assigned a special orienting value, all the pitches and intervals in the observables can be assigned values relative to the orienting value, so that the relationship between any pitch and any other pitch can be expressed economically.

Similar economies can be introduced into the description of rhythmic features. For example, the pulsations inferable from the durational values in example 6.2 can be co-ordinated by orienting them about the first or last attack. (Parentheses

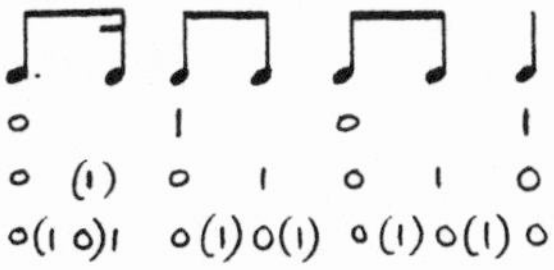

♩. ♪ ♪ ♪ ♪ ♪ ♩

```
o       i       o       i
o  (i)  o   i   o   i   o
o(i o)i  o (i)o(i)  o (i)o(i) o
```

6.2

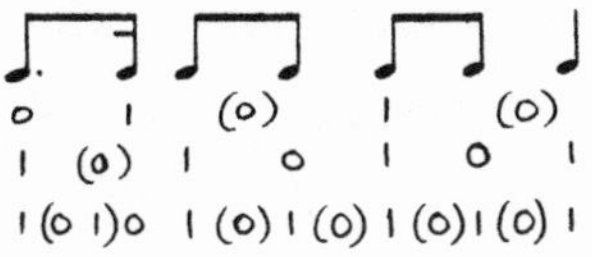

♩. ♪ ♪ ♪ ♪ ♪ ♩

```
o       i      (o)      i      (o)
i  (o)  i       o       i       o      i
i(o i)o  i (o)i (o) i (o)i (o) i
```

6.3

| ♩ ♩ | ♩ ♩ | 𝅸 |

```
o   i   o   i   o
```

6.4

indicate values that have no direct correlates in the observables but are implied by them.) Once again, any moment can be considered orienting and labelled 'o.'

Although the assignment of an orienting value to a class of pitches, moments, or intervals can be arbitrary, it may also be strategic, adding to the interpretation's unity. For instance, the hierarchical assignment of orienting values described in example 6.2 obviously unifies the interpretation more than the scheme of example 6.3. In this type of hierarchy, values at a higher level (e.g., line one of example 6.2) imply values at a lower level. In an oriented structure, 'o' is defined as the orienting value, that which implies other values. In a true hierarchy, as in example 6.2, o at a higher level implies o at a lower level. This makes the interpretation economical by introducing redundancy. In example 6.2, these economies are maximized; in example 6.3 they are minimized.

By means of a referential value, a mode and a measure can be distinguished from a gamut or a scale on the one hand and a pulsation on the other. For example, the pitches of the C-major mode can be numbered as in figure 6.3 and measures of 2–4 can be notated as in example 6.4. At this point, however, the effect is still rather superficial. The real justification for singling out one class of pitches or moments as orienting is to be found in the new relationships that it adds to the interpretation. One of these new relationships is that between a melodic dissonance and its resolution.

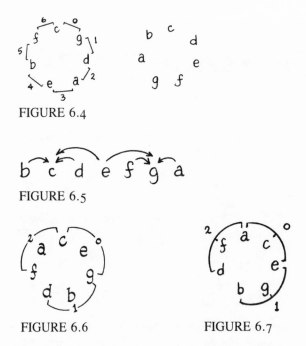

FIGURE 6.4

FIGURE 6.5

FIGURE 6.6   FIGURE 6.7

In the cycle shown in figure 6.4, if interval c–g is termed 0, g–d is termed 1, etc., a special property of seven-tone scales is revealed. Since $1 + 6 = 7$ (the modular interval of intervals), interval g–d ($= 1$) is the symmetrical partner of f–c ($= 6$). Similarly, d–a ($= 2$) and b–f ($= 5$) as well as a–e ($= 3$) and e–b ($= 4$) are symmetrically placed. In terms of figure 6.4, pitch class f (from interval 6) is adjacent to g and pitch class d (from interval 1, the symmetrical partner of 6) is adjacent to c; b (from 5) is adjacent to c and a (from 2) is adjacent to g; and e (from 4 and 3) bisects the interval c–g: in other words, symmetrical pairs correspond to symmetrical adjacency relationships. Note also that f is lower than g, and d is higher than c; similarly, b is lower than c and a is higher than g. Such a correspondence is indicative of a high degree of symmetry in seven-tone modes.

This symmetry can be exploited in the definition of special sets of pitch classes within a mode. These sets can be termed *voices*. Each member of the referential sonority (c and g, in this instance), together with the adjacent degrees described above (b and d, and a and f, respectively), as well as the bivalent bisector (e) constitute a voice. The two voices of the c, or Ionian mode, above, are thus b–c–d–e and e–f–g–a. The tonic dyad can be defined as orienting for the piece,

6.5

6.6

6.7

that is, *c* and *g* can be considered resolutions for the other pitches. If an arrow is used to represent the relationship between melodic dissonance and its reso- lution, the symmetrical arrangement of figure 6.5 emerges. Examples of places where such voice-leading is found include the familiar late medieval and Renaissance cadences. For example, in a cadence to *c* and *g* (example 6.5), the pitches *d* and *b* are resolved into *c*, and *f* is resolved into *g* (cf. Rahn, 1978c, 1981b).

If a triad, rather than an interval or dyad, is considered the focus of the mode, special features of the major-minor system become apparent (figure 6.6). Here, the triads *g–b–d* (1) and *f–a–c* (2) are symmetrically arranged around the tonic triad *c–e–g*. Strikingly, the intervals in all three triads are identical: *c–g* = *g–d* = *f–c* = 7/12 or 4/7; *c–e* = *g–b* = *f–a* = 4/12 or 2/7; and *e*, *b*, and *a* bisect *c–g*, *g–d*, and *f–c*, respectively, at the levels of both the gamut (twelve semitones to the octave) and the scale (seven degrees to the octave). Again, symmetry is revealed: *a* (from triad 2) is adjacent to and above *g*, whereas *b* (from triad 1) is adjacent to and below *c*; *f* (from 2) is adjacent to and above *e*, and *d* (from 1) is adjacent to and below *e* (example 6.6). An analogous situation holds for the minor mode (figure 6.7). Here all three triads are also identical: *a–e* = *e–b* = *d–a* = 7/12 or 4/7; *a–c* = *e–g* = *d–f* = 3/12 or 2/7; and *c*, *g*, and *f* bisect *a–e*, *e–b*, and *d–a*, respectively. A similar symmetry is revealed: *f* (from 2) is adjacent to and above *e*, and *g* (from 1) is adjacent to and below *a*; *d* (from 2) is adjacent to and above *c*, and *b* (from 1) is adjacent to and below *c* (example 6.7).

The orienting pitch (o) can be termed the *tonic* and the orienting interval or triad can be termed the *tonic sonority*. The remaining pitches, intervals, and triads can be defined as *dissonant* and can be considered *resolved* into these orienting pitches, intervals, or triads.

ABSOLUTE ORIENTATION

Precedence
Until now, moments have been arranged linearly and cyclically in terms of adjacency and derived notions. In this way, the pitch succession *a, c, e* has been considered identical to its retrograde, *e, c, a*, since all relationships based on adjacency (e.g., next to, between, and beyond) are preserved in the reversed version. Moreover, though the assignment of an oriental value (e.g., o) to a pitch or moment gives rise to special relationships of symmetry, the description of one event as earlier or later does not change the relationships inferable: the relationship 'earlier than' embodies a form of absolute (i.e., not relative) orientation.

To introduce the notion of precedence, one need only define the relationship of 'before.' Such a relationship is irreflexive (a moment cannot be before itself), antisymmetric (if A is before B, B cannot be before A) and transitive (if A is before B, and B is before C, then A is before C).

The relationship of precedence in combination with that of adjacency gives rise to a considerable number of corollary relationships. For example, one moment can be just before another if it is both before and adjacent to the other moment. Two or more moments can be before one or more moments. And in a given span, the extreme that is before all other moments is the first. Other relationships result if, in the above statements, the term 'span' or 'duration' is substituted for 'moment,' 'after' replaces 'before,' and 'last' fills in for 'first.'

Altitude
Just as one moment can be described as before or after another, one pitch can be described as higher or lower than another. As has already been observed, any piece can be turned upside-down without affecting syntactical relationships. Nevertheless, in many repertoires (i.e., groups of pieces), altitude is treated in a consistent manner. The finalis in Gregorian chant almost invariably corresponds to the lower version of the tonic pitch class, not the higher. There are recurrent overall downward trends in much of the music of preliterate societies, but no

recurrent upward trends have been reported. The Yuman rise is just that – a rise, not a fall, in the middle of a song. Whether this is the result of cultural conventions or psychological principles is quite beside the point here, and, in any event, probably unprovable at present. What is important is that similar pieces often betray an asymmetry with respect to altitude. Descents are often preferred at ends of pieces; melodies are often located in the upper registers of homophonic pieces; and rises often occur in the middle of pieces. To ignore such regularities would be to miss important aspects of several repertories.

As was the case with precedence, a number of corollary relationships can be posited once 'higher than' has been introduced. A pitch can be just above another by being both adjacent to and higher than the other pitch. Two or more pitches can be above one or more pitches. And in a given band, the extreme that is above all other pitches is the highest. Other relationships result if, in the above statements, *band* or *interval* is substituted for *pitch*, *below* replaces *above*, and *lowest* fills in for *highest*.

LOUDNESS

Much that has been said about pitch and time could well be claimed for loudness. As was true of pitches and moments, loudnesses have no proper parts, can be identified, and are describable as adjacent to other loudnesses. Bands (or 'strips') of loudnesses can be identified. However, beyond this point, the parallel breaks down. If one considers two pitches or moments, it is not difficult to find a mathematical scale by which an interval or duration can be compared with another; for example, a geometrical progression for pitches, and an arithmetical progression for moments. However, there appears to be no useful scale for identifying 'intervals' of loudness. Consequently, there appear to be no modular intervals for identifying 'classes' of loudnesses. Thus, the functions of loudnesses seem generally to involve emphasis or interference with relationships already present in pitch-time structures and articulation of foreground events. The latter is achieved, for instance, by differences in loudness between the beginning and subsequent portions of a tone. Even here, however, there is a typical skewing in favour of louder values: the commencement or attack of a tone is marked by a sharp increase in volume rather than a decrease. In a similar way, timbral distinctions can serve to segment a span into subspans.

TIMBRE AND SONANCE

Timbre and sonance have not been taken as primitive because a timbre, or 'an envelope,' is really a composite of pitch, time, and loudness. In other words, timbres, unlike the three primitive qualities, do have proper parts. For example, a vibrato is a periodic succession of pitches within a given band, and a tremolo is a periodic succession of loudnesses within a loudness band. Similarly, a formant is a group of pitches within given bands of pitch and loudness, and a spectrum (or a timbre, in the narrow sense of the word) is a set of pitches of various loudnesses.

Just as sets of pitches, loudnesses, or moments can be identified and compared, so too can timbres. For example, an *a* (ah) sound can be identified as such, can be considered adjacent to other phonetic variants of *a*, or adjacent to *o* (oh) and *e* (eh), and can be placed into the pitch continuum: *i* (ee), *e* (eh), *a* (ah), *o* (oh), *u* (oo). The basis for ordering consists in the altitudes of pitch bands that define the formant in each case. In a similar way, vibratos and tremolos can be identified and compared according to their pitch or loudness widths as well as their frequencies. Finally, attacks and releases (or decays) can also be identified by their pitch and loudness qualities and compared in terms of their times and loudnesses. However, just as in the case of loudness, there appears to be no basis for ordering timbres in terms of intervals. This is because a suitable scale for complex qualities is lacking, and no pieces have been found that suggest or encourage the use of such a scale.

PROXIMITY

One conclusion to be drawn from the preceding sections is that almost any part of the observables can be compared with another part. If this is done according to adjacency or an intervallic scale, one finds that degrees of proximity obtain among the observables. The corollary notion of proximity has considerable importance for the theory presented here. It clarifies a number of recurrent issues. It also yields some anomolous (but nevertheless valid) interpretations that rear their heads because of the multiplicity of different but interrelated scales on the basis of which the relative proximity of events can be assessed. In example 6.8 one can see a conflict between pitch and band conceptions of measurement. In terms of the twelve-semitone gamut of pitch bands from which these tones are drawn, intervals x and y are identical in size; that is, *f♯* and *c♯* are in equal proximity to *g* and *c*, respectively. However, at the level of nuance (cf. Rahn 1978b), the *f♯* and *c♯* are both raised in pitch in their functions as leading tones, so that *f♯* is closer to *g* than *c* is to *c♯*.

In example 6.9 a clash between gamut- and scale-degree bases for determining proximity is evident. In terms of the twelve-semitone gamut, intervals x and y can be considered equal (three semitones each). But *e–g* represents an interval of two scale degrees and *c–d♯*, represents an interval of only one scale degree. In this sense, x is larger than y.

6.8

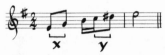

6.9

6.10

6.11

6.12

Mer-ri-ly we roll a-long

6.13

Relationships of bisection also give rise to ambiguities. In example 6.10 intervals x and y can be considered equal because pitch *d* bisects the interval *g*–*g*¹. Nevertheless, x is larger than y in terms of scale degrees and gamut steps.

Finally, cycles of pitch classes give rise to multivalent situations. In example 6.11, interval y is larger than interval x in all the respects just discussed, but in terms of the cycles of semitones and scale degrees, it is smaller. Similarly, if example 6.12 is interpreted modally in g-Dorian, interval x, the members of which belong to the same voice, is smaller than interval y, the pitches of which are drawn from different voices.

All that has been said of pitch intervals could be said of durations. With respect to loudness, mensural conflicts arise if individual loudnesses and bands are compared.

If an entire span is compared with another, the several possible scales give rise to constellations of proximities. In example 6.13 proximities can be posited between spans x and y, and x and z. Span x is farther from z if pitch, pitch class, gamut, or scale degree is taken as the criterion, and also if moment is taken into account. However, in terms of membership in the orienting sonority (g–b–d) and the orienting hierarchy of pulsations of eighth-note and quarter-note time intervals, x is closer to z than y is. If the relationships between x and y and y and z are considered, one finds an instance of a recurring type of relationship known as a *process*.

The pitch of x is higher than the pitch of y by two gamut degrees and one scale degree, and the same relationships obtain between y and z. Since similar relationships hold between pairs (x and y, and y and z) that succeed each other immediately (since x is before y, which is before z), a 'process of measured descent' can be inferred. Interestingly, in terms of timbre, the formants of the vowels of x, y, and z are related processively as well: the formant of E (in mer-) is lower than the formant of I (in ri-), which in turn is lower than the formant of i (in -ly). This gives rise to the inference of an ascending formant process, which is in contrary motion to the pitch process (example 6.13). In later chapters, one will find a number of examples of processes.

SUMMARY

A survey of the ground covered thus far is now in order. Truth-logical predicates and pre-syntactic concepts (set and identity) have been assumed from the outset. Notions that have great importance for music (pitch, moment, loudness, and timbre; adjacency; precedence and altitude) have been introduced. Of these notions the first four are phenomenally distinct. Although loudness relationships are similar to pitch and time relationships, no parallels have been found to the notions of, for example, interval, duration, gamut, and pulsation with regard to loudness.

The notion of adjacency has been found to be extremely fruitful because one can derive from it many of the rich relationships in both the theory and interpretation of music. The absolute notions of precedence, altitude, and intensity

6.14

give orientation to individual pieces and explain regularities within repertories (as in rises and falls in pitch).

Thus a number of notions have applications far beyond music; one notion, adjacency, is essential to interpret pieces; another, precedence, is desirable to interpret pieces; and the remainder are desirable to interpret repertories. Throughout the remainder of this study, then, I will restrict myself to these concepts and their derivatives.

In order to summarize the ideas introduced so far, interpretations of the entire children's song is offered (example 6.14). These interpretations could be extended further to reveal other features of the piece, but such elaborate analyses will be reserved for later. Moreover, the piece was chosen for its high degree of ambiguity: in accordance with this ambiguity, competing interpretations will be offered as a test of the approach developed above to evaluate interpretations. As will be seen, the result is a stalemate between two interpretations. This, in turn, is a situation that recurs so often that an explanation of how to deal with it will be offered as well.

TWO INTERPRETATIONS OF A CHILDREN'S SONG

The gamut from which the pitches are selected consists of twelve pitch classes to the octave. The scale selected from this gamut can be considered as consisting of either (a) *g–a–b–c–d–e–f♯* according to a cycle of seven-and six-semitone intervals [i.e., seven pitch classes selected from twelve by means of a cycle of seven and six semitones, or more briefly expressed, 7 from 12 by 7 (and 6)] (figure 6.8), or (b) *g–a–b–d–e* according to a cycle of seven- and eight-semitone intervals [i.e., five pitch classes selected from twelve by means of a cycle of seven and eight semitones, or 5 from 12 by 7 (and 8)] (figure 6.9). Under the first interpretation, *g–b–d* can be considered an oriental triad according to the symmetrical arrangement in figure 6.10. Here each triad consists of intervals of four scale degrees (*g–d, d–a, c–g*) and two scale degrees (*g–b, d–f♯, c–e*). Four degrees bisect seven, and are bisected by two. Furthermore, the four-degree

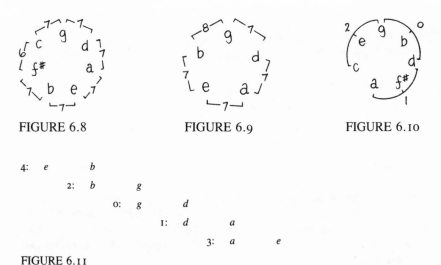

FIGURE 6.8   FIGURE 6.9   FIGURE 6.10

```
4:    e         b
         2:    b         g
              0:    g         d
                   1:    d         a
                        3:    a         e
```

FIGURE 6.11

intervals uniformly consist of seven semitones (which bisect twelve) and the two-degree intervals are all made up of four semitones (which bisect seven semitones).

According to the second interpretation, *g–d* could be considered the oriental dyad as shown by the symmetrical arrangement in figure 6.11. Here each triad consists of an interval of three scale degrees (*g–d, d–a, b–g, a–e, e–b*). Furthermore, *b* bisects *g–d* in terms of both scale degrees and the gamut. Thus, *g–b–d* can be considered an oriental triad.

If the pulsations in example 6.15 are considered referential, a striking correspondence with the oriental triad of both interpretations can be observed. With the exception of the circled moments, degrees that do not belong to the tonic triad (e.g., *a* in m. 3) are found only on the second (1) of a periodic pair (0 1). Thus, members of the tonic triad appear at any moment (0 or 1) but non-members generally appear only at odd moments (1). The inconsistent spots (which are circled) can be resolved by inferring a change of orientation to the dominant triad (4 in heptatonic, or 3 in pentatonic) at the points where they occur (example 6.16). In the heptatonic interpretation, 1 or 6 (*a–c–e* or *f♯–a–c*) might have been chosen as the temporary referential triad, rather than 4 (*d–f♯–a*), and in the pentatonic interpretation 4 (*a–e*) might have been selected instead of 3 (*d–a*). However, the intervals of 4/7 in heptatonic and 3/5 in pentatonic play such a large role in the interpretations that the dominants are chosen for the sake of unity and economy. Furthermore, the notions of hierarchy, proximity, and ori-

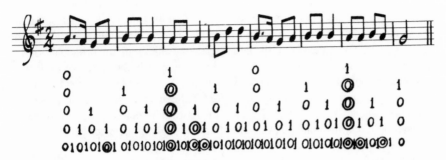

6.15

6.16

6.17

entation lead one to prefer to posit the more central triads of the cycle that is based on the hierarchically superior interval of four or three scale degrees in heptatonic or pentatonic, respectively. The reason for the 'fifth's' hierarchical superiority is its status as the bisector of the modular interval of an octave.

In both interpretations, final extremes (or ends) play a large role. The final pitch of the piece is g (0), whereas the last pitch of the first half is d, the dominant (4 in heptatonic, and 3 in pentatonic), which bisects the modular interval on the tonic ($g-g^1$). Thus, the end of the larger span coincides with the principal oriental pitch class of the piece, whereas the next shorter span in the hierarchy ends with the next principal pitch. Similarly, descending one more level in the hierarchy, two-measure units end with the bisector of the interval formed by these two principal pitches (i.e., b that bisects $g-d$). Also to be noted is that a processive pulsation of quarter-note attacks is presented throughout the piece but interrupted at the end (circled in example 6.17).

Finally, foreground adjacency plays a large role in the piece, whichever of the two interpretations is chosen. According to the heptatonic interpretation, temporally adjacent tones are, with two exceptions, also adjacent in terms of scale degrees. The two exceptions (mm. 4–5) involve members of the tonic triad that are already resolved in any case. According to the pentatonic interpretation, all temporally adjacent tones are also adjacent in terms of scale degrees.

The advantage of the heptatonic interpretation is that it defines an isomorphism among the triads. In the pentatonic interpretation, there is only one triad posited, albeit a special, oriental one. The advantage of the pentatonic interpretation is that it provides a closer fit to the observables: a construct of only five tones is posited to account for relationships among four tones in the piece, whereas a construct of seven tones is posited in the heptatonic interpretation. However, despite the fact that only four of the seven tones in the diatonic collection appear, 'Merrily We Roll Along' would seem to belong to a song type that (a) is found in the English-speaking children's repertoire and (b) depends for its musical definition on a formulation cast in terms of seven rather than five tones (cf. Rahn 1981c: 44–8).

One can observe the possibility for ambiguity between heptatonic and pentatonic interpretations. However, this need not be considered a sign of weakness of either the system of interpretation or the pieces themselves, for ambiguity properly understood does not imply vagueness or indeterminacy: it merely means that two equally valid interpretations can be derived from a single set of observables. Just as in a pun one gets two meanings for the price of a single word or phrase, so too in much music that encourages various pentatonic and heptatonic interpretations one can derive two or more interpretations from a single set of observables. An interpretation that neglected such determinate ambiguity would be similar to an interpretation of works by Joyce or Shakespeare that left out the plays on words: only half the story would be told about the observables.

The principal function of loudness in this piece appears to consist in the patterning of tone attacks. The interrupted pulsation in quarter notes has already been dealt with. Another pattern is the succession of attacks in example 6.18, which coincides with measures of two quarter notes in the rhythmic hierarchy.

6.18

6.19

Timbres function similarly in that successions of timbres coincide with metrical units (example 6.19). The syllables 'roll along' coincide with one-measure units, and the sentence 'Merrily we roll along' coincides with two-measure units of the hierarchy. Interestingly, the latter units are found at the beginnings of the piece's two halves, whereas the distinction between tonic and dominant is highlighted at the ends of sections: here, timbre articulates beginnings in a repetitive way, whereas tonality distinguishes endings in a non-repetitive manner.

Additional determinate statements could be made about this piece, and these would unify the interpretation still further. Nevertheless, the analysis will stop here for the present because the point has been reached, which seems to occur in any interpretation, where the main course of analysis has been sufficiently established for further observations to suggest themselves in great numbers. The main problem in interpretation always seems to be to get off on the right foot at the outset: once this is done, the other steps fall readily into place.

The question of evaluating different interpretations has already arisen with regard to the children's song that has served as the principal musical example for the last two chapters. This question is pursued further within a different framework during the next chapter. There, specific pieces that have had considerable importance recently in ethnomusicology will be interpreted and, to a certain extent, the resulting analyses will be compared with those that have been offered in the past. In many of the pieces, traditional problems in analysis will be clarified and several will be seen for what they really are: pseudo-problems rather than true perplexities.

It might seem odd to devote such concentrated attention to individual pieces, given the emphasis in ethnomusicology on groups of pieces rather than individual works. Nevertheless, I think that there are two justifications for this course. First, a piece is logically prior to a repertoire, just as individual people, sentences, and chemical elements are implied by societies, paragraphs, and compounds, respectively. A second and more important justification is that one can offer a formal definition of a piece in terms of interpretation itself, which strongly suggests that one should deal with pieces before repertoires. According to such a definition, a piece is a set of observables among which relations of logic, identity, and adjacency are posited. This is in contrast with repertoires where such relationships are either not posited at all – as in the extreme case of a repertoire being a mere collection of unrelated pieces – or are posited less extensively. In other words, the observables of a piece are interrelated, whereas in a repertoire such interrelationships need not be advanced. For example, if an a^b is found in two sets of observables and a relationship of identity is posited between the two instances, the two pitches are considered to belong to the same piece. Otherwise, the two sets of observables are considered to represent two pieces that may or may not be grouped into a corpus. In effect, this means that two sets of observables might be considered to belong to the same piece with regard to aspects of tempo and timbre, and to two different pieces with regard to certain features of pitch and loudness. Since unity rather than diversity is sought in any interpretation, be it of a piece or a repertoire, the first place to find it will be in the individual piece where there is an interpretive imperative to seek unity. Accordingly, the central preoccupation of the following chapter will be with pieces regarded as sets of observables that are interrelated as intensively as possible.

PART III
APPLICATIONS

7

Some Pieces Reinterpreted

The present chapter offers interpretations of three pieces: a sweathouse song of the Flathead; a Hukwe song, ' Du:,' for voice and musical bow; and a *taqsim* for the *nai* in the Egyptian tonal system called *maqam nahawand*. Each of these has been transcribed and analysed before.

As far as possible, the transcriptions have been checked by me against the original recordings and revised where necessary. By and large, the differences between the transcriptions that appear here and those previously published are either non-existent or slight. By 'slight,' I mean that if the interpretations resulting from the various transcriptions are compared, one finds that the more background, deep, or global aspects are similar, for the discrepancies between transcriptions merely correspond to relatively foreground, superficial, or local features of the analyses. (Interestingly, the most profound differences in transcription are to be found in ' Du:,' which is the only one of the three originally transcribed by scholars who were rather unfamiliar with the music of the culture concerned. By contrast, Alan Merriam, and Bruno Nettl and Ronald Riddle had long and intimate contact with music of the Flathead, and of the Middle East, respectively, when they transcribed the examples that appear here.) Not only are the pieces retranscribed but, more importantly, they are reinterpreted and previous analyses are reassessed. For the most part, interpretive shortcomings similar to those discussed in previous chapters (especially 2 and 3) are not belaboured here; more subtle problems are dealt with.

A number of analytic traps await the unwary interpreter of individual pieces. Two of these traps occur with such frequency that they deserve special discussion. These are the pitfalls of negative formulation and confusion of levels.

By 'negative formulation,' I mean the description of a thing in terms of what it is not, rather than what it is. In Western music theory, there are several terms that embody such a negative approach. For example, a *non-harmonic* tone – as its name suggests – is considered to be one that does not belong to the chord that is orienting at the time. Chromatic tones are often described as though they were simply non-diatonic. Syncopation is considered to be a deviation from the oriental metrical organization. And so forth. But if a tone is non-harmonic, chromatic, or syncopated, one still wants to know what kind of tone it is, rather than merely what kind of tone it is not. This is not to deny the importance of recognizing such dichotomies as those between harmonic and non-harmonic, diatonic and chromatic, or commetric and syncopated. Rather it is to encourage making further distinctions within these categories in order that further dichotomies can be established. Such distinctions are not merely classificatory, in the narrow sense of the word; rather, when functionalized, they give rise to extra levels of the hierarchical constructs by which the piece is interpreted. In this way, far from being otiose, they enhance the richness of an interpretation. Another way of viewing such distinctions is to regard them as determining contexts in which unresolved dissonances can be considered resolved by intensifying the hierarchical constructions.

The second peril, 'confusion of levels,' really amounts to 'putting the cart before the horse,' for when levels are confused, a foreground phenomenon is assigned a background function, or vice versa. This frequently occurs with respect to timbres and loudnesses. For instance, it is a common practice to slice a piece into spans on the basis of distinctions between solo and choral singing, vocal and instrumental performance, loud and soft passages, and so forth. The problem with such an approach is that the notion of interval appears not to be applicable to timbres or loudnesses. Thus, the latter cannot yield relationships, such as those of bisection, in terms of which the richness of the hierarchical relationships in a piece can be most economically accounted for. One cannot, of course, negate the potential importance of such foreground features as changes of dynamics or patterns of timbre, but they should be assigned to their proper place in an interpretation. Indeed, relatively superficial phenomena should be accounted for as well as deeper structures and, in fact, often represent the most challenging aspects of a piece.

As one accumulates experience in interpreting pieces, one finds that each work presents unique challenges. For example, if one is used to dealing with works that feature only tones from the seven-tone diatonic collection, the experience gained will probably facilitate one's handling of pieces of this type, but new questions will inevitably arise. One's progress as an interpreter appears never to cease, for new questions continually emerge from the observables. For this reason, the following analyses will be presented in terms of problems that I have attempted to solve.

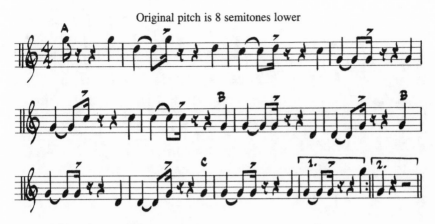

7.1 Sweathouse song (Merriam's version)

7.2 Sweathouse song (Kolinski's version)

SWEATHOUSE SONG OF THE FLATHEAD

The first piece to be discussed is a sweathouse song of the Flathead Indians of western North America. The song was originally transcribed and analysed by Alan Merriam (1967: 192–205; see example 7.1). Later, in a review of Merriam's study, Mieczyslaw Kolinski reanalysed Merriam's transcription and suggested a different barring (1970: 89–90; see example 7.2).

The barring of a piece is a matter of interpretation rather than of transcription,

7.3 Sweathouse song (Rahn's version)

since bars need not correspond to anything directly observable in the sounds. Thus, examples 7.1 and 7.2 convey a single transcription under two metrical interpretations. Finally, I myself retranscribed the piece (example 7.3).

As one can observe by comparing the three notations, Merriam did not notate the percussion accompaniment, which consists of sticks beating against rocks in the ritual sweathouse. Moreover, the meaningless syllables of the text and slight discrepancies which appear between the strophes were also ignored, as well as the registral distribution of voices. (Strophes can be defined here as the longest spans that resemble each other most closely.) Furthermore, I fail to discern any observable correlates to the loudness accents that appear in Merriam's transcription. What I do notice is that the tones marked with accents (by Merriam) are of relatively short duration, but that increases in loudness observed by me tend to coincide with rises in pitch rather than forming the periodic pattern that Merriam's accents suggest. However, these differences among the transcriptions are, for the most part, of little structural import, since here timbral, durational, registral, and loudness values do not yield a deep hierarchical organization as compared with pitches and moments. All the same, Kolinski bases his revised barring of the piece on the distribution of loudness accents in Merriam's transcription, preferring to have the stresses coincide with downbeats of measures. However, the stresses notated by Merriam are, as I have said, not particularly evident – to me at least. Furthermore, there need be – as Kolinski himself has pointed out (1973: 495–7) – no one-to-one correspondence between stress accents and a metrical hierarchy. Finally, his reading does not take into account the accompanying percussion part, which does not appear in the transcription by Merriam that was used as a basis for his analysis, nor does it account for the pitch organization, which, because of its possibilities for hierarchical depth in co-ordination with rhythmic relationships, one would expect to loom large in a metrical interpretation. One of the problems to be dealt with in this piece, then, consists in determining the best barring for the piece, in other words, orienting the observables metrically.

Only three pitches and their octaves are presented in the piece: g, c, and d. This set of pitches can be considered a section from any of the following cycles:

Cycle of twelve-semitone gamut:

$b\flat$–7–f–7–c–7–g–7–d–7–a–7–e–7–b–7–$f\sharp$–7–$c\sharp$–7–$g\sharp$–7–$d\sharp$–7–$a\sharp$ ($b\flat$)

Cycles of heptatonic scales derived from twelve semitones:

f–7–c–7–g–7–d–7–a–7–e–7–b–6–f

$f\sharp$–6–c–7–g–7–d–7–a–7–e–7–b–7–$f\sharp$

f–7–c–7–g–7–d–7–a–7–e–6–$b\flat$–7–f

f–7–c–7–g–7–d–7–a–6–$e\flat$–7–$b\flat$–7–f

f–7–c–7–g–7–d–6–$a\flat$–7–$e\flat$–7–$b\flat$–7–f

Cycles of pentatonic scales derived from twelve semitones:

c–7–g–7–d–7–a–7–e–8–c

c–7–g–7–d–7–a–8–f–7–c

c–7–g–7–d–8–$b\flat$–7–f–7–c

Merriam, by describing the piece's pitch collection as 'tritonic' or, more properly, 'tritypic' [i.e., a section of 3 from 12 by 7 (and 10)], appears to consider the first cycle to be referential for the piece, but as will be shown presently, this and the following heptatonic cycles would not enhance the interpretation as much as the intermediate inference of a five-cycle.

If one of the pentatonic cycles is considered referential, a number of interesting properties of the song emerge. First, there is a determinate relationship between the section c–g–d and the various cycles of five. If c–g–d is considered a scale that is derived from a pentatonic cycle by taking a section of three adjacent pitch classes therefrom, one finds that intervals of one degree (e.g., g–c, c–d, d–g) correspond to one or two degrees of the five-tone scale, and intervals of two degrees (such as g–d, c–g, and d–c) correspond to three or four degrees in pentatonic. Thus there is a determinate co-ordination of interval sizes expressed in terms of the three- and five-tone scales. Furthermore, there is a co-ordination of bisectors when the sizes of intervals are expressed in terms of the five-tone scale and the three-tone scale derived from it:

c bisects g–d into 1/3 + 1/3 and 2/5 + 1/5
d bisects c–g into 1/3 + 1/3 and 1/5 + 2/5
g bisects d–c into 1/3 + 1/3 and 2/5 + 2/5

Accordingly, with regard to bisection there is a strict correspondence between the three- and five-tone scales. This, however, is not the case with respect to seven- and twelve-tone cycles. For example, c divides g–d into 3/7 + 1/7 and 5/12 + 2/12, and neither of these divisions represents a bisection. There is no isomorphism in such interpretations and they are, accordingly, weaker in this regard. Thus, it appears preferrable to view the three pitch classes as the result of a selection of three from five (by 3 and 4) from twelve (by 7 and 8). (Note that c, g, and d represent a section rather than a cycle, because 4 does not bisect 5.)

If the three pitch classes are viewed in this way, g can be considered the tonic (o), and d the dominant (1). Also g–d can be considered the oriental dyad. From these interpretive decisions, the following points of co-ordination between the pitch and time structures of the song can be understood.

In the rhythmic scheme that dominates the piece (example 7.4), x can be considered oriental (i.e., the downbeat, or o), y the bisector of the modular interval x–x¹ (i.e., the upbeat of the whole measure, or 1° – read one of zero), and z the bisector of y–x¹ (i.e., the upbeat of a half measure, or 1¹). Moment y can also be considered the downbeat of the second half (0¹) (see example 7.5). Each downbeat (0°) is coterminous with a member of the tonic dyad (g–d),

♩. ♩. ♩ *w*
x y z x'

7.4

♩. ♩. ♩ *w*
x   y z (x')
0^0 1^0 (0^0)
    0^1 1^1 (0^0)

7.5

save in measures two and five. The latter represent a shift of the oriental dyad to *c–g*. (It is noteworthy that *g–d* and *c–g* are the only intervals in the scale that are of the same size: $2/3 = 3/5 = 5/12$). This is followed by a return to the tonic dyad, *g–d* from measure six to the end.

The overall rhythm of the piece can be considered next. The work divides into two halves, the second of which is extended by immediate repetition (figure 7.1). The last half is worth considering in more detail. Here the tonic dyad, *g–d* is oriental for the first two measures. The next two measures are an extension of the latter by means of immediate repetition, and the last measure is an extension of the penultimate, again by immediate repetition.

This interpretation of the piece's form is quite similar to Merriam's, who considers sections to be defined by precise repetition (cf. example 7.1). However, there is in his analysis no co-ordination of metrical, tonal, and repetitive aspects of the piece. (For example, A, B, and C are equated as sections though hierarchically distinct with regard to metre.) Kolinski's trisection of the piece into 4 + 4 + 3 measures is in great contrast to a bisection of it into 5 + 6 measures. All the same, Kolinski refers to the last three measures as 'coda-like' (1970: 90), suggesting the role that immediate repetition plays in the extension.

One of the central problems in interpreting this piece has been the fact that it presents both a collection of pitches that do not form a gamut or a cycle of bisection and a set of moments that are neither periodically nor cyclically arranged. Generally, it is not too difficult to analyse a piece the pitches of which consist of a simple pentatonic or diatonic collection, such as *c–d–e–g–a* or *c–d–e–f–g–a–b*, or that is commetric within a periodic or cyclic framework, such as ♪♩ ♪♩ *w* or ♪♩ ♪♩ ♩ *w*. In the present work, this was not the situation. Nevertheless, an interpretation in terms of cycles of moments and pitch classes was possible. The *g–c–d* set could be understood as a segment of adjacent members of a pentatonic cycle – such as the following: *f–c–g–d–a–(f)* – and the rhythmic pattern similarly can be understood as a section of adjacent members of the following cycle:

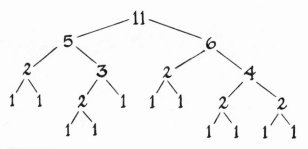

FIGURE 7.1

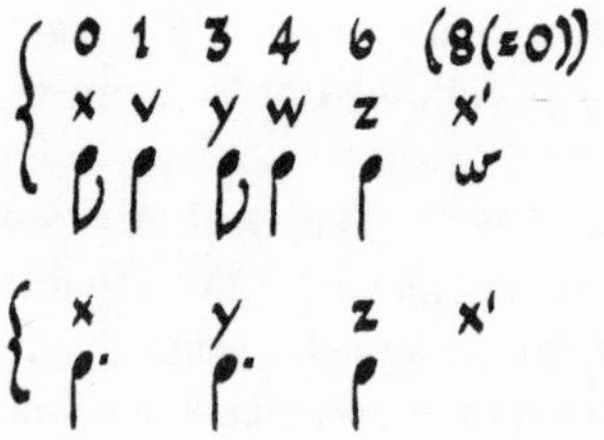

FIGURE 7.2

0   4   1   6   3   [8 (= 0)]
x   w   v   z   y   x¹

which can be rewritten as in figure 7.2.

The two sets of moments are only subsets of cyclic collections, but they also turn out to have certain properties that set them apart as special. There is a co-ordination of interval sizes expressed in terms of the derived or original scales, so that there is a determinate connection between three-tone and three-moment 'scales' on the one hand, and the five-tone and five-moment cycles on the other. Since interval sizes in the latter also correspond unambiguously to interval sizes in the twelve-semitone gamut and eight-eighth-note pulsation, each interval in the 3-sets has a clear correlate in the 5-, and 12- or 8-sets. Furthermore, there is a co-ordination of bisection in terms of the 3- and 5-sets. This means that the bisector of an interval in terms of a 3-set is also the bisector of the same interval expressed in terms of the 5-set. Since the same relation holds between the 5-sets and the 8- and 12-sets, g–c–d can be regarded as a gamut that has been transformed by various selection procedures, and the rhythmic pattern, ♩·♩·♩, can be viewed as a 'pulsation' that has similarly been transformed. In effect, this means that the interval between g and c is the same as the interval between *c* and *d*, and the interval between *d* and *g*. Similarly, *g–d* is equivalent in size to *c–g* and *d–c*. It follows that either *c* or *d* can be considered to bisect the modular interval *g–g¹* and *c* can be considered to bisect *g–d* just as *d* can be considered to bisect *c–g¹*.

These features of the set are exploited in the piece itself. A bisector (*d*) of the octave on the tonic (*g–g¹*) functions as the 'dominant' in the tonic dyad *g–d*. For much of the piece these tones alone are used on strong beats, the pitch *c* being introduced on a weak beat as a 'passing tone' between *d* and *g*. Consistent with this is the appearance of the dyad *c–g* as oriental for the second, or less accented, of two measures (i.e., m. 2) and the third of three (m. 5).

Where the dyad *c–g* is oriental, an isomorphism of interval sizes in the 3-set, 5-set, and 12-set is exploited, for of the three one-degree intervals in the 3-set, only *g–d* and *c–g* are equivalent in size according to all three metric systems: they correspond to one degree in the 3-set, two degrees in the 5-set, and seven semitones in the 12-set. By contrast, the *d–c* interval corresponds to one degree in the 3-set, but to only one degree in the 5-set and only two semitones in the 12-set. Thus, when there is a 'modulation,' it is made to a dyad that is thoroughly identical to that of the tonic. [A similar preference for thoroughly identical dyads can be found, for example, in late medieval modal music where 'modulations' (or more properly, commixtures) are made to dyads of precisely a perfect fifth (e.g., *a–e, c–g, d–a, e–b, f–c,* and *g–d*), rather than to a dyad of a diminished fifth (e.g., *b–f*) (cf. Rahn 1978c, 1981). Indeed, this avoidance of non-identical intervals can be found in the music of other cultures as well.] For these reasons, a tritonic interpretation of the piece in which the three tones presented in the work are accounted for in terms of a pentatonic collection based in turn on a twelve-tone gamut excels Merriam's interpretation of the piece as tritonic (in the sense of 'tritypic') where a direct leap is made between the tones of the piece and the twelve- semitone system. By positing an intervening pentatonic construct one can establish further isomorphisms in the piece and thus enhance the interpretation.

With regard to form, the present interpretation catches the repetitions described in Merriam's analysis and goes further, for the repetitions are placed into a tonometric context. In this way, a relatively foreground aspect of the piece, namely, its motivic form, is positively related to deeper pitch-time structures. Accordingly, the interpretation interrelates more aspects of the piece and is thus better.

Finally, one can note that the percussion pattern coincides with the downbeats in this interpretation – it would not do so in Kolinski's barring – and the upbeat/downbeat dichotomy is co-ordinated with the opposition between the syllables 'a' and 'he.' In this way, retranscription leads to relationships between aspects of the piece as originally notated and other features that had not previously been set down on paper. Accordingly, retranscribing can enhance an interpretation. On the other hand, it was found that the accents in the original transcription seemed to be illusory. If the piece had not been retranscribed and the accents removed, these accents would have coincided with upbeats of the interpretation and would have been considered to articulate the metrical unit of a measure in the present interpretation. However, in the retranscription, such accents are co-ordinated with a more superficial level of the hierarchy, coinciding as they do with rises in pitch, and hence duplicating relationships based on altitude that are directly inferable from the pitches of the transcription and do not correspond so consistently with the deeper tono-metric structure of the piece. In these ways reinterpretation can enhance the richness of an analysis and retranscription can lead to a reassessment of foreground features.

Until now, tonal systems have been characterized as either gamuts or scales. From the present example, one can see the efficacy of recognizing yet another type of tonal system which might be termed a *subscale*. A scale can be viewed as a selection from a gamut by means of cyclic bisection, whereby (a) alternate members of the cycle are adjacent; (b) there is a determinate co-relation between interval sizes expressed in terms of scale degrees and the gamut; and (c) bisectors of intervals between scale degrees are also bisectors of the same intervals expressed in terms of the gamut. A subscale consists of a section of adjacent members of the bisection cycle by which a scale is defined. Since subscales are not cyclic, they do not feature property (a). Nevertheless, they do manifest properties (b) and (c). The 3-set found in the present example is not an isolated case, for as chapter 8 reveals, the pentatonic scale can be considered a subscale of the heptatonic 7 from 12 by 7 (and 6) collection. As will be seen, this is but one instance where the interpretation of even a single piece from a given culture can lead to insights that help one to interpret music from other cultures.

'ꞌDU:,' A HUKWE BOW SONG

Transcriptions of 'ꞌDu:,' the next song to be considered, appear in a 'Symposium on Transcription and Analysis' in the journal *Ethnomusicology*. Nicholas England recorded the song and provided a summary of its place in the culture of the Hukwe, a people of southern Africa. Four scholars – Robert Garfias, Mieczyslaw Kolinski, George List, and Willard Rhodes – transcribed and analysed the song (all 1964). Their transcriptions differ to a certain extent, but since a recording of the piece was fortunately made available with their reports, I am offering a fifth transcription (example 7.6). For the most part, my notation is closer to that of Kolinski than to that of any of the other scholars. I, like the earlier transcribers, have, with one exception, not notated the text: the recording's low fidelity would

7.6 ,Du:

7.6 (continued)

7.6 (continued)

7.6 (continued)

seem to prevent any but an expert in Hukwe from underlaying the melody. However, on the basis of England's reconstruction of the text (1965: 151–2), it is possible to discern clearly the recurrent phrase 'ta-nu djó ré' (approximately, 'Are they waterbucks of another country?'), and the attacks of the remaining tones notated in the vocal part appear to coincide with the beginnings of syllables in this largely syllabic song. Since it is difficult to discuss five interpretations at the same time, I will present my own interpretation and then my comments on the others' efforts.

The central problem which this piece poses is that of determinate ambiguity. More specifically, there are two candidates for the role of downbeat, and neither appears preferable. Such a situation has consequences for a theory of interpretation, and these will be dealt with later. Also to be confronted is the question of variability in interval size, for it is found that the piece's structure would not be changed greatly if certain pitches were to be substituted for those found in the piece. This in turn is related to the nature of the instrument on which the piece is played.

Four pitch classes (*b, c, e,* and *g*) are presented in the song. These imply a scale of seven pitch classes derived from a gamut of twelve by mixed cyclic bisection involving the intervals 7/12 and 6/12. Thus, *c–d–e–f* (or *f♯*)–*g–a–b* could be considered the referential diatonic collection for the piece.

The four pitch classes form a symmetrical group of three pairs: *c–e, e–g, g–b*. The first and last intervals are identical in size and contrast with the central interval, *e–g*. In terms of scale degrees, *e* bisects *c–g* (4/7) into *c–e* (2/7), and *e–g* (2/7), and *b* bisects *g–c* (3/7) into *g–b* (2/7) and *b–c* (1/7). Similarly, *c* bisects *b–e*, and *g* bisects *e–b*. In this sense, the interval *e–b* can be considered to bisect *c–g*, and vice versa.

Pulsations are of great importance to the piece: a series of eighth-note durations and a modular series of six eighths. The six eighths are grouped into 3 × 2:

(cf. Kolinski: 1964, 249). The measures of dotted halves are grouped into threes:

♩. ♩. ♩.

and these in turn are grouped into pairs:

♩. ♩. ♩. ♩. ♩. ♩.

Thus the hierarchy of pulsations in example 7.7 holds for the piece.

Nevertheless, there are ambiguities that are central to the work. First, the interval *c–g* can be considered oriental (o), and *e–b* can be viewed as its bisector, or vice versa: *c–g* can be considered to bisect *e–b*, which can be considered

7.7

oriental. Second, either *a* or *b* (see example 7.6) can be considered to represent the oriental class of moments. Thus, two readings are possible and of equal merit: (1) *a* is the downbeat and *c–g* is the tonic dyad, bisected by *e–b*; (2) *b* is the downbeat and *e–b* is the tonic dyad, bisected by *c–g*.

According to the first interpretation, level 3 (starting at *a*) of the periodic hierarchy has the following pitch values (strophes 1 and 2):

o i o o i o o i o o i o etc.

giving rise to level 4, as follows:

o   o   o   o   etc.

This is interrupted at the end (strophe 9):

o i o o i i(!) i(!) o (the syllable '˗Du:')

According to the second interpretation, level 3 (starting at *b*) of the pulsation coincides with the following pitch values:

i i o i i o i i o i i o etc.

This is extended at the end (strophe 9, again):

i i o i i o o(!)

Pieces like this can be described as 'pendular' processes. In the movements of a pendulum one can distinguish right and left extremes, but there is no reason to favour either as oriental for the whole. Similarly, in a pendular process such as the present instance, there is no reason to prefer interpretation (1) or (2).

The piece unfolds in strophes roughly corresponding to pulsation no. 5 (example 7.7). In the transcriptions, these are labelled one to eight. Two rather exceptional strophes occur. In the eighth, the first six measures are extended by immediate repetition of the last half (cf. Kolinski 1964: 249). The relationships between the duration of this strophe and the duration of the 'normal' ones is 3 : 2. In other words, strophe 8 bisects (i.e., is one half of) the duration of strophes 7 and 8. This example of controlled extension, where repetitions give rise to longer spans, which are nevertheless hierarchically related to shorter spans by bisection, is similar to what has been found in the Flathead song discussed earlier.

Strophe 3 presents a more complex situation. According to the first interpretation, the first three measures of a normal strophe present the following pattern (where the second half of a measure in the interpretation begins at the downbeat in the transcription): o–o I–o o–I, which is extended to four in strophe 3 by doubling the last two half measures to full measures:

Strophe: o–o   I–o   o – I   mm. 7–9
Strophe 3: o–o   I–o   o–o I–I   mm. 13–16

The last half features similar extensions. According to (1),

o   I   o   of mm. 9–12

is extended to

o o   I I   o I o   in mm. 17–23

where mm. 18 and 20 represent extensions by immediate repetition of the content of mm. 17 and 19 and the last two measures form an extension by immediate repetition of the content of the preceding two measures. (Note the imbricative relation between measures 19–20 and 20–21: this is an example in which imbrication can be considered to represent succession as opposed to simultaneity. Much the same holds in some Western music – for example, by Mozart – where the end of one phase is the beginning of the next.)

According to (2), the content of the first measure is repeated in the second measure, the content of the third measure is repeated in the fourth, and the last two measures repeat the immediately preceding two measures. In this way, three measures are extended to seven:

Strophe 2: I   I   o   mm. 9–12
Strophe 3: I I   I I I o   I o mm. 17–23

In sum, neither interpretation (1) nor (2) appears preferable.

Altogether, the eleven measures of stophe 3 bisect the seventeen measures of strophes 2 and 3 (or 3 and 4). This is similar to the situation in strophe 8, which, though an extension, fits into a scheme of bisection.

In the light of these two interpretations, one can assess those offered by the four scholars in 1964. The groupings of interpretation (2) are consistent with List's transcription, and the other authors' notations accord with interpretation

𝅘𝅥𝅮𝅘𝅥𝅮𝅘𝅥𝅮 𝅘𝅥𝅮𝅘𝅥𝅮𝅘𝅥𝅮 𝅗𝅥
a   a   a

7.8

(1). This shows that barring is a matter of interpretation, but differences in barring can be moot. Garfias's observation that the class of moments represented by *a* coincides with slightly longer durations in the bow part (example 7.8) tends to support interpretation (1) where the *a*'s are special by virtue of their positions at oriental moments and might be expected to be treated in a special way durationally. But the same author's observation that the *e*'s of the last two measures of six-measure groups are presented simultaneously in both the bow and voice parts (in contrast to the general case where simultaneous bow and vocal pitches differ) supports interpretation (2) (1964: 239). Both of these observations – I do not hear the fermatas – refer to relatively foreground aspects of the piece and hence are of little consequence to the interpretation as a whole. Accordingly, the fact that they support opposite readings of the piece is of little interpretive importance.

List notes a basic correlation between timbre and duration: the vocal line displays many more types of durations between attacks than does the bow part (1964: 262). One can add that the voice part emphasizes the overall 3-4 metre, whereas the bow part articulates 6-8 groupings. In accordance with this, List describes three vocal motifs as A, B, and C, and Garfias writes of motifs A and B, where his A corresponds to List's A and B, and his B to List's C. A general remark can be made about these motifs: A coincides with measures 1 to 3 of the six-measure unit (i.e., the first half); B coincides with measure 4 (the beginning of the second half); C corresponds to measures 5 and 6 (the end of the whole unit). The only exceptions are strophes 2 and 3, where A is used at measures 5 and 6 (i.e., a half-phrase later than usual) and C is employed at measure 3 (i.e., a half phrase earlier than usual). In this way, formal aspects of the piece can be related to tono-metric structure as these authors failed to do.

In contrast to the overall triple organization, the bow part intermittently articulates 6-8 groupings (cf. Kolinski 1964: 250; List 1964: 261), as in example 7.9. In each part of the example, altitude plays a role. In (a), each group of three tones is arranged as follows:

first ⩾ second > last

In (b), the following arrangement is observed:

first < second = last

(a) mm. 4–5 of (1)

(b) mm. 9–10 of (2)

7.9

Relying as they do on altitude, these intermittent 6-8 measures can be considered a source of ambiguity in metrical structure between the foreground (temporarily in 6-8) and the background (consistently in 3-4). In a hierarchical interpretation this is clear, as it is not in Kolinski's analysis.

Finally, Kolinski's description of *e–g* as the 'tonal center' (1964: 246) is consistent with the aforementioned symmetry of the intervals *c–e, e–g, g–b*. However, it should be noted that this symmetry is not exploited in the piece but lies dormant throughout. As a point of metatheory, it should be noted that a piece need not exploit all the relationships of the system that interprets it. This is borne out in several contexts. For example, in early Western music, it is often true that a piece in Ionian or Aeolian does not exploit the symmetrical arrangement of triads characteristic of these modes. Indeed, one can distinguish between pieces that are in Ionian or Aeolian and those that are more properly described as major or minor on the basis of whether triads or dyads are exploited in them. (Conversely a major piece need not exploit the modal resources of Ionian.) Furthermore, though List's description of the piece as bitonal (1964: 264) approximates the notion of a pendular process, his method for arriving at that conclusion (by applying Hindemith's deterministic theories while turning a blind eye to the simultaneous major sevenths that occur) indicates that the appropriateness of his conclusion is a fortuitous coincidence.

Finally, it should be noted that much the same relationships would hold if the tones *e♭* and *b♭*, or *d* and *a*, were substituted for *e* and *b*. If this were done, *e♭* or *d* could be considered to bisect *c–g* into 1/5 + 2/5 according to a pentatonic scale, and *b♭* or *a* to bisect *g–c* into 1/5 + 1/5, according to the same system. (In a similar way, *g* could be considered to bisect *e♭–b♭* or *d–a*, and *c* to bisect *b♭–e♭* or *a–d*.) With regard to the instrument itself such alternations would amount to stopping the bow three or two semitones above the fundamental rather than four semitones, since the variable tones are produced by a single stopped position on the bow. In this manner, there is a considerable amount of leeway at the performer's disposal within which much the same piece can be produced in different renditions. Such renditions would be the same in terms of bisection and different in terms of interval identity.

TAQSIM

The pieces considered thus far have had a restricted tonal vocabulary (four pitch bands at most per octave) and a highly periodic metrical organization. However, in example 7.10, a *taqsim* in *Maqam Nahawand*, which was originally transcribed by Bruno Nettl and Ronald Riddle (1973: 30–3), the following pitches appear within an octave: g, $a\flat$, a, $b\flat$, $b\natural$, b, c, $c\sharp$, $d\flat$, d, e, $e\flat$, f, and $f\sharp$. Furthermore, there appears to be no oriental set of pulsations for the piece as a whole. Nevertheless, one can cite a number of features that might provide clues for analysing the work. First, there are several spans (e.g., a, in example 7.10) where pitch attacks are organized periodically. Also several tones are considerably longer than adjacent tones (e.g., tones marked x). Note in the original transcription that the broken double bars represent rests of from one to three seconds, and the duration of a tone is considered to be the time interval between its attack and the beginning of the next pitch. Moreover, the melodic movement appears to be predominantly a scale pattern: temporally adjacent tones are also adjacent in terms of scale degrees. The articulation is predominantly legato: the spans of successive tones tend to be contiguous. Finally, pitch class g coincides with the piece's temporal extremes: its beginning and end.

These clues – which in themselves are of heuristic import only – can be put to work in the following way. Leaps and rests can be considered special, as can pitch class g and tones that are longer than those surrounding them. One can also add the notion of hierarchy to account for the observables.

Several pitch classes can be considered to form the referential diatonic collection: g–a–$b\flat$–c–d–$e\flat$–f (not $f\sharp$: see below). This collection has a number of features, including cyclic bisection and co-ordination of cyclic and linear orderings of scale degrees and the gamut of twelve semitones from which it is derived, as well as mapping of intervals expressed in terms of the gamut onto intervals expressed in terms of the scale. In Western music, the symmetry of identical minor triads is exploited in voice-leading. The symmetrical arrangement of figure 7.3 gives rise to the pattern of voices in figure 7.4. In modal music, the symmetrical arrangement of fifths is exploited in analogous fashion. A symmetrical arrangement of fifths (figure 7.5) gives rise to the disposition of voices, as shown in figure 7.6 (cf. Rahn 1978c, 1981). In the present piece, however, only the latter feature is exploited. The dyad g–d can be considered orienting and, with the bivalent third degree ($b\flat$), to constitute the upper reaches of the tonal hierarchy. Other scale degrees (f, a, c, $e\flat$) are adjacent to members of this triad.

Durational relationships between adjacent tones seem to emphasize pitches of the diatonic collection, especially at the outset of the piece (sections 1 to 6).

7.10 Taqsim

7.10 (continued)

7.10 (continued)

The tonic triad is emphasized at the very beginning (sections 1 to 3). As an illustration of pitch emphasis, one can consider the first section. Here tones that are longer than those adjacent to them are marked x: *g, b♭, c, d, a, a, g.* The emphasized non-triadic pitches (*c* and *a*) are all diatonic, and are found between members of the triad: *c* appears between *b♭* and *d, a* between *d* and *g.* Furthermore, the pitch that immediately follows each non-triadic pitch is a member of the tonic triad: *d* of the triad follows *c; g* follows *a.* This can be summarized as in figure 7.7, where braces join members of the referential triad, and arrows connect non-triadic pitches to the triad members that follow immediately.

If the second section is schematized in this way, figure 7.8 results. Once

```
c    eᵇ    g
         ┌─────────────┐
         │  g    bᵇ    d  │
         └─────────────┘
              d    f    a
```

FIGURE 7.3

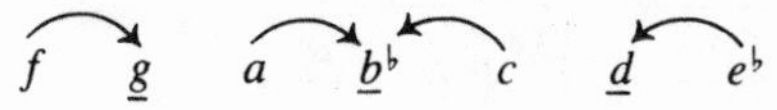

```
 f    g    a    bᵇ    c    d    eᵇ
```

FIGURE 7.4

```
bᵇ    f
      f    c
           c    g
              ┌──────────┐
              │  g    d  │
              └──────────┘
                   d    a
                        a    eᵇ
                             eᵇ    bᵇ
```

FIGURE 7.5

again, non-triadic pitches are followed immediately by an adjacent member of the triad. Here, however, a new twist is added: the pitch $f\sharp$, which does not belong to the diatonic collection, is also emphasized. This constitutes a type of chromaticism. The important word here is 'a', for there are many types of chromaticism possible. Here if $f\sharp$ substitutes for $f\natural$ as the seventh degree, the resulting collection, $g–a–b\flat–c–d–e\flat–f\sharp$, lacks two features of the referential diatonic collection. It lacks a determinate relationship between intervals measured in terms of the gamut and of the scale, since, for example, three semitones can correspond to an interval of one degree (e.g., $e\flat–f\sharp$) or two (e.g., $g–b\flat$). Also, the bisection of intervals in terms of the gamut and in terms of scale degrees is not co-ordinated. For instance, $e\flat–g$ is bisected in terms of scale degrees by $f\sharp$ into $1 + 1$; in terms of the gamut, this is not a bisection: $e\flat–f\sharp = 3$ semitones, $f\sharp–g = 1$ semitone, and 1 is not a bisector of the sum (4).

Nevertheless, two features of the diatonic collection are preserved, namely, cyclic bisection ($g–7–d–7–a–6–e\flat–7–b\flat–8–f\sharp–6–c–7–g$), and co-ordination of linear and cyclic orderings. With regard to the latter, one can note that g and a

FIGURE 7.6

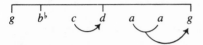

FIGURE 7.7

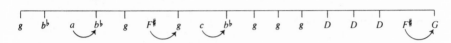

FIGURE 7.8

are two steps away in the cycle described above, and adjacent to each other in the collection. Similarly, d and $e\flat$, a and $b\flat$, $e\flat$ and $f\sharp$, $b\flat$ and c, $f\sharp$ and g, and c and d share these characteristics. Since two features of the original scale are lost, one can term this a 'third degree' chromaticism.

The $f\sharp$s, which are special pitches, are also treated in a special way. They are preceded and followed by adjacent scale degrees in successions such as g, $f\sharp$, g, and g, $f\sharp$, $e\flat$ (or $e\sharp$, see below) even when they are not emphasized. When emphasized, they are treated like other non-triadic tones encountered thus far in that they are resolved into an adjacent member of the triad, g. Among chromatic pitches, indeed, these $f\sharp$s rank very high in the pitch hierarchy. Not only do they disrupt the features of scale construction only slightly, but also they are closely allied to the lowest level of the tonal hierarchy: the tonic g.

In the third section, the pitches g, $b\flat$, and d are emphasized again. Altogether, the first three sections represent a recursive pattern: in the first and last sections, the pitches g, $b\flat$, and d are emphasized as well as neighbouring diatonic pitches, which are resolved into adjacent scale degrees. In the middle section, G, D, g, and $b\flat$ are emphasized, yielding a lower range that is imbricatively related to the ambitus of its neighbours. Here not only diatonic neighbours are emphasized, but also the third-degree chromatic pitch $f\sharp$. Despite this tonal excursion, these non-triadic pitches are resolved to their referential neighbours as before. Throughout the three sections, $f\sharp$ also appears in unemphasized form: relatively brief in duration and surrounded by neighbours. Appended to one $f\sharp$ is an $e\sharp$, which

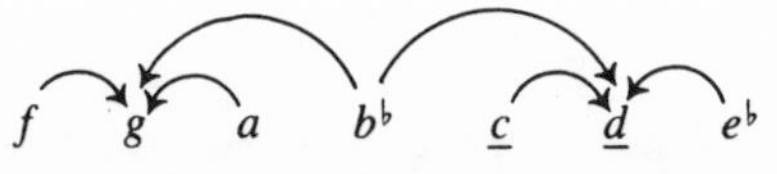

f g a b♭ c d e♭

FIGURE 7.9

constitutes a fourth or ultimate degree of chromaticism: if $e\sharp$ is substituted for $e\flat$, and $f\sharp$ for f, the following collection results: $g–a–b\flat–c–d–e\sharp–f\sharp$. This cannot even be expressed as a cycle of bisectors since the interval $e\sharp–b$ is less than half an octave: five semitones, rather than six, seven, or eight. It is treated even more carefully than $f\sharp$ for it only appears as a lower neighbour to that pitch: $f\sharp–e\sharp–f\sharp$. Both these pitches are examples of 'chromatic leading tones,' phenomena that will be discussed later. Suffice it for now to point out that $e\sharp$ forming as it does a leading tone to $f\sharp$ is on a lower level of the tonal hierarchy.

As mentioned before, the general trend is for stepwise progression. By and large, this is true of the first three sections, where leaps mostly occur between subsections articulated by rests (example 7.11). Such leaps are analogous to the 'dead' intervals between the end of one phrase and the beginning of the next. Nevertheless, an exceptional case of a 'live' interval deserves mention. At the beginning of the third section, there is a jump from g to c. The g, which belongs to the tonic dyad $g–d$, is already resolved. The c, which does not belong to the referential interval, is resolved immediately to d. In terms of the model for modality described above (figure 7.9), this is not only a resolution to a neighbour, (d), but also a resolution in terms of structural voice-leading (example 7.12).

In the next three sections, leaps are more frequent. For example, section 4 begins with a series of leaps between members of the tonic dyad: $g–d$. Thereupon, less central members of the tonal hierarchy are emphasized. Up to this point, non-triadic pitches with emphatically long durations have appeared only one at a time. In sections 4 to 6, however, groups of two or three of them form dyads and triads. For example, there is a long stretch where $e\flat$, c, and a are emphasized in pairs, whereas pitches of the tonic triad are emphasized only one at a time. In this way, the roles of triadic and non-triadic tones are reversed: the non-triadic tones constitute oriental constructs on their own and the emphasized triadic pitches function as passing, or neighbour, tones between them (example 7.13).

Throughout sections 4 to 6, the triads and dyads formed in this way are made up exclusively of members of the diatonic collection: $e\flat–c–a; \ c–a; \ g–E\flat;$ $F–C; \ E\flat–B\flat$.

With due allowance for the tonal functions of leaps, the skeletal version of these three sections can be described as in figure 7.10.

Once again, the three sections represent a recursive form. The first and

7.11

7.12

skeletal version: *e♭ c c e♭ d c b♭ c a c b♯* etc.

7.13

7.14

last sections lie higher and are tonally less ambitious than the middle part. The latter transcends the normal procedure whereby relatively non-oriental triads appear one at a time between statements of the tonic triad, for *F–(A)–C* and *E♭–(G)–B♭* are presented in immediate succession (i.e., without *G–B♭–D* intervening). This is carried out by means of a melodic sequence that establishes a process interrupted only on the return to the tonic (example 7.14). As are frequently found in music, such processes serve to extend the normal boundaries of tono-rhythmic structure. This was also the case in the two previous pieces.

Finally, a certain amount of determinate ambiguity is introduced into the piece by the emphasis on *E♭* in the fifth section. Up to this point, all sections had begun and ended on the tonic triad. Here, however, only *g* and *b♭* are presented at first, and *E♭* is thereupon emphasized. Thus, the section can be read in two ways (figure 7.11). According to the first reading, the *g* triad is referential for the whole section, the *E♭* triad for the middle of the section, and the *F* triad represents a neighbour to the *E♭* triad. With regard to the entire piece, where other sections begin and end on the tonic or its triad, the first interpretation makes better sense. But in terms of the section itself, the absence of an emphasized *d* and the presence of an emphasized *E♭* are in the second interpretation's favour.

In the remaining sections, chromaticisms of various kinds continue to play a

Section 4

Emphasized tones	d	e^b–c–c–e^b–d–c–b^b–c–a–c
Referential triads	⌐(g–b^b)–d⌐	⌐———— a–c–e^b ————⌐

Emphasized tones	b^b–c–d–b^b–b^b–g–b^b–a–g–F♯–g–g–d–g–d–b^b
Referential triads	⌐————— g–b^b–d ————————⌐

Emphasized tones	c–a–c–d–d–c	g–g
Referential triads	⌐a–c–(e^b)⌐	⌐g–(b^b–d)⌐

Section 5

Emphasized tones	b^b–a–b^b–g–F–g	E^b–F–C	E^b–B^b
Referential triads	{ ⌐—g–b^b–(d)—⌐	⌐f–(a)–c⌐ }⌐e^b–(g)–b^b⌐
	⌐————e^b–g–b^b——⌐⌐f–(a)–c⌐}	

Emphasized tones	D–G–C–B^b–A–G–FF♯–A–G–G
Referential triads	⌐————g–b^b–d————⌐

Section 6

Emphasized tones	g–D–a–g–g–g
Referential triads	⌐g–(b^b)–d⌐

FIGURE 7.10

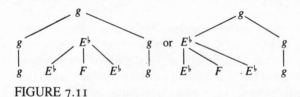

FIGURE 7.11

role. In section 7, c♯ is introduced: here it functions similarly to f♯, but it forms a leading tone to the dominant, d, rather than to the tonic, g. About halfway through the section, a more striking development occurs: the pitches e, b, and a^b are introduced and the triad c–e–g is emphasized. This can be interpreted as a move to a new mode with the tonic triad g–e–c as the oriental triad and the

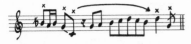

7.15

diatonic collection: *g f e d c b a♭*. Immediately following this passage, the basic diatonic collection reappears, and the tonic triad *g–b♭–d* is emphasized. The tonal form of this segment is recursive. It begins in *nahawand*, moves to the new mode, and returns to *nahawand*.

In sections 8 and 9, a gamut of twenty-four quarter tones is implied. The diatonic collection becomes *g–a–b♭–c–d–e–f* and the tonic triad is *g–b♭–d*. In the tonic triad, the third degree bisects the dyad *g–d* (= 14 quarter tones) exactly into halves: 14 = 7 + 7. However, a certain amount of consistency of cyclic bisection is sacrificed. Two deviant intervals (of thirteen quarter tones) are present whereas only one (of six semitones) was present before:

g–14–*d*–14–*a*–14–*e*–13–*b♭*–13–*f*–14–*c*–14–*g*

Given this inconsistency, it is not surprising that the only pitches that are emphasized two at a time are members of the diatonic collection: the tonic triad (*g–b♭–d*) and *a–c*. In the ninth section, an interesting case of octave displacement occurs (example 7.15): pitch-class *c* is presented emphatically in the register below its resolution (*d*). However, because of the co-ordination of cyclic and linear orderings, this is not unexpected, for the degree-class *c* is adjacent to the degree-class *d* regardless of the registers in which they are presented. Although such melodic dissonances and their resolutions are usually registrally adjacent – as would have been the case if *c* were presented an octave higher – there is no reason why they need be, for the scale represents an ordering of all *g*'s, all *a*'s, all *b♭*s, etc., rather than merely those that appear within a given octave; in other words, all *c*'s are neighbours of all *d*'s in the collection.

In section 10 there is an emphasis on *d*, for this part – unlike any other sections in the work – begins on the dyad *d–f*, rather than on the tonic triad (*g–b♭–d*). Eventually, the tonic triad is reached and this is followed by a return to the original mode of *nahawand* and its tonic triad.

The final section (11) also begins as the last concluded: with an emphasis on the tonic, by means of an initial leap from *g* to *d*. However, of the tonic triad only *b♭* and *d* are emphasized at first, with *e♭*, *c,* and *a* appearing in neighbouring dyads (figure 7.12). In this way, the *b♭–d* dyad could be considered to belong either to the tonic triad *g–b♭–d* or to the mediant *b♭–d–f*. This ambiguity is driven home in the following passage where *d♭* and *e* make their appearance. The third and fifth scale degrees, *b♭* and *d* (altered to *d♭*), are again emphasized

(g)   d   e♭   c   d   d   c   b♭   c   a

FIGURE 7.12

b♭–d♭–e–d♭–c–d♭–b♭–b♭–c–b♭   c–a   b♭–g–b♭

(g)–b♭–d♭   a–c   g–b♭–(d) [!]

FIGURE 7.13

until finally the tonic is reached by way of the dyad *a–c* (figure 7.13). The resulting collection (*g–a–b♭–c–d♭–e–f*) lacks determinate correlation between interval sizes with regard to the gamut and scale degrees, and a co-ordination of bisection at the levels of gamut and scale. Accordingly, the collection is more 'weakly' structured than the scale of *nahawand*. Nevertheless, it features cyclic bisection and co-ordination of linear and cyclic orderings. Throughout the remainder of the piece, the two scales alternate in pendular fashion. Much emphasis is given to *b♭* and *d* (or *d♭*) with an occasional statement of *g*, and despite the emphatic ending on *g*, the conclusion is ambiguous, for the fifth degree is last presented in its lowered form (*d♭*). Such an inconclusive ending is similar to that found in the sub-Saharan song discussed above.

Two procedures dominate the organization of the piece. First, there is an overall tendency to increased chromaticism and exploration of more remote tonal regions. Emphasized tones that do not belong to the tonic triad are introduced first singly, then two and three at a time. At first, only diatonic scale degrees are presented and emphasized, but eventually chromatic pitches are introduced, first as relatively short tones then with emphatic durations. By section 7, such chromatic pitches are emphasized in conjunction with others to form dyads as the diatonic pitches had done. In the same section, the tonal centre is shifted and chromatic leading tones are introduced at the same time. In the next section, the twelve-semitone basis gives way to a twenty-four-tone gamut and a structurally less consistent scale. At the end of the piece, there is an oscillation of modes centring around the third and fifth degrees and even the tonic triad is not immune to alteration!

Coterminous with this progressive exploration of remote tonal realms there is a tendency to recursion. The piece as a whole starts and concludes on *g*. Changes of mode are made one at a time: they are preceded and followed in rondo fashion by emphasis on the tonic triad of *nahawand*. In each section, the tonic triad is emphasized by leaps or relatively long durations at the beginning and end. And within sections, non-triadic pitches form dyads or triads which generally appear one at a time between emphatic statements of the tonic. In this way, the 'linear' tendency towards more remotely related tonalities is combined with a 'cyclic' tendency continually to revert to the tonic. Nowhere is this better exemplified than in the oscillations between d and d^b which conclude the work.

At this point the analysis presented by Nettl and Riddle (1973) can be viewed in fairly clear perspective. The original transcribers' goal was to analyse several such *taqasim* in *nahawand* in order to discern regularities throughout the repertoire. Much of their analysis of the *taqasim* depends on slicing each piece into sections (e.g., sections 1 to 11 in example 7.10 see 1973: 15). The basis for their slicing was their observation of rests of from one to three seconds (indicated by a broken double bar above; cf. 1973: 30; note, however, the reference to 'one to five seconds' on p. 15). Such a rest was considered to separate one section from another. A number of theoretical difficulties arise from such a definition of sections. Most importantly, the definition depends on an absolute value (one to three or five seconds) which is left unrelated to the rest of the observables. One should also note that this absolute criterion would give rise to further subdivisions than the authors in fact recognize. The half rest at the beginning of the first section would have to be considered to define a very short section of three tones (example 7.16,1a). The quarter rest towards the end of section 7 might also be considered to split the segment into sections 7a and 7b, though in the absence of a precise metronome marking in the transcription, this passage is not clear. In this way, such an analysis raises the question of how long a 'long' rest is.

One need not resort to the apparently objective approach of Nettl and Riddle, for the piece can be sliced into sections on the basis of its tono-metric structure alone. Sequences of durationally emphasized tones yield segments that begin and end on g, the tonic. Between the extremes of such segments appear less oriental, albeit emphasized, pitches. The relation between relatively oriental and less oriental pitches is accordingly co-ordinated with the relation between extreme and medial tones so that the pitch and time structures go hand in hand. Generally, the segments defined in this way coincide with the sections defined by Nettl and Riddle, but in this formulation the hierarchical organization is clearer: rather than asserting that rests define sections, one can observe that they coincide with (or 'articulate' at the foreground) tono-metric segments that emerge at a higher level of the interpretation.

Finally, one can observe an analogy between the status of the relatively long durations that mark emphasized tones and the function of relatively accented moments in a metrical hierarchy based on pulsation. In the latter case, a relatively accented moment can be considered oriental for moments immediately preceding

7.16

7.17

7.18

and following it (i.e., adjacent to it). For instance, in example 7.17, moment a_1 can be considered oriental for moments b_0, c_0, d_0, b_1, c_1, and d_1. Indeed, a_1 can be considered oriental for all moments between a_0 and a_2. Since a_1 coincides with a certain level of the hierarchy (represented by a_0, a_1, and a_2, above), it is oriental for those moments next to it that correspond to lower levels. In example 7.17, its level corresponds to a pulsation in whole notes: a_0–a_1, a_1–a_2. Its function as an oriental moment applies to all moments within a whole note before and after it, that is, within the duration defined by the span consisting of whole notes whose extremes coincide with a_1.

Similarly, a relatively long duration (as opposed to a relatively accented moment) can be considered oriental for durations immediately preceding and following it (i.e., adjacent to it). Such a duration defines durations adjacent to it (a_0 and a_2, in example 7.18) that are coextreme with the shorter, adjacent durations (b_0 and b_2). In both instances, the functional relation is between 'included' and 'including': on the one hand, short durations are included in durations implied by the relatively oriental, longer duration; on the other hand, less oriental moments are included in durations defined by the level of a relatively oriental moment in the metrical hierarchy.

CONCLUSIONS

The central question to be answered by an interpretation of a piece is 'Why is it so?' or better phrased, 'Why is it *just so*?' This question can be asked about any observable or set of observables in the work: a pattern such as ♩. ♩. ♩, alternation between *c* and *e* in an instrumental part, and a sixteenth-note *f*♯. The sense in which the question can be answered is not the causal one; that is, one cannot, as yet, determine in any convincing way what brought the work or a part of it into being in all its detail. Nevertheless, one can account for why a certain set of observables are 'just so' in the sense of the following questions: 'How do they fit in with other parts of the piece?' or 'How are they related to other parts of the piece?'

Although in interpretation each work is considered to be a unique entity because of its 'just-so-ness,' this does not mean that the analysis of one piece is unrelated to that of another. The interpretation of one piece often results in the formulation of concepts that are useful in other contexts. For example, in this chapter, the notion of controlled extension was found to emerge from the observables of two very different works, the Flathead sweathouse song and the Hukwe bow song. Such a concept can be applied fruitfully to pieces of the most diverse backgrounds which have arisen independently of one another, as one must presume the North American and African pieces did. Ideas like 'controlled extension' provide convenient summaries of complex relationships which are found over and over again. Indeed they are much like the concept of bisection that is similarly useful. They are even comparable to primitive concepts, such as adjacency, but with one important difference: the latter are logically prior to the former, that is, controlled extension, bisection, etc., imply such notions as adjacency or interval, not vice versa.

As one builds up a body of such concepts, however, it is all too easy to employ them in a facile manner or inappropriately. For example, it takes no great imagination to label a piece in which only certain pitches appear (for example, *c, d, e, f, g, a, b*) as having a diatonic collection based on a selection of 7 from 12 by 7 (and 6). One should be more interested in specifying just what features of such a 'white-note' scale are projected in the piece, for describing such a piece in terms of the 7 from 12 by 7 (and 6) collection without specifying what relationships embodied in that collection are in fact used is to stop short of deeper interpretation.

The 'perils of pigeon-holes' do not cease here, for there is always a danger of positing relationships of little consequence to a piece based on one's past experience. For example, if one were used to interpreting minor-mode works in the recent Western tradition, it would not be too surprising if one looked for tonic, dominant, and subdominant chords (in the narrow sense) in the *nai* piece just discussed, for much of it corresponds in pitch content to the European harmonic minor: *g, a, b*♭*, c, d, e*♭*, f*♯. But such an expectation would not be satisfied in the piece itself. Thus, there is a constant dialectical interplay between one's past analytic experience and the piece that one is currently interpreting.

The experience one has accumulated can be summarized by notions such as (cyclic) bisection or (controlled) extension, but their grammatical status as nouns should not lead one into the trap of considering them 'things' in themselves. The observables are the only things one is concerned with; concepts are means to ends. Even less should such concepts be considered 'universals' in the narrow sense. A piece does not have to embody cyclic bisection or controlled extension to qualify as music.

Nevertheless, such notions are useful for they help one to be ready for new pieces. In this sense, they predict the terms in which the next interpretation might be couched. And this predictive capacity helps one to transcend the individual piece and come to terms with groups of pieces, i.e., with repertoires.

8

Some Repertoires Reinterpreted

Thus far I have dealt with individual pieces. In this chapter I will be concerned with groups of works, that is, repertoires. In its broadest sense, the term *repertoire* denotes merely a set of pieces but here it means much more, namely, a musically unified set of pieces. The adverb 'musically' is an important qualifier, for though a repertoire might correspond to a cultural unit – as the repertoires to be considered here do – there is no implication that such must be the case. A set of pieces from diverse cultural backgrounds might be grouped together and found to be unified musically, in which case the set would still be termed a repertoire. This is not to deny that frequently there is a close correlation between cultural variables and musical features.

The ways in which a group of pieces can be considered unified are many. First, if there is at least one feature common to all the pieces, they can be considered to constitute a class. Second, if each piece shares features with at least one other piece in the group, and the latter shares another feature with a third, and so on, the repertoire can be considered 'connected.' Third, if numbers can be assigned to the values that musical variables take and the frequencies of these values form an approximately normal, Poisson, or other type of distribution, the pieces can be considered to exhibit 'regularity.' Fourth, if at least one type of value is never found in the pieces, they can be considered to have a 'boundary.' Finally, and most importantly, if a single system provides the best interpretations of all the pieces, they can be considered a 'systemic unit.'

The last criterion, systemic unity, would seem to be a *sine qua non* for defining repertoires. If the system that explained the unity of a repertoire differed from that which best explained individual pieces in the group, there would be no link between the interpretation of a piece and the comparison of several pieces. Through a system of interpretation, individual pieces are linked to others. Indeed, one can go further and assert as a criterion that the terms in which a group is

8.1 Asaadua: percussion part

described as a class, connected, regular, or bounded should be terms of the unifying system, otherwise they would be meaningless in the sense of being unconnected with the interpretation of an individual work.

ASAADUA OF THE AKAN

The first group of pieces to be considered is known as *Asaadua* (examples 8.1, 8.2). Seven examples of this genre from Ghana have been collected, transcribed, and published by Kwabena Nketia (1963). In his introductory remarks, Nketia says that the intervals as sounded correspond quite closely to those of equal temperament, that his use of bars does not imply stress accents on the downbeats, and that the absolute pitches of what was notated as *c* range from *f* to *b*♭ (1963:

8.2 Asaadua: vocal and castanet parts of seven songs

8.2 (continued)

2–6). The comment about the pitches is interesting as it reflects a restriction, which means that the songs are bounded. A similar boundary is found in the absolute tempos of the pieces, for *M.M.* ♩ = 94–108 applies throughout the songs.

The last observation is even more significant because all of the songs feature a single ostinato pattern in the percussion parts, and this corresponds in duration to six quarter notes. Other features that unify the group are the alternation of solo (i.e., leader or cantor) and chorus parts, and a restriction in pitch selection to the white-key scale. Thus the corpus represents a class that is bounded in various ways. The extent to which these class and boundary features are systemically meaningful remains to be seen, however. Much of what follows is devoted to this problem.

4. ♩. = 96

A- baa- baa- wa ee pɛ a-du-ro yɔ Wo-ya-ree a- kyɛ oo.

Pɛ a-du-ro yɔ___ma o-bi nware wo. Pɛ a-du-ro yɔ _____

'ba- baa- wa ee pɛ a-du-ro yɔ. Wo- ya-ree a- kyɛ oo. Pɛ a-du-ro

yɔ ma o-bi nware wo. Pɛ a-du-ro yɔ _____ 'ba- baa

wa ee, pɛ a-du-ro yɔ. Wo- yaree a kyɛ oo. Pɛ a-du-ro yɔ ma o-bi nwaa

wo. Pɛ a-du-ro yɔ _____ 'ba- baa- wa ee, pɛ a-du-ro

yɔ. Wo-ya-ree a- kyɛ oo. Pɛ a-du-ro yɔ ma o-bi nware wo.

8.2 (continued)

Since the percussion parts are conceptually separable from the vocal parts –
though contextually interrelated with them – they will be considered first. In
connection with these patterns, three terms will be used which thus far have not
been formally defined: commetricity, cross rhythm, and polyrhythm. Once defined, they will be found to embody important distinctions in interpreting individual pieces and the repertoire as a whole. Later on, when questions of tonal
organization are raised, two more terms, 'chain of thirds' and 'appoggiatura,'
will be defined to interpretive advantage.

Percussion Patterns
The notion of *commetricity* can be illustrated by the rattle-castanet ostinato
(example 8.3). In a thoroughly commetric passage, the presented upbeats (1)

8.2 (continued)

are preceded and followed by (i.e., resolved by) presentations of the adjacent downbeats (o) on the same level of the metrical hierarchy (cf. Rahn 1978d). Upbeats that are not presented (in parentheses in example 8.3) need not be resolved, of course.

Accordingly, three types of *contrametricity* (i.e., syncopation) can be distinguished: (a) a presented upbeat is resolved by the following downbeat at its level (→) but not by the preceding downbeat (↤), signifying lack of resolution, as shown in example 8.4; (b) a presented upbeat is resolved by a presentation of the preceding downbeat but not the following downbeat (example 8.5); (c) a presented upbeat is resolved by presentations of neither the preceding nor the following downbeats (example 8.6).

In terms of adjacency, types a and b are identical, since the relationship of adjacency does not distinguish between preceding and following events. In terms of sequence, types a and b are different: both share one feature with the thoroughly

8.2 (continued)

8.2 (continued)

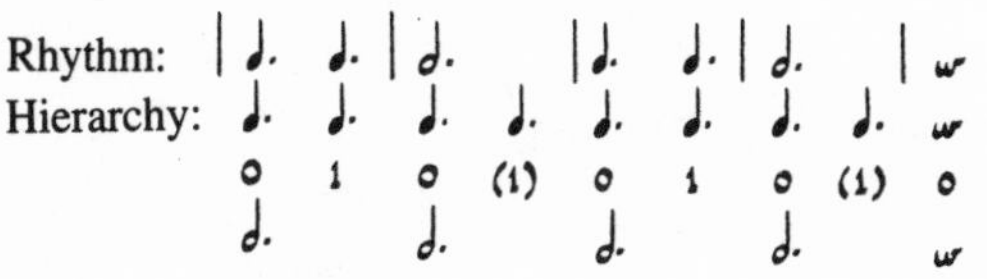

Rhythm: | ♩. ♩. | ♩. | ♩. ♩. | ♩. | w
Hierarchy: ♩. ♩. ♩. ♩. ♩. ♩. ♩. ♩. w
    0   1   0 (1) 0   1 0 (1) 0
    ♩.   ♩.   ♩.   ♩.   w

8.3

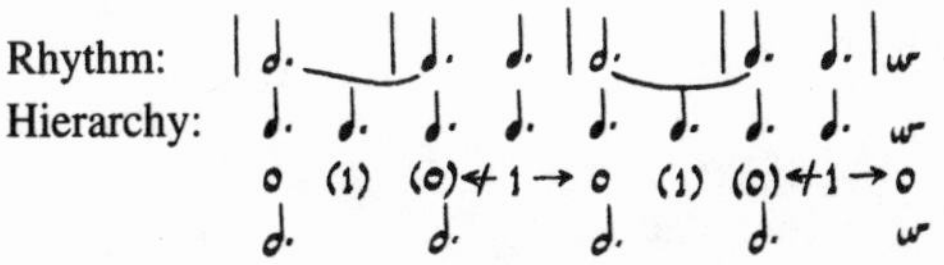

Rhythm: | ♩.___ | ♩. ♩. | ♩. ___ | ♩. ♩. | w
Hierarchy: ♩. ♩. ♩. ♩. ♩. ♩. ♩. ♩. w
    0 (1) (0)←1→0 (1) (0)←1→0
    ♩.   ♩.   ♩.   ♩.   w

8.4

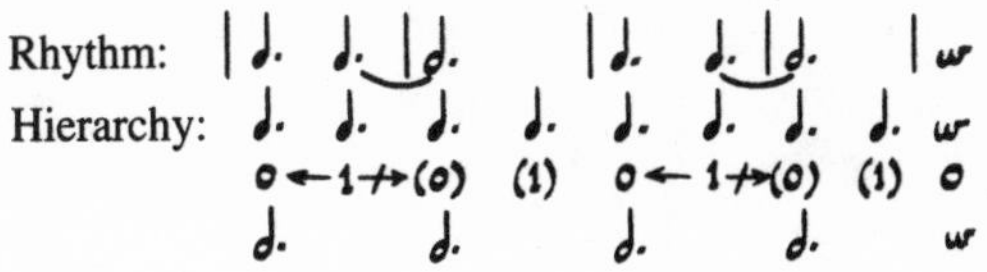

Rhythm: | ♩. ♩. | ♩. | ♩. ♩. | ♩. | w
Hierarchy: ♩. ♩. ♩. ♩. ♩. ♩. ♩. ♩. w
    0←1→(0) (1) 0←1→(0) (1) 0
    ♩.   ♩.   ♩.   ♩.   w

8.5

♩. ♩.|♩. ♩.|♩. ♩.|♩. ♩.| w
♩. ♩. ♩. ♩. ♩. ♩. ♩. ♩. w
0 1→(0)←1→(0)←1→(0) 1→(0)
♩.   ♩.   ♩.   ♩.   w

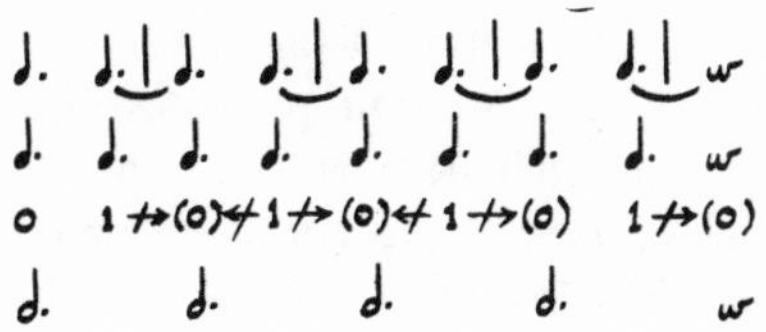

8.6

commetric case and with the thoroughly syncopated case (type c), but none with each other. Thus, the four types (A, B, C, D) can be arranged as in figure 8.1. In this cyclic arrangement, opposite members (A and C, B and D) share no features, and adjacent members (A and B, B and C, C and D, and D and A) share one feature.

In Western music, one often groups A and B together as commetric in opposition to C and D, which are considered syncopated. There is no reason, however, why any of the four typologies in figure 8.2 should not be adopted, for each is internally consistent. Category A is undeniably commetric, B is doubtful: it can be considered either syncopated or commetric. If a distinction is to be made between A and B, it is that B includes all commetric rhythms that are 'dotted' or that feature an anacrusis, whereas A is 'four-square.' This distinction between dotted or anacrustic and 'plain' rhythms is sometimes signifi-

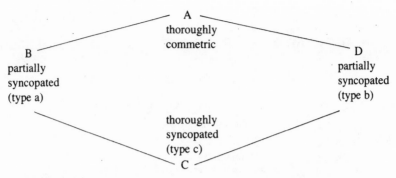

FIGURE 8.1

	Commetric	Synocopated
1	A	B, C, D
2	AB	C, D
3	AD	B, C
4	ABD	C

FIGURE 8.2

cant. For example, the music of the Huguenot psalter can be distinguished from other French monophony of the sixteenth century by its uniform 'plain-ness' (cf. Rahn 1977b). Interestingly, C and D are distinguished by Renaissance theorists, for syncopated passages that begin according to type D are considered more easily perceivable and easier to perform than those of type C. Type D is also recognized in the West under the headings *Scotch snap* and *feminine cadence*, rhythms that are considered distinctive but not clearly recognized as syncopated or strictly commetric. That these latter forms are ambiguous in European theory is probably a reflection of the West's preference to view all types of 'dissonances' (including upbeats) as being resolved by following rather than preceding events. This in turn is a reflection of the stylistic tendency among Western musicians to consider as oriental the ends of pieces or sections, rather than beginnings. Regardless of how the four types of pattern are grouped into categories – a matter that depends in each situation on the observables and their interpretation – it is evident that the rattle-castanet part is undeniably commetric.

In general, one attempts to interpret patterns as commetric rather than syncopated if at all possible. Why this is interpretively desirable can be understood if two possible barrings of the rattle-castanet part are compared (example 8.7). According to the first interpretation, two moments (a and c) of the pattern belong to the upper level of the hierarchy (o) and one (b) to the lower level (1); in the

8.7

8.8

second, only one (b) belongs to the upper level and two (a and c) to the lower. Thus, the first interpretation matches more observables with higher levels of the hierarchy. In this way, more of the relatively local events are directly related to more of the relatively farflung or global events (cf. Rahn 1978d). Table 8.1 illustrates those presented moments that are directly related to any given presented moment by being adjacent to it according to the two possible hierarchies. As can be observed, interpretation 1 features far more direct relationships than interpretation 2. Since the interpretations are otherwise identical, one can assert that 1 is the better of the two, accounting as it does for more relationships than the second.

A more complex case is represented by the hourglass drum's part. Here two pitches are involved. In this style of music, such percussion pitches function as

TABLE 8.1

Moment	Adjacent moments in the hierarchy
According to interpretation 1	
a	b, c
b	a, c
c	a, b, d
d	c, e, f
e	d, f
f	d, e
According to interpretation 2	
a	b
b	a, c
c	b
d	e
e	d, f
f	e

8.9

8.10

8.11

timbres: only the identities of the pitches are significant, not the intervals between them. In the present instance, there is a correlation between pitches and the metrical positions at which they occur: the high pitches coincide with o-moments, and low pitches with 1–moments (example 8.8; an upward stem indicates the low pitch, a downward one the higher).

In both the parts considered so far, there is no problem in barring the pattern: one orientation is critically better than the other possibilities. That the o's of both patterns coincide (example 8.9) means that they can be considered oriental for the other patterns, where no single orientation qualifies as the 'best.' This can be observed most closely in the case of the medium frame drum's part. If the pattern is isolated from its context, two orientations qualify as best (example 8.10). In both orientations the two pitches coincide with specific metrical positions at a single level: in the first barring, the low pitch coincides with o, the high with 1; in the second, the opposite holds: o is high, 1 is low. At the next higher level, there is no co-ordination between pitch and metrical position. Rather the pitches marked x 'anticipate' the following tone. Such anticipations can be defined by the appearance of a given pitch content on an upbeat immediately before the same content appears on the next downbeat (example 8.11). In this instance, regardless of whether interpretation 1 or 2 is followed, tones *b* and *e* are anticipations of *c* and *f*, respectively, because at the level where they occur *b* and *e* are 1 to the o of the *c* and *f* that follow (example 8.12). Of the two

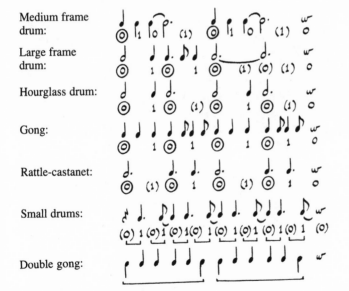

8.12

8.13

8.14 Braces indicate spans articulated by small drums and double-gong parts. Circles indicate coincident zeros.

Rattle-castanet:

Hourglass drum:

8.15

Rattle-castanet:

Small drums:

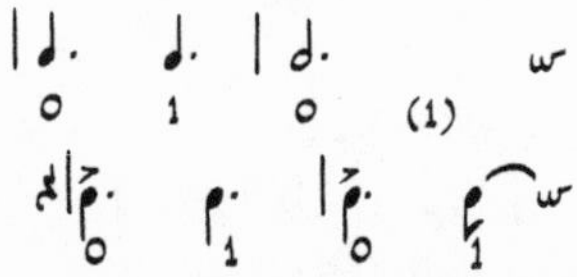

8.16

Level 3

8.17

Rattle-castanet: hierarchy

Small drums:

8.18

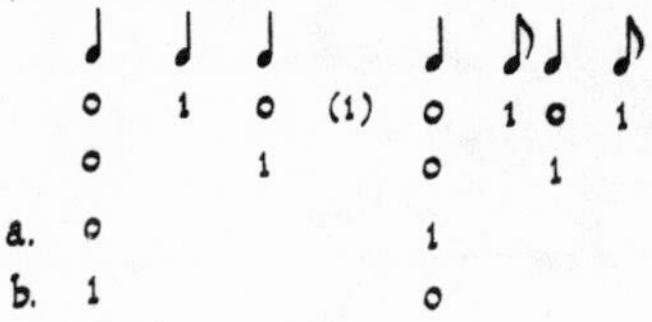

8.19

possible orientations the first is the one in which o's of the highest level coincide with o's of the highest levels of the rattle-castanet and hourglass-drum parts. Thus, following the logic employed in distinguishing between the two possible orientations of the rattle-castanet part, the first is to be preferred as the better interpretation in the context of the other parts. One can also note that low tones (e.g., *a* and *d*) coincide with o's, as was found in the hourglass-drum part (example 8.13). Similarly, the other instrumental parts can be arranged as shown in example 8.14 (circles indicate coincident zeros). In its first measure, the large frame drum coincides metrically with the hourglass drum; in its second, with the rattle-castanet pair; in its fifth, with the hourglass drum again; in its sixth, with the small drums. The latter coincide with the double gong's first measure and the (single) gong's third measure. In this way, all the parts are hierarchically interrelated through the rattle-castanet and hourglass-drum parts.

Also evident is the use of 'cross rhythm,' which can be defined as the simultaneous presentation of different bisectors of a given modular interval. In the rattle-castanet and hourglass-drum parts, for example, measure 5 appears as in example 8.15. In the rattle-castanet part, the six-eighths' duration is bisected into $6 = 3 + 3$ $(2 = 1 + 1)$; in the hourglass part, into $6 = 4 + 2$ $(3 = 2 + 1)$.

The small drums provide an instance of 'polyrhythm' which can be defined as the simultaneous presentation of differently oriented metrical hierarchies. If their part is compared with that of the rattle-castanet, one can observe that their respective o's are not coincident (example 8.16). Accordingly one can distinguish between cross rhythm, which has to do with the non-coincidence of 1's, and polyrhythm, which involves non-coincident o's.

The hierarchical metrical structures considered so far have been based on the coincidence of o's. In the present instance, the attacks of the small-drums part bisect the pulsation established in the rattle-castanet part, so that the former coincide not with the o's of the rattle-castanet as in previous instances but with the 1's. Such a relationship represents what might be described as a 'first degree' polyrhythm. In hierarchical terms, the small-drums part presents a pulsation every moment of which coincides with a bisector of the pulsation that appears at the same level (2, in example 8.18) in the rattle-castanet part. Each moment marked o in level 3 can be considered oriental for that level: in a sense, moment a (example 8.17) stands for (i.e., is oriental for) the durations marked x and y (see chapter 7 concerning the *taqsim*). Accordingly, moments b and c, as the bisectors of durations x and y, respectively, can be considered to stand for them as well. Thus, the small-drums part articulates both moments and the durations implied by moments that appear in the hierarchy (example 8.18).

The rhythmic complexity of such ensemble patterns can have great consequences for the vocal parts, since the latter can be co-ordinated with any of the various cross rhythms and polyrhythms at any given time. Nevertheless, in the genre being considered here, the sung passages are for the most part monometric, though they do 'cross over' from one type of bisection to another. Most important for the vocal parts is the prevailing pulsation in dotted halves that is found in the percussion ensemble, as well as the two-measure patterns in all but the small-drums part. These two-measure patterns are, however, not specifically oriented. Thus, for example, the gong part can be read in either of two ways (a or b, example 8.19). Nevertheless, they do provide an articulation (or grouping) of pairs of measures that can be – and is, in fact – exploited in the vocal parts.

Deeper Levels of the Metrical Hierarchy
In the sung portions, the two-measure phrases are grouped in twos and threes to form units of text or music. These in turn are grouped to form even larger units, and so forth. A good example of this hierarchical organization based on the percussion can be seen in 'Oye adee yie Nana Safo ee.' Here each line of text corresponds to two statements of the two-measure percussion pattern. Pairs of lines are parallel in construction, beginning with the same words:

Oye adee yie Nana Safo ee
Oye adee yema n'amo oo

Pairs of these pairs are grouped timbrally by the distribution of the solo and chorus parts:

S1   C/   S2   C/   S3   C/   S4   C/

Between four-line groups, there is further parallelism, since the solo part is varied and the chorus part is rendered in much the same way each time:

S1   C   S2   C   S3   C   S4   C

In each of the songs, this hierarchical type of scheme is worked out in a slightly different way. But common to all of them is the following overall scheme (listed from lower to higher levels):

1 Percussion pattern
2 Textual unit or parallelism
3 Textual unit or parallelism
4 Textual unit or parallelism
5 Alternation of leader and chorus
6 Musical parallelism through variations in leader's part
7 Textual parallelism

In some songs, where only three or four levels appear, the hierarchy is rather shallow. In others it is deeper, five or even six levels being found. Throughout the songs, there are levels corresponding to numbers 1, 5, and 6, above. Levels corresponding to numbers 2 to 4 are optional, but when they occur they fill in the hierarchy between 1 and 5. The musical strophe, the section that is repeated in toto, always corresponds to number 5 or 6 above.

Thus, though each song has an hierarchical structure, the specific kind varies from item to item. Some types of levels are common to all examples, and others are added in their appropriate places. That there is a basic format (i.e., percussion pattern, alternation of leader and chorus, variation of leader's part) unifies the corpus. That levels added to this scheme are ordered in a specific way contributes to the repertoire's unity as well. Also to be noted is that a number of the levels are distinguished by musical rather than textual patterning. The nature of these patterns can be described in terms of tonal organization.

Tonal Organization
A number of regularities in pitch organization mark the songs. First, only tones of the 7 from 12 by 7 (and 6) scale appear: c, d, e, f, g, a, b. Second, in ambitus the songs as a group range from c to e^1: $c, d, e, f, g, a, b, c^1, d^1, e^1$. Third, there is a considerable number of simultaneous thirds in the chorus sections. These thirds appear singly or in pairs or triples (example 8.20). Finally, the songs end in the bottom region of the range, on $c, d,$ or e (with or without a group of thirds above these tones).

Considered in isolation, these individual observations appear interesting but not very coherent. Considered from the point of view of what can be called 'chains of thirds,' they seem more closely related.

Since the diatonic collection features co-ordination of interval sizes between scale and gamut, all of the thirds can be considered equal in size. Thus, for example, the interval from c to e is the same as that from e to g. Moreover, since the scale features a co-ordination of bisection with respect to both the gamut and the diatonic collection, each third can be considered to be bisected by the intervening scale degree; for example, c–e is bisected by d, d–f by e. These are ideal conditions for organizing pitches into two complementary chains of thirds (figure 8.3).

Each chain forms a 'scale' of its own in the sense that each member is a given distance from the next member, and members of each chain bisect adjacent members of the other. As can be seen, however, pitches that might otherwise be considered to belong to the same class of pitches (e.g., c and c^1, d and d^1, and e and e^1) are assigned to different sets: c belongs to chain A, c^1 to chain B; d to chain B, d^1 to chain A; etc. Thus, these chains of thirds constitute an

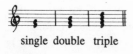

single double triple

8.20

anomaly: the modular interval of twelve semitones is significant in defining the diatonic collection of pitch classes, but there is another organization that cuts across this ordering, namely, the partitioning of the set of pitches (not scale degrees!) into two chains of thirds.

In addition, one can note that the ranges of all the songs are an octave or more. In this way all pitch classes in the diatonic collection are presented in each song. All of this produces a systematic ambiguity between pitch-class organization and the chains of thirds.

Finally, one aspect of the relationship between the gamut and the cycle is manifest in the songs, and in turn reflects on the chain-of-thirds organization. Of the fifths in terms of which the diatonic cycle is defined, all but one are perfect, that is, correspond to seven semitones. The exception, *b–f*, consists of four degrees but only six (not seven) semitones. It is the only ambiguous interval in the collection. Either a fourth (*f–b*) or a fifth (*b–f*) can be six semitones in size. All other intervals when expressed in terms of the gamut correspond to only one interval expressed in degrees. (For example, all intervals of three semitones which are found in the collection are thirds.) Significantly, the *b–f* interval never appears in the chains of thirds that are referential for the songs. If it did, it would appear either at the bottom of chain B (figure 8.4) or at the top of chain A (figure 8.5). This is one instance where what does *not* happen in pieces illuminates the system on which they are based, for it reveals a consistency between the ordering of the diatonic collection and the chains of thirds.

This system of tonal organization is co-ordinated with the metrical hierarchy, yielding tono-metric patterns. This can best be illustrated by 'Mesu mefre agya Katakyie.' Here the first beat of each 6–8 measure can be considered oriental. If the members of chain A that coincide with the beginnings of such measures are labelled o and the members of chain B that similarly coincide are labelled I, the interpretation in figure 8.6 results.

Clearly section b is a repetition of section a. Section c which concludes the first half contains an extension of the preceding pattern (I I) (o o), which becomes (I I) (o I o I). With or without this controlled extension, it forms a parallel with the first two sections, differing from them only at its end (figure 8.7). Its close on I concludes the first half. The second half (d, e, f) concludes on o. (This is analogous to the case in Western music of the eighteenth century where

Chain A   c   e   g   b   d¹
Chain B   d   f   a   c¹   e¹

FIGURE 8.3

B   d   f   a   c′   e′

FIGURE 8.4

c   e   g   b   d′   f′

FIGURE 8.5

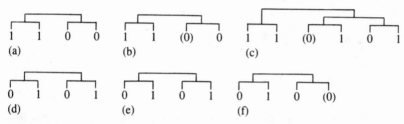

(a)   1   1   0   0

(b)   1   1   (0)   0

(c)   1   1   (0)   1   0   1

(d)   0   1   0   1

(e)   0   1   0   1

(f)   0   1   0   (0)

FIGURE 8.6

a   1 1 0 0
b   1 1 0 0
c   1 1 0 1 0 1

FIGURE 8.7

d   0 1 0 1
e   0 1 0 1
f   0 1 0 0

FIGURE 8.8

binary forms (such as dances) typically end their first halves on the dominant and their second halves on the tonic.)

In the second half, section e is a repetition of section d. Just as in the first half, the last section of the second is parallel to the others, differing only at its

8.21

1 Idiophone

2 Two idiophones

3 Pitches

4 Two-tone chords

5 Three-tone chords

8.22

end (figure 8.8). Its close on o concludes the second half and the piece as a whole.

Although each song presents its tono-rhythmic patterns in a special way, the principles of extension, immediate repetition, and parallelism all play a leading role in the interpretation of pieces in the repertoire. Also, the chain of thirds presented at the end of each piece is oriental (o) for the work as a whole.

One detail that deserves mention here is the use of appoggiaturas in the solo part. This occurs in sections b and c (figure 8.6), where appoggiaturas are marked by parentheses. Generally, the vocal rhythms are commetric, but one type of syncopation, the so-called Scotch snap (type c, figure 8.2), occurs frequently at the ends of textual lines. When it does, the first syncopated tone (circled, example 8.21) invariably belongs to a different chain of thirds than the following tone. (For example, in figure 8.4, *f* belongs to the *d–f–a–c–e* chain, in figure 8.5, *g*, to the *e–g–b–d* chain.) The following tone (e.g., *g*) is referential, and the first tone (e.g., *f*) forms a melodic dissonance which is resolved to the referential tone. (Such appoggiaturas can then be defined by the appearance of a non-oriental pitch on a downbeat, that is, an oriental moment, followed by its resolution to a referential pitch on a succeeding upbeat.) The significance of appoggiaturas is that the normal co-ordination of pitch and moment orientation is temporarily reversed. When this occurs, the parallelism of the line which features syncopation with the preceding further encourages such an interpretation if only on grounds of economy (example 8.21).

By way of a long disgression, a basic distinction will be developed at this point between reference and orientation, for a passage of music can be organized referentially – that is, each event can be profitably referred to a construct – without the passage being oriented. Simple instances of this occur in example 8.22. All the events, be they undifferentiated strokes on one (1) or more (2) idiophones, or pitches (3) or chords (4, 5), can be referred to a single construct, a pulsation. In such passages, the pulsation binds each event to the passage as a whole, but there are no intervening units: only the whole and its smallest parts are accounted for. Such schemes have been described as 'flat' hierarchies (Meyer 1973: 90–7, esp. n.6, p. 90).

In more complex cases, such as those in example 8.23, two values are arranged periodically (observe the correspondence of 3 and 4 to the Hukwe and Akan pieces, respectively). In these passages, there is a pulsation of attacks:

and two pulsations (2 and 3 as in example 8.24) each corresponding to one of the values, that is, for example, one of the two idiophone tones, pitches, or chords. Example 8.24 shows a hierarchy of sorts: level 1 is uppermost in the hierarchy levels, 2 and 3 form the middle, and the passage as a whole constitutes the lowest level. Since there are intervening levels in these patterns, one cannot say that the hierarchy is flat. Neither is it strictly oriented: the members of level 1 could be oriented to either level 2 or level 3 (example 8.25). One can describe such patterns as hierarchical and oriented in a determinately ambiguous manner.

If a pattern is not strictly periodic (in contrast to those considered thus far), the issue of commetricity arises. Whenever a pattern can be described as commetric, one is dealing with an unambiguously oriented hierarchy. Thus, for example, the pattern:

♩ ♩ ♩ ♩ ♩ ♩ ♩ ♩ ♩ ♩ ♩ ♩ ♩ w

can be read commetrically, as in example 8.26, which implies a hierarchy, shown in example 8.27, in which the uppermost level (a) is oriented to the next lower level (b). Between level b and the whole passage there are no intervening levels. Such patterns are minimally oriented. The terms *metre* or *measure* (in the sense of 2–4, 3–4, etc.) could profitably be restricted to passages that are at least minimally oriented rather than being merely periodic and flatly hierarchized.

8.23

8.24

8.25

♩ ♩ ♩ ♩ ♩ ♩ ♩ ♩ ♩ ♩ ♩ ♩ ♩ ♩ ♩ 𝅝

0 1 0(1) 0 1 0(1) 0 1 0(1) 0 1 0(1) 0 1 0(1) 0

8.26

♩ ♩ ♩ ♩ ♩ ♩ ♩ ♩ ♩ ♩ ♩ ♩ ♩ ♩ ♩

(a) ♩ ♩ ♩ ♩ ♩ ♩ ♩ ♩ ♩ ♩ ♩ ♩ ♩ ♩ ♩ ♩ ♩ ♩

(b) ♩ ♩ ♩ ♩ ♩ ♩ ♩ ♩ ♩ ♩

8.27

♩ ♩ ♩. ♩ ♩ ♩. ♩ ♩ ♩. 𝅝

1 ♩ ♩ ♩ ♩ ♩ ♩ ♩ ♩ ♩ ♩ ♩ ♩ ♩ ♩ ♩ ♩ ♩ ♩ 𝅝

2 ♩ ♩ ♩ ♩ ♩ ♩ ♩ ♩ ♩ ♩ ♩ ♩ ♩ 𝅝
  0   1 0 (1) 0   1 0 (1) 0   1 0 (1) 0

3 ♩. ♩. ♩. ♩. ♩. ♩. 𝅝

8.28

Though duple metres provide the simplest examples, one could also describe triple patterns that are minimally oriented, as in example 8.28. Here there is a certain ambiguity between the first and second levels, since quarter-note durations function as unit intervals on level 1 and as halves of the units on level 3.

As long as only simple contents (such as idiophone strokes of a single timbre or pitch) are involved, the relationship between rhythm and content is simple too. As soon as the contents are differentiated, possibilities arise for complex relationships between temporal and tonal hierarchies. For example, two timbres (1), pitches (2), or chords (3, 4, 5) might be found in a similar passage (example 8.29).

The rhythmic organization of attacks forms a minimally oriented hierarchy, as it did in the undifferentiated example. The differentiation of contents leads to a determinately ambiguous structure. For example, the pitches of (2) can be oriented around *g* or *d*. If they are oriented around *g*, the most elegant interpretation would be as in example 8.30. Since *g*'s appear at the beginning of every fourth measure and *d*'s at the point that bisects these four-measure groups (the downbeats of mm. 3 and 7 above), the passage can be understood as an oscillation between 0 (*g*) and 1 (*d*). Within these two-measure spans, the following applies: the orienting pitch occurs on downbeats and the non-orienting pitch on upbeats. In this way, the interpretation is enhanced through a pitch-

8.29

8.30

8.31

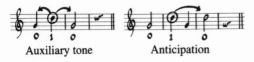

Auxiliary tone   Anticipation

8.32

8.33

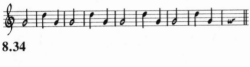

8.34

8.35

time isomorphism by the appearance of oscillations at the levels of both one and two measures.

With g as o, the interpretation in example 8.30 is better than another that might be offered, namely, the one in example 8.31. In the latter interpretation, there is no isomorphism between one- and two-measure levels. Another way of stating this is to say that the first interpretation is preferable because it features 'auxiliary' tones rather than the 'anticipation' in the second reading (example 8.32). Just as commetric interpretations are preferable to syncopated ones, so too auxiliaries are to be preferred to anticipations. All such non-harmonic tones can be defined as tones in which there is not an exact co-ordination of tonal and rhythmic orientation. In other words, non-harmonic tones include all tones except those that are assigned the value o with respect to both the pitch and temporal organizations. These can be classified as in figure 8.9. In a harmonic tone, the pitch and the moment of attack are both oriental, that is, all other values are oriented towards them. In an auxiliary, the pitch and moment of attack are both non-oriental. A tone is an appoggiatura if its attack is temporally oriental and its pitch is tonally non-oriental. Finally, if the tone is temporally non-oriental and the pitch has the same function as that of the next temporally oriental tone it is an anticipation. In sum, harmonic and non-harmonic tones arise from passages that are differentiated in content and at least minimally oriented. All the

8.36

8.37

8.38

same, such passages need not be unequivocally oriented at lower levels, for the passages outlined above could be read as in example 8.33. In other words, *d*, rather than *g*, could be considered the oriental pitch. Similarly, the other examples cited above can be read in two ways: *c–g* or *e–b* is oriental (3); *c–g* or *e♭–b♭* is oriental (3a); *c–g* or *d–a* is oriental (3b); *c–e–g–b–d–* or *d–f–a–c–e* is oriental (4); *c–e–g* or *g–b–d* is oriental (5). Whichever pitch or chord is considered oriental, there are two possible readings, of which one is preferable because it features auxiliary tones, which embody an isomorphism between levels, rather than anticipations, which – in this case – yield a less elegant reading. In each situation there are four likely readings, of which two are equally elegant. These

Harmonic: rhythm   ⎛0⎞ 1 ⎛0⎞ 1 ⎛0⎞
               pitch   ⎝0⎠ 1 ⎝0⎠ 1 ⎝0⎠

Auxiliary: rhythm   0 ⎛1⎞ 0 ⎛1⎞ 0
               pitch   0 ⎝1⎠ 0 ⎝1⎠ 0

Appoggiatura: rhythm   0   1 ⎛0⎞ 1 0
               pitch   0   x ⎝1⎠ 0 1

Anticipation: rhythm   0   1 0 ⎛1⎞ 0
               pitch   0   1 0 ⎝0⎠ 0

FIGURE 8.9

patterns are accordingly minimally oriented with respect to their attack rhythms and determinately ambiguous with regard to their contents, which create lower levels of the hierarchy, levels of two and four measures rather than one-half or one measure.

Such differentiated patterns need not be ambiguous, however, for the contents can be arranged quite unequivocally. For example, the type of passage in example 8.34 can be most elegantly read in only one way, that is, as shown in example 8.35. In this interpretation, groups of two measures form the next higher level of the hierarchy which is marked by anticipations (circled). Had the passage been read as in example 8.36, the circled tones could have had two significances: they could be considered either anticipations of the following non-oriental tones or resolutions of the d's which could then be regarded as appoggiaturas. The situation would thus have been ambiguous. Although one is often forced to acknowledge ambiguity in a pattern, reasons of economy lead one to prefer an unambiguous reading when possible.

For all of the passages considered so far, I have assumed that multiples of two or four measures were presented, as in example 8.37. If this were the case, the bottom level of the hierarchy would begin in a different way than it ended. If, however, the passage began and ended with the same pitch or chord, new possibilities – as illustrated in example 8.38 – would emerge for orientation. A passage can be viewed, not as a succession of contiguous spans (0 1 0 1 etc.), but as a durational hierarchy in which non-oriental spans are included in an overall oriental span (figure 8.10). In such an interpretation, the non-oriental

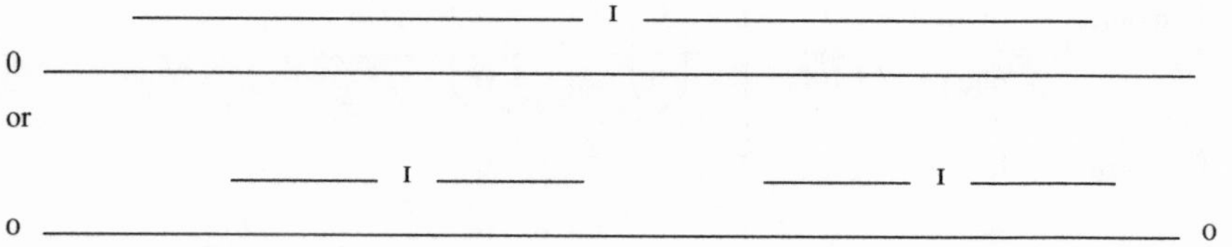

FIGURE 8.10

spans are considered to be within oriental spans or superimposed on them, rather than merely *between* them.

In all such patterns it is preferable to consider as oriental the extreme values (first and last) rather than the included values, a consideration that is consistent with the view that lower levels of a temporal hierarchy (i.e., those which correspond to longer spans) are preferably associated with lower levels of the tonal hierarchy. Lower levels account for more of the piece than higher levels both temporally and tonally. That this is true with regard to rhythm is evident from the conventions of hierarchical notation itself. That it is true of tonality is obvious if one remembers that all the pitches of a piece are related to the tonic sonority by transposition and inversion. This allows one to assert that all the pitches of a piece having a tonal centre are accounted for most economically by the tonic sonority and operations (or transformations) that can be directly performed on it.

In brief, the superficial rhythm of a passage can give rise to a single temporal orientation, but the coterminous pitches need not be considered oriented. If the contents of the passage's extremes are identical, one is encouraged to view these contents as oriental and other values as non-oriental and included in the whole.

At this point, an objection might be raised that non-oriental anacruses and escape-tones, which occur at the beginning or end of a piece, might play an undue part in determining the interpretation. For example, suppose piece 1 of example 8.38 was varied as in example 8.39. Would *d* have to be considered oriental? Common sense rebels at the thought, as does the theory presented here. Indeed, only a pseudo-objective approach would endorse such an interpretation; when one selects the pitches that one might consider oriental, one is always concerned with the largest spans in the piece. The oscillation between *g* and *d* takes place at the level of the commetric pulsation in half notes. The anacrusis and escape-tones do not contradict this pattern but are included within it. Had the first *d* and the last *g* been a half note in duration, *d* might have been considered oriental. As it stands and in terms of the oscillation in half notes, the piece begins and ends on *g*. In such instances, *g*, by its periodic recurrence on downbeats, can be said to 'control,' or 'be referential for,' a pulsation in whole notes

8.39

8.40

which forms the deepest level of the structure (apart from that of the entire piece).

Example 8.40 describes the tonal hierarchy of this variant. The upper level (1) represents all that happens at the very surface of the piece, the notes themselves, which yield a pulsation in quarter notes. The next level (2) represents the commetric pulsation in half notes. The bottom level (3) stands for the whole pulsation of *g*'s. One can read this from bottom to top, so that tones that control progressively shorter spans are added at each level. (Values that are implied – by the pulsation – but not presented are in parentheses.) In this way, the foreground (1) of the piece can be regarded economically as an embellishment, ornamentation, or elaboration of more background levels (2 and 3). Another way of putting this is to say that the immediate details of the piece can be viewed as insertions into or projections from its deeper structure.

LIN YÜ'S MUSIC FOR THE CONFUCIAN TEMPLE

The pieces to be considered in the present section (example 8.41) consist of the sixteen songs in Lin Yü's *Music for the Confucian Temple* (Provine, 1974). The songs exhibit a number of class and boundary features. For example, each song consists of precisely thirty-two tones corresponding to eight four-syllable lines of text which are set syllabically throughout. Within the four-tone phrases, pitches that are temporally adjacent to each other differ. The only instances of immediate repetition of a pitch (or a pitch class defined by the octave) occur between lines: at times the last tone of one line and the first tone of the next line are the same.

8.41 Sixteen songs in Lin Yü's music for the Confucian temple

8.41 (continued)

8.41 (continued)

In other words, the only temporally adjacent tones that are identical in terms of pitch class are extremes.

Some of the songs are to be repeated in performance. Thus, it is not surprising that the first and last tones of these songs are identical, since, on repetition, the last tone of the last line is temporally adjacent to the first tone of the first line. Moreover, this identity between first and last tones is found not only in the songs that are repeated but in all of the others as well.

The pitch-class content of each song consists of members of the heptatonic collection [7 from 12 by 7 (and 6)]: all (and only) these pitches are used. If one considers the pentatonic subsets that compose the heptatonic scale, one can observe how this regularity is related to the previous observation that all of the songs begin and end on the same pitch. For instance, the heptatonic scale, $f\ c\ g\ d\ a\ e\ b$, contains three pentatonic subsets:

1 $f\ \ c\ \ g\ \ d\ \ a$
2 $\ \ \ c\ \ g\ \ d\ \ a\ \ e$
3 $\ \ \ \ \ \ g\ \ d\ \ a\ \ e\ \ b$

With allowances for transposition to a different 'key,' the pitch of the first and last tones always belongs to subset 1 rather than subset 2 or 3. In thirteen cases, this tone corresponds to f, which is peculiar to subset 1 since it is not found in 2 or 3. In the remaining three instances, it corresponds to c, d, or a, which are also found in subset 2 or 3. Never, however, does it correspond to e or b, which are found only in subset 2 or 3.

The last observation can be restated probabilistically: the pitch of the extremes is always a member of subset 1 and in a significant majority of cases corresponds to the only member of 1 that is special to it. In other words, the special case of a general rule is most likely to be found. Had the reverse held, one would be less willing to advance the general rule, for the absence of b and e as extremes might have been fortuitous.

The language of classes and boundaries is rather austere: one speaks in an all-or-nothing manner of what always happens or never happens in a group of pieces. By contrast, the theory presented here emphasizes that anything can happen in a single piece. Between these two extremes, the probabilistic approach stresses that though anything might occur in a single piece, some things tend to happen more often than others in a group of pieces that constitute a repertoire.

With regard to the Confucian songs, I will be concerned with what happens most often (i.e., in the majority of cases) or more often than comparable events (i.e., in a plurality of instances), and also how different aspects of pieces co-vary. Majorities and pluralities are rather straightforward and can be exemplified by the fact that most of the songs begin and end on a pitch corresponding to f. Co-variation (or correlation) is epistemologically more complicated. For example, if it is found – as it is – that non-members of subset 1 tend to occur on odd tones (i.e., the first or third of a group of four) rather than even tones, there is considerable latitude for interpretation. In orthodox statistics, such a co-variation is usually not mentioned unless the probability of its having occurred by chance is less than a given amount. For instance, in the social sciences, findings that might have occurred by chance according to odds of twenty-to-one or less are generally rejected; that is, if the probability that the finding was due to chance is more than 1/20, the co-variation is generally not reported. This, of course, is an arbitrary restriction and other criteria, such as odds of 10 : 1 or 100 : 1, have been employed. Indeed, any odds greater than 2 : 1 would seem to be episte-mologically acceptable. Furthermore, such conventional restrictions give rise to the possibility that the only findings reported are those that may have occurred by chance. It is not too difficult to imagine that of twenty experiments, the very one that might have been a result of chance would also be the only one reported! However, from a pragmatic point of view it seems best to report the statistic that represents the chances of a finding being fortuitous, if only to distinguish between how much is explained by a given model and how much might be the result of chance. (In each table below, the odds are 200 : 1.)

An added criterion is that the finding be meaningful, in other words, that it relate to other observed relationships in the pieces. That the findings are consistent with the system used to account for individual pieces and the collectivity of a repertoire is the ultimate criterion for their worth.

At the beginning of this chapter, another criterion, namely, connectivity, was advanced as a requirement fulfilled by repertoires but not necessarily by mere collections of pieces. It was stated there that a group of pieces could be considered connected if each shared at least one systematically defined feature with another work. In the Confucian songs, there is a group of pieces that appear – intuitively, at least – to resemble one another or to be variants of one another.

The relationship of resemblance is non-transitive (since if A resembles B and B resembles C, it does not necessarily follow that A resembles C). This non-transitivity is a highly dangerous quality of the resemblance relationship, for ultimately any two pieces might be considered to resemble each other or else to be joined by a 'chain' of resemblances. In order to make such a relationship meaningful, one must specify its systemic status and also recognize that there are degrees of resemblance.

A final consideration concerns the very observables themselves. The surviving notations for the Confucian songs are highly ambiguous. An 'original' Chinese version and a revised Korean version survive. Two systems were used for the original, and there are discrepancies between them. To a considerable extent, this is of little consequence, since the deviations in the two notations consist of different registral versions of the same pitch class (e.g., one notation reads d^1 and the other d^2). Since the following analyses are couched in terms of pitch classes rather than their specific registral versions, such discrepancies are irrel-evant. For other notes, two symbols which are virtually homonyms (i.e., $t'a$ and $t'ai$, i.e., d and $d^\flat$ or $c^\sharp$) are interchanged. However, these can be rectified easily because they involve contradictions of the conventional scale designations that are found at the beginnings of the pieces. Finally, almost all of the other discrepancies can be accounted for in terms of the style of the songs; as will be seen in the analysis that follows, the typesetter's mistakes appear to have been idiomatic. Songs 1d, 2, 3, 6, 7, and 13 provide instances of such idiomatic variants as indicated by the asterisks in the transcription of example 8.14.

Where variants are found, individual songs must be analysed according to the different possible readings since no criteria exist to decide between the two versions in any given instance. Furthermore, statistical tables based on such analyses should also reflect this indeterminacy by distinguishing between tones and intervals that are interpretable in one and more than one way. (Statistics in the following material are based on the determinately notated tones; figures arising from the inclusion of indeterminately notated tones are indicated in parentheses.) One should note, however, that the situation is not one of chaotic observables but rather of a choice between two possible readings. The manner in which the problem of two possible readings is settled leads to a consideration of relations between music and culture in which some rather severe restrictions are placed on the correlation of the two.

Statistical Regularities

Earlier it was pointed out that chromatic pitches (e.g., b and e vis-à-vis the f-collection described above) tended to occur on odd-numbered tones. There is little difference between the frequencies of degrees 6 and 3 at the respective tones. Similarly, there is little difference between the frequencies of chromatic pitches on tones 1 and 3, or 2 and 4. Table 8.2 describes the frequencies with which chromatic-pitch classes ($b = 3$ and $e = 6$ in the f-collection) appear as the first, second, third or fourth tones of four-tone phrases. The first thing to be observed is that chromatic tones are found much less frequently than diatonic tones. All things being equal, one would expect these chromatic tones to occur in 2/7 (0.29) of the cases, since there are two in the seven-tone collection. However, the ratio is closer to 1/9 (0.11) (table 8.3). Moreover, there is a difference in the frequencies with which chromatic tones are found on odd- or even-numbered tones. Where one would expect chromatic pitches to occur with equal frequency, they are found in a ratio of about 5 : 1 (table 8.4). This is in great contrast to diatonic pitches which are found in about equal proportions on odd and even tones (table 8.5).

Table 8.5 suggests that there is a basic dichotomy between the pentatonic subset and the other members of the heptatonic collection, and between odd- and even-numbered members of the four-tone phrases. Accordingly, one might consider subset 1 as oriental for the heptatonic collection, and the four-tone phrases as consisting of two two-tone phrases. This approach to the songs is further confirmed by findings with regard to melodic succession, i.e., the intervallic relationships between temporally adjacent tones. In the pentatonic sub-

TABLE 8.2

Chromatic tone	Number of tone in four-tone phrase				Total
	1	2	3	4	
6 (= e)	12	4	11	3 (4)/	30 (31)
3 (= b)	10	2	13	0 (1)/	25 (26)

TABLE 8.3

Chromatic	56 (0.11)
Diatonic	456 (0.89)
Total	512 (1.00)

TABLE 8.4

Odd	46
Even	10
Total	56

TABLE 8.5

	Odd	Even
Chromatic	46	10
Diatonic	210	246

$\chi^2 = 25.98$, significant at 0.005 level

TABLE 8.6 Tones of four-tone phrase

1–2	2–3	3–4	4–1
2	6(5)	0	8

TABLE 8.7

	Between	Within
Heptatonic	13 (14)	2
Pentatonic	226 (227)	254

$\chi^2 = 9.13$, significant at 0.005 level

TABLE 8.8

	Frequency
Step	422 (451)
Leap	132 (146)

TABLE 8.9

Odd	147 (166)
Even	407 (431)

TABLE 8.10

	Step	Leap	Odd	Even
Within	372 (396)	90 (102)	103 (120)	359 (378)
Between	50 (55)	42 (44)	44 (46)	48 (53)
	$\chi^2 = 29.0$, significant at 0.005 level		$\chi^2 = 25.7$, significant at 0.005 level	

TABLE 8.11

	Step	Leap
Within	223 (243)	18 (21)
Between	49 (53)	72 (81)

$\chi^2 = 116.76$, significant at 0.005 level

set, only two types of intervals (and their inversions) are found. These consist of two and three, and four and five semitones (and their inversions of ten and nine, and eight and seven semitones respectively). In the heptatonic collection, two more interval classes appear, consisting of one (or eleven) and six semitones. If one compares the frequencies with which these specifically heptatonic intervals appear between consecutive members of four-tone phrases, one finds that they are unevenly distributed (table 8.6). This regularity is analogous to the fact that immediately repeated tones only occur between four-tone phrases. However, heptatonic intervals in general tend to appear between two-tone phrases, that is, between consecutive second and third, or fourth and first tones rather than within phrases (table 8.7).

Not only scalar interval-type (pentatonic versus heptatonic) but also interval size and type within the scale are correlated with relative position in the four-tone phrases. First, steps (intervals of one or four scale degrees) are substantially more frequent than leaps (intervals of two or three scale degrees) (table 8.8). Second, even-numbered intervals (i.e., intervals of two or four scale degrees counting upwards) are much more frequent than odd-numbered intervals (of one or two degrees) (see table 8.9). Third, neither of these observations applies to intervals between four-tone groups (table 8.10). Fourth, within four-tone phrases, leaps are more frequent than steps between tones two and three (i.e., between two-tone phrases) (table 8.11).

In summary, a typical four-tone phrase might be that in example 8.42, where (1) a chromatic pitch (e.g., *b*) appears on an odd-numbered tone; (2) within subphrases, movement is by step and even-numbered interval (*b–a*, *d–c*); and (3) between subphrases, movement is by leap and even-numbered interval (*a–d*). Such a typical case is, however, only an abstraction. How, then, can these tendencies be understood systematically?

8.42

Systematic Interpretation
The first thing to be noted is that several of the regularities considered so far have to do with relationships between temporally adjacent pitches, i.e., melodic progressions. Matters of melodic progression can be accounted for in terms of arpeggiation when the successive pitches can be considered members of the same 'sonorities' (or 'chords'), and voice-leading when the pitches involved belong

to different sonorities. Other regularities involve relationships between collections (e.g., the f-subset and the heptatonic scale). A possible link between such regularities could be posited if the relationships between sonorities and the collections to which they belong were clarified. Finally, many of the regularities have to do with temporal position. These can be linked to the former two aspects if some relationships between temporal and tonal organization can be established.

In order to describe the position of the tones one need not resort to numbers, such as 32, 8, and 4, as was done above. The position of every tone in a song can be specified by invoking the hierarchy in figure 8.11. Each tone (T) in the top level is an extreme of a pair of adjacent tones that constitute a subphrase (S). Each such subphrase is the extreme of a four-tone phrase (P). And so forth. The restriction on immediate repetition can then be couched in terms of the levels of tones, subphrases, and phrases.

In each pair of adjacent tones, the second can be considered oriental, for in a span of adjacent moments, only one extreme need be considered last and all will be ordered in terms of before and after. Similarly, all of the subphrases, phrases, etc. can be grouped into relatively accented and unaccented pairs, the latter of each pair being considered oriental. The pitch equivalence of the first and last tones can thus be expressed not only as an identity of temporal extremes, but also of the most- and least-accented tones in the piece (last and first, respectively).

The pentatonic and heptatonic collection can be developed as before. If this is done, two voice-leading schemes can be constructed for the pentatonic scale. The first results from a symmetrical arrangement of intervals of three pentatonic degrees as in figure 8.12. This gives rise to the scheme of voices in figure 8.13 (as above, figure 6.5, chapter 6). If the complementary interval of f–c (i.e., f–a) is chosen, the schemes shown in figure 8.14 result. The majority of progressions within subphrases can then be described in terms of schemes that specify relationships of resolution between adjacent scale degrees (e.g., a–c, d–c, etc., in 2; d–f, g–f, etc., in 4). These correspond to the most frequent progressions in the songs: up one or four scale degrees.

In the f–c and f–a constructions (1 and 3), c forms an interval of two pentatonic degrees with f, (c–f), and constitutes the most frequent type of leap in the songs. The same can be said of g–f vis-à-vis d–f: g lies on the same side of f as c in the f–c and f–a constructs, and forms with f a more frequent type of progression than does d. This tendency in progression can be seen, then, as a skewing to one side of the symmetrical arrangement. This skewing is even more pronounced at the ends of phrases than at the beginnings, and still more so at the ends of sentences and entire songs (table 8.12). Note that if paragraphs are disregarded, there is a strict rank-order correlation between hierarchical depth and the relative

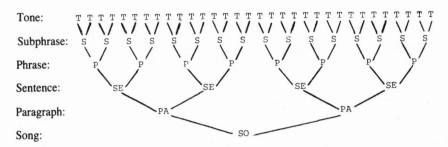

FIGURE 8.11

1   *d – a*

    a – f

        $\boxed{f - c}$

           c – g

             g – d

FIGURE 8.12

2   *a   c   d   f   g*

FIGURE 8.13

3   *g – c*

    c – f

        $\boxed{f - a}$

           a – d

             d – g

4   *d   f   g   a   c*

FIGURE 8.14

TABLE 8.12

Interval in pentatonic degrees	Subphrases	Phrases	Sentences	Paragraphs	Songs
	Frequency at ends				
1	40 (44)	12 (14)	4 (6)	9	1 (2)
2	8	2 (6)	2	0	1
3	5	0 (1)	0	0	0 (1)
4	70 (76)	45 (48)	24 (26)	7	13
	Percentage of g–f (4-degree) type of cadence at ends				
	57	76	80	44	87
	$r_{rank} = +0.40$ (if the figure for paragraphs is disregarded, $r_{rank} = +1.00$)				

frequencies with which odd-numbered intervals are employed. This suggests that the hierarchical organization is disrupted tonally at the ends of the first halves of songs.

Individual Songs

When applied to individual songs of the Confucian group, this systematic perspective clarifies their structures considerably. For example, most of the first song can be understood as a series of progressions from an *a–e* dyad to tones and dyads higher in the hierarchy of orientation (example 8.41). In the first four-tone phrase, *a* and *e* are in accented positions, forming the resolutions of 1–0 cadences: *c–a, g–e*. In the next phrase, *e* is presented again – this time as the resolution of a 4–0 cadence (*d–e*) – and the dyad is arpeggiated (*e–a*) and resolved on *g* at the end of the first sentence. The third phrase parallels the first, with a change in subset from C to D. Significantly, the cadences in phrase 1 consist of progressions that are identical in terms of the twelve-semitone gamut: *c–a* and *e–g* both consist of three semitones. This identity is maintained in the third phrase despite the shift to the *d*–subset, where both cadences involve progressions of two semitones. (Had the shift been to the *g*-subset, the intervals would have differed: *b–a* (2 semitones) and *g–e* (3 semitones). In the last phrase of the second half, a return is made to the *C*-subset and the *a–e* dyad resolves to *g–d*: *g* and *d* are presented in accented positions, preceded by tones that form 1–0 and 4–0 cadences, the intervals of which are again identical in terms of semitones. In sum, the first half is characterized by two progressions from *a–e* to *g* or *g–d*.

By contrast, the second half consists of a single progression from *a–e* to *g–c* and its complement *c–e*. Whereas each progression in the first half covers a sentence, the single progression in the second half is unfolded over an entire paragraph.

In the first sentence of the second half, the C-subset is referential for the extremes, and the D-subset is in the middle. The pitches *a* and *e* are accented, and *a* is prolonged by its neighbour tone, *c*. Finally, both dyads on *c* are presented.

At the next higher level, the progressions appear to be from *e* to *g* and *d* in the first half, and from *c–e* to its complement *c–g* in the second. At the highest level, the progression is from *d* to *c*. If *c* and dyads that bisect the octave, such as *c–e*, are considered oriental, all of these progressions represent resolutions or cadences in the broad sense: less-accented tones being associated with lower levels of the oriental hierarchy.

Variants

Between the levels of piece and repertoire lie variants: pieces that resemble each other more than they do other pieces in the repertoire. A set of eight such pieces can be isolated in Lin Yü's songs (example 8.43). These appear to constitute two basic subgroups and an intermediate case.

If one compares the thirty-two tones of songs 6 and 7 one finds that about one-half correspond (indicated by vertical lines in example 8.43). This is particularly marked in the first and last phrases. In the second measure, one can observe that the $g\sharp$–$f\sharp$ cadence in 6 corresponds to the a–$f\sharp$ cadence in 7. The first is a 1–0 cadence to $f\sharp$ in the E-subset; the second, a similar cadence in the A-subset. Apart from the difference in subsets, the tones correspond. In the last phrase (b), a 4–0 cadence to $f\sharp$ occurs in 6 where a 1–0 cadence to the same tone appears in 7. Much the same comparison holds for the last two tones of the previous phrase (c). In the third phrase (d), a sequence of cadences to $c\sharp$ and *a* in 6 is found reversed in 7 (indicated by a cross). A similar relationship obtains between 6 and 7 in the fifth phrase (e). And if the sixth phrase (f) of 7 is read *b–a*, $f\sharp$*–e*, much the same can be said. Finally, if the seventh phrase of 7 (g) is read as *e*–$f\sharp$, $c\sharp$*–b*, its parallelism with 6 is evident. In sum, with the exception of two tones at the beginning of the fourth phrase (h), the melody of song 6 can be transformed quite simply into the tune of song 7, if provision is made for shifting from one subset to another, substituting 4–0 cadences for 1–0 cadences and vice versa, and reversing even-numbered tones within a phrase. (The latter transformation is, of course, consistent with considering second and fourth tones separated by two or three degrees as 'chords' in the interpretation of individual pieces.)

If these provisions are made, one can observe that song 10 corresponds in all but two tones (k) to 6 or 7. (On the basis of comparisons with 6, one would read the corresponding tones in 7 as *b–a*; with 10, as *a–b*. Since repeated tones

8.43 Variants in Lin Yü's songs

8.44

are otherwise never found in these positions and would preclude the possibility of interpreting a given progression as a cadence, one can rule out *a–a* and *b–b* as readings.) Accordingly, 6, 7, and 10 can be considered the core of the set of variants discussed here.

Following the procedure for comparing songs 10 and 6 with 7, one finds fewer but still striking parallels between these three songs on the one hand and 8 and 9 on the other (indicated by circles). Furthermore, if songs 8 and 9 are compared, one finds several tones shared by them but not found at similar positions in 6, 7, or 10 (indicated by lines). Finally, the remaining discrepancies between 8 and 9 in the first sentence disappear if both are considered to outline a b–$f\sharp$ dyad (indicated by circles and braces in example 8.44).

If song 4 is compared with songs 6, 7, and 10 in this way, even more correspondences are found, but none with 8 and 9. Thus, there appear to be three families of songs: 6, 7, 10; 8, 9; 4.

When song 12 is compared with 6, 7, and 10, the circled correspondences appear; if it is compared with 8 and 9, those shown by squares. In the notation for 3, circles mark correspondences with 6, 7, and 10, and squares, correspondences with 8, 9, and 12.

In sum, songs 6, 7, and 10 resemble each other considerably; 4 is closest to this group but shares features with 3, which in turn shares features with 12, 8, and 9, which are closely related among themselves. If one supposes that songs 6, 7, and 10 form a group, as do 8, 9, 12, and 3, then the problem of alternate readings can be resolved somewhat. In 6, b of the b–$f\sharp$ alternates seems the most appropriate reading to judge from 10, though either is idiomatic. In the fourth phrase of song 3, the a–b succession seems more appropriate if 12 is anything to go by. In the sixth phrase of 7, a–b–e–$f\sharp$ corresponds to 10, and its opposite b–a–$f\sharp$–e corresponds to 6. Either alternative is possible, and the variant readings might have resulted from the overall similarities of the three songs. In the following subphrase, e–$f\sharp$ seems called for: 6 and 10 are in agreement here.

Making such a decision involves a musico-cultural assumption, namely, that culturally proximate behaviour is also musically proximate. In many cases, this is not an assumption but merely an hypothesis to be falsified or not. In the study of genres (i.e., repertoires with which patterns of cultural behaviour are positively associated), it is so prevalent as to represent a 'standing hypothesis.'

By emphasizing 'behaviour,' one avoids the vagaries of mentalistic language and guarantees that one will remain in the realm of observable phenomena. In this case, the observable phenomena consist of the facts that songs 6, 7, and 9 form the extremes of the 'First Offering' section of the liturgy, and beyond this, that the concordant songs are all found in the middle of the service (3–12).

One fact that might be coincidence is that the absolute pitches of the concordant songs agree: all are in Fa of A. Is this to be interpreted as a musical fact or as a liturgical one? Absolute pitch is usually of little musical relevance since one is mostly concerned with relationships among tones rather than their absolute values. All the same, Robert Provine (1974: 10), though reluctantly, compares the A modes as a group with those on C and E especially in the matter of phrase final frequency. However, one can object that the distinctive distribution of phrase finals that Provine finds for the pieces in Fa of A is more a reflection of the eight songs in this group being close variants of one another than of a special 'tonal structure' for A modes.

Though the musico-cultural assumption might be of value in deciding between readings, two things should be emphasized. First, in order to 'predict' the appropriate reading on the basis of this assumption, a great deal of purely musical interpretation has to be carried out independently of the assumption itself. Second, such an assumption is supernumerary to the analysis of the songs. As such it and others like it are to be avoided as much as possible, since every assumption involves a risk, namely, that it is false. In any case, the only justification for making such an assumption is that it leads to new findings. In the present case, the pieces in question are found to be more proximate under the assumption, but this only begs the question. As it stands, the assumption itself is 'terminal.' Were the choices which result from it found to correlate with further, independent findings, there would be some justification for it.

Nomenclature

A final cultural matter worth considering is that of pitch nomenclature. In the Chinese seven-tone solmization system for Fa of C, the pitches are named as follows (in old style romanization):

c d e $f\sharp$ g a b (c^1)
kung shang chiao pièn-chih chih yü pièn-kung kung

The notable thing about this list of names is that $f\sharp$ is considered as a *pièn* form of g, and b, a *pièn* form of c. What *pièn* means in this context seems never to have been determined. Some authors equate *pièn* with 'filler,' apparently because $f\sharp$ and b appear between members of the c-pentatonic scale:

c d e $(f\sharp)$ g a (b) c^1

This however raises the question why $f\sharp$ and b rather than, for example, f and $b\flat$ are specified. In both cases a 7 from 12 by 7 (and 6) collection is formed, and the filler tones are found between members of the pentatonic scale:

c d e (f) g a $(b\flat)$ c^1

The difference between having $f\sharp$ and b and having f and $b\flat$ intercalated is that in the first case, the addition of the two tones allows for the transposition of c-

```
c   d   e   g   a
        g   a   b   d   e
                d   e   f#  a   b
```

FIGURE 8.15

```
              c   d   e   g   a
        f   g   a   c   d
bb  c   d   f   g
```

FIGURE 8.16

	Corresponding pairs	Size in semitones	Size in pentatonic degrees
1	f#–d	4	2
	g–d	5	2
2	f#–e	2	1
	g–e	3	1
3	f#–a	3	1
	g–a	2	1

FIGURE 8.17

	Corresponding pairs	Size in semitones	Size in pentatonic degrees
1	b–d	3	1
	c–d	2	1
2	b–e	5	2
	c–e	4	2
3	b–g	4	2
	c–g	5	2

FIGURE 8.18

pentatonic up three or six (= one) pentatonic degrees (figure 8.15), whereas the second case allows for transposition down three or six (= one) degrees (figure 8.16). This, then, is another instance of skewing to the dominant rather than the subdominant side of a potentially symmetrical arrangement.

It follows from this that the term *filler* is not precise enough here. What I would suggest is *dominant alternate*, for *b* and *f♯* are on the dominant side (as are *c* and *g* in the voice-leading arrangement discussed above) of the *c*-pentatonic scale and are alternates for *c* and *g*, respectively. The sense in which they are alternates is as follows. Any interval formed between *f♯* and another member of the seven-tone collection that is expressible in terms of pentatonic-scale degrees (i.e., not a minor-second or tritone) is of the same size (in pentatonic degrees again) as the corresponding interval formed by *g* and vice versa (figure 8.17). The same can be asserted of *b* and *c* (figure 8.18).

In figures 8.17 and 8.18, the interval *f♯–b* has been left out. However, if *f♯* is an alternate for *g* and *b* for *c*, one can conclude that *g–c* is the interval corresponding to *f♯–b*. When expressed in terms of pentatonic degrees, both are of size 2. What this means is that any interval within one of the three subsets can be translated into an interval of the same (pentatonic) size in either of the other two subsets by means of the alternate versions of a given degree. In this sense, *f♯* is a kind of *g* and *b* is a kind of *c*. Such an interpretation is consistent with findings in the repertoire as a whole, individual pieces, and variants thereof. In the latter case, the positing of, for example, *g–e* and *f♯–e* as equivalent 1–0 cadences has led to regular results. Furthermore, that *c* and *g* are basic and *b* and *f♯* are variants of them seems borne out by the strategic positions that subset 1 (*c*–pentatonic) assumes at the extremes of the pieces.

THE HORNPIPES IN HARDING'S COLLECTION

One can make a number of observations about the tune 'Harvest Home' (example 8.45,1). It is heptatonic and major in tonality. Its melody (the upper part) contains all (and only) the pitch classes of the heptatonic collection. The metre is thoroughly duple. Both parts, melody and accompaniment, are commetric in the strictest sense of the word. The upper part consists solely of two durations between adjacent tones, one of which is half as long as the other. Similarly, the lower part consists solely of two durations, of which one is half as long as the other, but the shorter of the two durations in the lower part is equal in length to the longer duration of the upper part. (In order to facilitate discussion, the durational unit common to the upper and lower parts will be termed the *beat*). The piece as a whole is divided into halves, each of which is repeated. Not counting these repetitions, each half consists of thirty-two beats. The accompaniment presents a periodic succession of beats that is interrupted by the larger duration at the end of each half. At the ends of these halves a succession of three beats appears in the upper part. Finally, each half begins with an anacrusis of one beat in the melody.

1. **Harvest Home**

6. **College Hornpipe**

8.45 Hornpipes in *Harding's Collection*

11. Mountain Hornpipe

17. Devil's Dream

8.45 (continued)

20. Soldier's Joy

23. Fisher's Hornpipe

8.45 (continued)

30. Rickett's Hornpipe

33. Bridge of Lodi

8.45 (continued)

35. Liverpool Hornpipe

49. New Century Hornpipe

8.45 (continued)

55. Durang's Hornpipe

65. Vinton's Hornpipe

8.45 (continued)

69. Favorite Hornpipe

170. Flowers of Edinburgh

8.45 (continued)

Recurrent Traits

One could go on pointing out features of 'Harvest Home' ad infinitum. What is interesting about the features already cited is that each is found in a majority of the pieces considered in this section: the hornpipes in *Harding's Collection of Jigs, Reels, and Country Dances* (1891/1932). Table 8.13 outlines the distribution of these features in the fourteen hornpipes in this anthology. As can be seen, though one feature (major tonality) is common to all of the pieces, and each feature is common to fifty per cent or more of the repertoire, all of the features are found in only three pieces (nos. 1, 17, and 35). If one disregards the feature of major tonality, one can observe that each hornpipe shares at least four of the traits with every other piece in the group. Thus, the repertoire is a class, by virtue of major tonality, and it is bounded, continuous, and marked by a number of majority features. Accordingly, one can consider this set of ten features to be fairly definitive of the repertoire as such.

What remains to be seen is how these features are interrelated with one another and with interpretations of individual pieces. Furthermore, one would like to know how the exceptions (where a feature is absent) are related to the regular pieces. Do the exceptions represent little havens of stylistic anarchy? Or extensions of the practice found regularly?

In order to achieve these ends, one can return to 'Harvest Home' to discern what sense the features make in the context of a single piece. It can be noted that the piece is thoroughly binary in its metrical organization: from the shortest duration to the song as a whole, something special happens at every level of the metrical hierarchy. The level of eighth notes coincides with most of the melody's attacks, whereas the next higher level is marked by the majority of attacks in the accompaniment. Moreover, in mm. 3 and 11, the chord progressions take place at this level. In mm. 7 and 9, and 10 and 15, the harmonic rhythm coincides with the level of half notes, and melodic repetitions coincide with this level in measures 9 and 10, 4 and 12, and 5 and 13. Single chords are presented for a whole measure in measures 4 and 12, and 8 and 16, and for two measures at the very beginning of the piece. Motivic repetitions articulate four-measure spans throughout the hornpipe. Finally, eight-measure units are repeated to form sixteen-measure spans which constitute the halves of the dance as a whole.

From such a hierarchical perspective, the durations employed in the upper and lower parts can be considered to articulate two levels each. In the melody, the two lowest levels ($\flat$ and $\flat$) are presented. The periodic successions of the accompaniment overlap those of the melody: the beat ($\flat$) is common to both, and the next higher level is found only in the accompaniment. The spans during which the periodic succession of beats in the accompaniment is interrupted coincide with the spans at which the melody shifts from half-beat durations to

TABLE 8.13 Distribution of majority features in hornpipes in Harding's Collection

	1	6	11	17	20	23	30	33	35	49	55	65	69	170
Major	x	x	x	x	x	x	x	x	x	x	x	x	x	x
Duple	x	x	x	x	x	o	o	x	x	x	x	x	o	x
Anacrusis	x	x	o	x	x	x	x	x	x	x	x	x	x	x
Ending figure	x	x	x	x	x	x	x	x	x	x	x	x	o	x
Strictly commetric	x	x	o	x	x	x	x	x	x	x	x	x	x	x
Halves repeated	x	x	x	x	o	x	o	x	x	x	x	x	x	x
32-beat halves	x	x	x	x	x	x	x	x	x	x	x	x	o	x
Interrupted only at halves	x	o	x	x	x	o	x	o	x	o	x	o	o	o
Melody unit one-half accompaniment unit	x	x	o	x	x	x	o	x	x	x	o	x	o	o

the beat itself as in example 8.46 (from 'Harvest Home'). The spans during which there is a shift in the pulsations coincide with the extremes of the piece's halves. In other words, special events at the lowest levels of the metrical hierarchy coincide with the extremes of spans at the upper levels. The three-note figure (a) in example 8.46 appears in the melody at the end of each half, and coincides with the parts of this shift when the melody and accompaniment present the same durations. Finally, the anacrusis that appears at the beginning of both halves represents a fusion of the two parts of the texture, for just where the pulsation of beats in the accompaniment is interrupted, it is introduced in the melody so that the pulsation in quarters is maintained throughout the passage in the texture as a whole, although it is broken in the lower part.

Given this hierarchical conception of one of the 'regular' hornpipes, one can appreciate 'irregularities' found in other pieces of the collection. Some of these have sixty-four beats in each half, rather than thirty-two. This merely represents a further continuation of the binary hierarchy discussed previously. In some hornpipes, the accompaniment's pulsation in beats is interrupted not only at the extremes of halves (i.e., every eight measures) but elsewhere as well. But these interruptions emphasize rather than defy the overall hierarchical organization, for they occur at the ends of spans of four, two, or one measures (example 8.46 from 'College Hornpipe').

In one of the pieces, three durations are found in the melody. However, the third duration is twice as long as the larger of the other two and is handled commetrically. Indeed it appears at the end of a four-measure span and thus emphasizes this level of the hierarchy in the same way as halves are normally articulated (example 8.48, from 'Flowers of Edinburgh'). In two other cases where a third duration appears in the tune, a triplet figure: ♩♩♩ is involved.

8.46

8.47

8.48

8.49

8.50

These nevertheless always appear as anacruses, whether to the halves of the song or to the next lower level (four measures; example 8.49, at the beginning of 'Fisher's Hornpipe'). These also constitute the only examples of non-duple durations.

The only other instance of three durations appearing in the melody involves a passage that is not strictly commetric (example 8.50 from 'Mountain Hornpipe'). Here the rhythm is dotted and thus involves an intermediate type of syncopation adjacent to commetricity: in strictly commetric passages, the moments adjacent to any given moment belong either to the same level of the hierarchy or the next-higher level: in dotted rhythms, a moment is preceded by

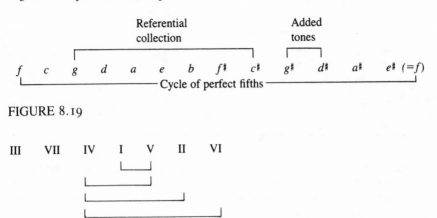

FIGURE 8.19

FIGURE 8.20

one belonging to the next-lower level but the immediately following moment belongs to the same or next-higher level. It thus represents a single degree of syncopation, unlike complete syncopation where neither of the adjacent moments belongs to the same or next-higher level. This syncopation is mild indeed, for – unlike the case with double dotting – the following moment belongs to the next-lower level rather than the second-lowest or one even more remote.

From the preceding discussion it should be clear that the bulk of exceptions can be considered to 'prove the rule,' since they represent deviations from it that are systematically consistent with it. Furthermore, the deviations represent transfers of typical phenomena to adjacent parts of the metrical hierarchy. Thus, the exceptions have the highest degree of proximity to the regular situations.

Of the few instances of deviation from strict diatonicism all but one can be accounted for in terms of the cycle from which the seven-tone scale is derived. The 7 from 12 by 7 (and 6) collection can be described as a cycle in its own right and also as a section of the cycle of perfect fifths. In all but one of the deviant cases, the chromatic tones which are introduced are adjacent to the referential set in the cycle of fifths. For example, in 'Durang's Hornpipe' (no. 55), g♯ and d♯ are introduced into a D-major context and g♯ is one perfect fifth away from c♯, and d♯ a perfect fifth from g♯ (figure 8.19).

Two further things are to be noted about such added tones: they are found on the dominant side of the tonic (in this case, d), and they form a continuous succession of perfect fifths with the referential collection (e.g., there are no breaks between the g–c♯ cycle and the chromatic tones as would be the case if d♯ appeared but g♯ did not.

TABLE 8.14 Distribution of chords in hornpipes in *Harding's Collection*

	1	6	11	17	20	23	30	33	35	49	55	65	69	170
IV	o	x	x	x	o	x	x	x	x	x	x	x	x	x
I	x	x	x	x	x	x	x	x	x	x	x	x	x	x
V^7	x	x	x	x	x	x	x	x	x	x	x	x	x	x
V/V	o	x	o	o	o	x	o	x	o	o	x	x	x	x
II	o	o	x	o	o	o	o	x	o	o	o	o	x	x
VI	o	o	o	o	o	o	o	o	o	o	o	o	o	x

Similar tendencies toward dominant skewing and continuity are found in the choices of chords in the hornpipes. The chords that appear in the dances are listed in figure 8.20. As can be observed, every piece contains I and V (or V⁷). Some also contain IV. Among these, some contain II (or V/V) and of the latter, one contains VI. The observed selections are outlined in table 8.14 (brackets include the chords chosen). As one can see, chords on the dominant side of the cycle of fifths (V, II, VI) are more frequently chosen than those on the subdominant side (IV, VII, III). Moreover, if a chord is introduced, its root forms a continuous series with the others selected. (For example, if I, V, and VI appear, II, which forms a link between V and VI, also appears.)

Comparisons with Other Repertoires

Until now the hornpipes have been discussed in isolation and defined in positive terms (i.e., with regard to features shared by the various pieces in the repertoire). The other, negative side of defining a repertoire is to distinguish it from other groups of pieces. Negative characterizations have already been encountered with regard to pieces and repertoires. One has been interested simply in what does not happen or what happens significantly infrequently within a given body of observables. When comparing repertoires, one is interested in what does not happen or only rarely happens in one repertoire, if it happens all the time, or significantly frequently in another. In the case of boundary features, such repertoires appear to be discrete or insular; with regard to merely statistically significant differences, they appear to overlap each other without coinciding (figure 8.21). The repertoire with which Harding's hornpipes are to be compared here consists of the highland flings (or strathspeys) that appear in the same collection.

Highland Flings

All of the highland flings have dotted rhythms (e.g., ♩. ♪). In this respect, a minority feature of the hornpipe is a class feature of the flings. In addition, most – more than seventy per cent – contain Scotch-snap figures (e.g., ♬.). Since no such first-degree syncopations occur in the hornpipes, a boundary

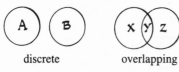

discrete   overlapping

FIGURE 8.21

feature of the latter turns out to be a majority feature of the former. Thus, a picture of rhythmic similarities and differences in the two repertoires emerges in table 8.15. In metre, a majority of the Highland flings, like most of the hornpipes, are consistently duple from the lowest to the highest levels, and the exceptions are duple at the second-highest level, though not at the first. Furthermore, the same relationship holds concerning the overlapping of durations in the melody and accompaniment, as shown in table 8.16. Finally, whereas a majority of Highland flings are in a major key and feature connectivity among chords according to the cycle of fifths, all of the hornpipes display these features, resulting in table 8.17.

From the present account, it would seem that the Scotch snap and dotted rhythms or their absence are more definitive of the differences between the two repertoires than are consistently duple metre, overlap of durational units, major tonality, and connectivity among chords. When this hypothesis is tested in a strictly statistical way (table 8.18), one finds that all of the differences in frequency are significant at the 0.10 or 0.05 levels or higher except one: the difference in frequencies with which there is overlap of durational units in the melody and accompaniment is not even significant at the 0.10 level. Two things can be learned from tables 8.15–8.18. First, the mere characterization of a trait as a majority, minority, class, or boundary feature, though it might serve well to explicate a single repertoire, can be misleading when applied to the comparison of two repertoires: in each case of comparison, a strictly statistical test is preferable. Second, features appear to be of different discriminating powers when repertoires are compared. In this respect, too, a statistical measure can sort out the differences in significance that might be attributed to different variables. Significantly, it was the features that represented the most foreground aspects of the pieces, namely, the variables of overlapping and consistency of duple metre, which turned out not to provide a statistically very significant difference between the repertoires. At the same time, however, it must be remembered that any comparison involves both similarities and differences, and that for the comparison to be musically meaningful the functional status of the variables should be explicated, as was done originally for the hornpipes.

Implicit in the foregoing discussion has been a distinction between melody

TABLE 8.15

	Boundary	Minority	Majority	Class
Hornpipes	SS	D		
Highland flings			SS	D

SS = Scotch snap; D = dotted rhythm

TABLE 8.16

	Majority	Class
Hornpipes	CD	O
Highland flings	CD, O	

CD = consistently duple
O = overlap of durational units

TABLE 8.17

	Majority	Class
Hornpipes		M, CC
Highland flings	M, CC	

M = major; CC = connectivity among chords

TABLE 8.18

	SS	No SS	Total	D	No D	Total
Hornpipes	0	14	14	1	13	14
Highland flings	10	0	10	10	0	10
Total	10	14	24	11	13	24
	$\chi^2 = 24.0$, significant at 0.005			$\chi^2 = 20.3$, significant at 0.005		
	CD	No CD	Total	O	No O	Total
Hornpipes	12	2	14	14	0	14
Highland flings	7	3	10	8	2	10
Total	19	5	24	22	2	24
	$\chi^2 = 1.54$, significant at 0.25			$\chi^2 = 3.01$, significant at 0.10		
	M	Not M	Total	CC	No CC	Total
Hornpipes	14	0	14	14	0	14
Highland flings	7	3	10	6	4	10
Total	21	3	24	20	4	24
	$\chi^2 = 4.80$, significant at 0.05			$\chi^2 = 6.72$, significant at 0.01		

and accompaniment. How can one make such a distinction and what is its theoretical status? First, it seems best to distinguish between a part (e.g., the bottom line) and a relatively melodic part (e.g., the tune). Generally, a part seems better defined if its timbre is consistent and differs from the tone qualities surrounding it. Moreover, a part stands out more if it is relatively loud. However, since differences of timbre or loudness are not specified in Harding's collection, one must turn to other criteria. Those pitches that (a) are closest to each other, (b) occupy the same relative position in the texture (e.g., top, bottom, or middle), (c) appear at the extremes of the texture (e.g., top or bottom), (d) are relatively distant from coterminous pitches, (e) feature pitch attacks that are closest in time, and (f) do not coincide in their attacks with the attacks of coterminous pitches, can be grouped to form a part. If this is done, the tones of 'Harvest Home' can be observed to align themselves in four parts to which one might be added or from which one might be subtracted at various points in the piece. Of these lines, the uppermost tones are best defined with regard to criteria b, c, d, e, and f. The lower parts are closer to each other in pitch (criterion a), but less partlike with regard to the other criteria. Furthermore, the highest part is less redundant and, hence, stands out more clearly as a melody (cf. Rahn 1982b).

As one can observe, the terms used to distinguish one part from another concern the foreground of the piece. In this way, the definition of parts and melodies is relatively asyntactic. All the same, the variables by which a melody is defined can interact with the deeper structures of a piece, so that a melody can be regarded as joining foreground to background.

All this having been said, one can return again to 'Harvest Home' for yet another view of the piece. The strategy employed here is to go through the work stopping at especially interesting moments. (These moments are indicated in example 8.45 by the letters a to i.) Along the way, the concepts of metre and phrase – so important for Western forms – are explored.

At moment a, the tone e appears in the melody. This is the first time a pitch not belonging to the oriental triad d–f♯–a is found. If the moment at which e occurs is considered to be an upbeat eighth note, the tone is absorbed into the metrical hierarchy. As a non-oriental value it is found where it belongs, namely, at a non-oriental moment. The same can be said of the following e and c♯. Furthermore, according to this interpretation the accompaniment becomes commetric at the level of a quarter note. Note, however, that there is nothing in the deep structure of the piece at this point to distinguish the levels of a half note, measure, etc.

Moment b introduces a conflict with the metrical hierarchy by being tonally non-oriental at a point that should, if the hierarchy is consistent, be oriental, the beginning of a quarter-note beat. Nevertheless, the three regular non-harmonic tones preceding b and the commetricity of the accompaniment argue against the *b* defining a revised hierarchy. More is accounted for if the beginning of each quarter-note beat is considered oriental.

Moment c appears to introduce a similar conflict at the level of a measure, for at the beginning of a measure, an oriental tonal value, such as a d–$f\sharp$–a chord rather than an a–$c\sharp$–e triad, would match the status of the downbeat as an oriental moment. However, this apparent conflict is absorbed at the level of two measures. As a moment, c stands as I to the o of the first *d* (m. 1).

One might consider moment d as the site of an imperfect, I–V cadence. With regard to voice-leading, the progression which concludes here represents a IV–I cadence transposed to V, where $f\sharp$ proceeds to *e* and *d* to $c\sharp$. However, the first four measures can be considered to be described best in terms of metre rather than phrase structure. It seems unnecessary to invoke the notion of phrase unless the last part of a span needs to be considered oriental in contrast to a preceding portion which is non-oriental. There is nothing to distinguish the latter part of the second pair of measures with regard to orientation, and the second pair of measures – presenting as it does V throughout – is certainly less oriental than the first if one is considering the first four measures as a unit.

Moment e seems to be analogous to b. However, in contrast, it represents an anticipation of the I to follow. In a span that is relatively non-oriental, there is no contradiction of the tono-metric hierarchy of oriental values. This point is brought out further by a consideration of moment f, where the $f\sharp$ could be considered a suspension were it not for the fact that as an oriental value belonging to the I chord it is already resolved.

At moment g, the $c\sharp$ serves to anticipate the V of the following measure. Moment h can be considered oriental for the measure before and after it. Hence, there is no contradiction here. When h arrives, its value as V is absorbed into the tono-metric hierarchy by the first measure of the piece. At the level of eight measures, it is non-oriental to the oriental moment represented by the first *d* of the work. In this way tonal events, with the exception of the *b* at moment b, are co-ordinated consistently with the hierarchy of moments.

Moment i represents quite a change. In the context of the second half it is less accented than h. Yet h and the span for which it is oriental are focused on V, whereas i and its span are centred on I. This represents a reversal of the usual co-ordination of metrical and tonal hierarchies. However, in the context of the piece as a whole, there is no contradiction, for h as noted before is absorbed by the first *d* of the piece and the span for which it is oriental, namely, the first half. Furthermore, the first half and last four measures of the work can be considered to define the extremes of the piece. As such they correspond to the oriental value of I in the *d*-tonality. In a certain sense, the piece ends at moment i, for in terms of the metrical hierarchy, all the preceding V's are resolved by this point. By prolonging the I chord through the last four measures, one achieves balance with regard to duration: two four measure phrases on I, one on V, and one on I. By and large, the metrical hierarchy is defined in terms of moments whose tonal significance might be modified by the contents of the spans for which they are oriental. These spans in turn are measured by the time-intervals between moments of the metrical hierarchy and serve to define the proportions and balance of a work.

CONCLUSIONS

Contemporary Western music theory has typically stopped at the level of the single piece, but there is no reason why the approaches of music theory need be restricted to such a set of observables. In this chapter, one can observe that there does not have to be a discontinuity between the systems that best interpret individual pieces and groups of pieces: features common to sets of pieces can be expressed in the same terms as are employed to describe the syntax of individual works. Since the criteria for admitting a piece to a repertoire are arbitrary, a given piece need not be described in the context of a single repertoire.Indeed, as has been shown in the case of the Confucian variants, one can discern repertoires within repertoires. This suggests the possibility of viewing groups of pieces hierarchically. Although the inclusion relationship (e.g., repertoire A includes repertoire B) is transitive and antisymmetric and thus encourages a hierarchical view of sets of pieces, there is no reason why repertoires – like pieces – cannot be related to one another fruitfully in a more open-ended manner through the relationship of resemblance which is non-transitive and symmetric. This would seem especially desirable if, as in the case of the Confucian variants, degrees of resemblance are posited.

Though the definition of repertoires is arbitrary from the point of view of the theory presented here, there is no reason why it cannot be strategic. In fact, the repertoires considered in this chapter correspond to determinate distinctions made in the cultures from which they were drawn: Asaadua, hornpipes, and flings are all recognized by name, and the latter two groups appear in a given collection, as do the Confucian pieces. Within the latter group one can discern a sub-repertoire corresponding to the named central portions of the liturgy. Thus, in these cases, sets of pieces that are musically unified correspond to units of cultural behaviour and can be considered genres.

The study of repertoires, and by extension, genres, seems to lead irresistably to a consideration of the cultural contexts of individual pieces. This shift of interest from purely musical structures to musico-cultural structures has an interesting counterpart in the aspects of musical structure that are considered. As one moves from pieces to repertoires, one seems encouraged to entertain non-structural, i.e., non-relational, absolute aspects of the observables. At the level of the repertoire, tempos, timbres, loudnesses, and before-after and higher-than-lower-than relationships can be treated not just as mere absolutes, but also as the sources of relationships among pieces. Though it would be tempting to deal only with such relatively absolute variables when one is considering pieces, there is no need to neglect relatively syntactical features. As the present chapter has shown, syntactical distinctions can serve to describe the unities to be found in repertoires. Furthermore, because of the potential depth of complexity that syntactical variables imply, it would be folly to neglect them in the interpretation of groups of pieces; if one were to do so, one would be avoiding the considerable unity and complexity that mark a successful interpretation.

As has been remarked, considerations of groups of pieces seem to lead beyond the confines of music theory in sensu strictu. In the following chapters, I will be concerned with showing how a music theoretical approach can be co-ordinated with findings from the realms of psychology and the social sciences. In each case, it will be seen that one need not make a fresh start when one enters these fields, nor need one reinterpret pieces that have already been analysed 'hermetically.' Rather it seems that a structural interpretation of the observables and the theoretical concepts which underly such an analysis are prior to perceptual and cultural studies of music rather than irrelevant to, or mere end-products of, such studies.

PART IV
BEYOND MUSIC THEORY

9

Perceptual Correlates

From the previous chapters, it should be evident that one can get a great deal out of a piece or a repertoire without going beyond the fields of music theory, logic, and mathematics. The latter two disciplines are non-specific: they have no special content, refer to nothing in particular, and are prior to, rather than products of, other studies, whether these be construed as humanities or sciences. It follows that a thoroughly empirical study of music can be undertaken without invoking concepts specific to other fields. Such a conclusion runs counter to a number of recent claims that one can study music only after preliminary studies (e.g., in human psychology and culture) have been carried out. According to these claims, it would appear that the study of music is a 'terminal' discipline: that it draws on other fields, but gives little or nothing in return.

It is not too difficult to discern how such a position might be adopted, for there is considerable overlap between the observables of music on the one hand and, for example, those of psychology and the social sciences on the other. What in an analytical study are regarded as the 'observables' could also be considered 'stimuli' in a psychological experiment or the immediate manifestations of 'human behaviour' in a study of culture. But the mere fact that there is overlap – that is, that the same phenomena can be observed from different perspectives – does not mean that the findings of one type of study are prior to those of another. Indeed, I would go so far as to reverse the usually advocated order of study and maintain that one must interpret a piece or repertoire musically before (in the logical, not the temporal, sense) one can attempt to correlate it with the activities, norms, values, etc. that are associated therewith.

As far as music is concerned, there are two types of studies: those that involve interpretation of the observables, and those that do not. The latter are not strictly musical, though they might be termed such because they deal with epiphenomena of music, such as musicians, musical institutions, and musical instruments (e.g., as a part of material culture). If a study involves such epiphenomena and is also musical, there are two choices open to the investigator. The observables can be studied separately from the epiphenomena and correlations made between the two sets of findings, or the two can be studied together. According to the first alternative, the observables might be interpreted according to the categories advocated earlier in this study. Thus, the interpretation would be reducible to basic concepts, such as pitch, interval, and adjacency, allowing for an operational interpretation of these terms. According to the second alternative, one might speak not of pitches but of perceptually discriminable pitches if one were undertaking a study in the psychology of music, or of culturally significant pitches (pitchemes?) if one were involved in a study of musical culture.

Problems arise if the latter approaches are adopted. As will be seen, both perception and culture are phenomena marked by a high degree of historicity, and both approaches encourage the positing of discrete values rather than the sort of determinate ambiguity that everywhere appears to raise its head in matters musical. Most importantly, such notions as 'perceptually discriminable pitch' and 'culturally significant pitch' are not ultimate concepts: both can be parsed into more primitive notions, such as 'pitch' or 'pitch band' (the latter by way of the notion of adjacency) and the undefined concepts of the behavioural and social sciences. They are not simple, undefined concepts but compound concepts subject to definition by stronger terms. Accordingly, they do not represent any epistemological advantage.

Several more problems arise if musical and extra-musical findings are to be co-ordinated. Some of these seem to arise from the fact that music theory – despite the familiar protestations to the contrary – is a far more mature discipline than those represented by the behavioural and social sciences. After thousands of years of development, music theorists can point to concepts and relationships that have been used to interpret widely varying phenomena. The concepts and relationships invoked here also have the advantage of being few in number and operationally definable. Furthermore, as has been shown, the interpretations themselves are subject to determinate evaluation, a step that marks the ultimate maturity of any field of inquiry. If one moves from this area of relative solidity into the fields of, for example, perception and culture, the contrast is almost overwhelming. From the introspectionists one is supposed to accept (on faith?) a host of concepts that are not operationally defined in a public manner; by the Gestaltists one is asked to accept a theory based on undefined notions such as 'good form'; the structural-functionalists want us to deal with 'motivations', undefined relations between the 'actor' and his 'situation,' 'systems of expectations,' 'meanings,' 'interaction,' 'cathexis,' 'cognition,' and so forth. (The latter are all from the opening pages of Talcott Parsons' classic text, *The Social*

System, 1951, where they are introduced along with many other terms and without any indication of how they might be defined operationally.) Much the same could be reported about other schools of inquiry into human activity, and the examples of theoretical flabbiness, imprecision, and general mystification multiplied. Suffice it for the present to assert that the move from music theory to social and behavioural theory is not so easy to make.

Two differences that music theorists might encounter when attempting to deal with extra-musical phenomena involve the types of structure to be confronted and the handling of complexity in other fields. In the field of music theory, one is used to hierarchical structures based on integer values that can be defined in terms of interval identity. In a pinch, one also has to deal with antisymmetric and transitive relationships, such as 'greater than' or 'before.' In the parlance of scaling theory, these types of relationships can be described as nominal, ordinal, and intervallic. The music theorist who then embarks upon the study of language, mythology, ceremonial, or taxonomy will be on familiar ground with respect to nominal and ordinal relationships, but will have little recourse to an intervallic scale that is the source of much of the relational richness that appears in musical interpretations. This is because it seems impossible to identify (or equate) the intervals between values in such systems, and consequently such operations as bisection are not available in these areas of study. (If the investigator is used to dealing with pieces where timbre and loudness, in addition to pitch and time, have functions, there could be a considerable overlap between the types of structures to be dealt with. Symptomatically, musical semioticians appear to favour dealing with pieces in which timbre and dynamics loom large or at least to treat pieces in a way that emphasizes nominal and ordinal relationships (e.g., Boilès 1973; Nattiez 1973a, 1973b; Naud 1975; Orlando 1975).)

In the quantitative social sciences, however, one often confronts structures (e.g., regression lines) that are based on rational values, though a methodological purist might insist that many of these might best be handled by 'non-parametric' statistics (i.e., by nominal or ordinal scale relationships). As far as music is concerned, rational relationships are far too strong for the types of structures that can best be attributed to the observables. Hence, a considerable methodological shift is required if findings from the two areas are to be co-ordinated.

The handling of complexity also differs considerably in the various fields of study. In musical interpretations, complexity is cherished, especially when it appears in a true form (i.e., founded on a simple basis). In the social sciences, complexity seems to be avoided: the details of phenomena are levelled so that the findings can be expressed in the simplest possible way. Hence the vague feeling that complex human characteristics or behaviour have been reduced in social scientific work to 'just a number,' and the recurrent apologies of social scientists that their findings apply only if one assumes that 'all other things are equal.' A similar sort of levelling occurs in musical analysis when a piece or repertoire is characterized by a single trait or group of traits, but this reduction or levelling of complexity takes place after the piece has been interpreted. No apologies are in order, because the relationships between the simple values and the complex interpretation is clear. For example, a trait such as 'pentatonic,' 'duple,' or 'commetric' is the end product of a long process of analysis and could only be meaningful after the best interpretation of the observables had been attained.

By contrast with the quantitative social sciences, studies of language and ritual seem to encourage structural complexity, and in this way represent less of a shock to the music theorist. Again, however, the degree of complexity seems to be limited, if only because the lack of availability of intervallic relationships prevents the generation of structures that are as richly interrelated as those that appear in musical interpretations.

Pursuing the general theme of compatibility between musical interpretations that result from the theory presented here and the findings of para-musical studies, one can recognize certain limitations of the relevance of other fields to an interpretation of music. Two areas that deserve discussion in this respect are the psychology of perception and cultural anthropology. In cultural anthropology, one would ideally discern how the findings of a musical interpretation correlate with cultural phenomena. One would like to know how the correlations are arrived at and how the observables are treated in reaching such correlations. These topics will be discussed in chapter 10. In matters of perception, one would like to know to what extent laboratory findings are relevant for a study of music. Let us begin with a consideration of the latter point.

LIMITATIONS OF PSYCHOLOGY

In the nineteenth century, the translation of acoustical data into percepts seemed to be a rather simple affair. Pitch percepts were considered to be direct analogues of the fundamental frequencies of sound waves. Sensations of timbre were regarded as simple correlates of the intensities of the harmonics in sound waves. And loudnesses were viewed as directly related to the amplitudes of such waves. Much has changed since then. Percepts can no longer be regarded as direct products of acoustical phenomena.

We now know that pitch varies with intensity (Mursell 1937: 74–5). The pitch associated with a wave of a given frequency appears higher if the wave is complex than if it is simple. Moreover, loudnesses change with the frequency of a wave's fundamental, and – for tones less than one-half second long – with duration.

Furthermore, the loudness of several simultaneous tones is not a simple sum of their individual loudnesses. Finally, the sensation of timbre depends not only on the spectrum of a tone's 'middle' or 'steady-state' portion but also on its attack and decay, which are products of changes in frequency and intensity (Roederer 1973: 4). In short, what were long considered independent sensations of tone (namely, pitch, loudness, and timbre) vary with each other. Indeed, the complexity of relationships among acoustical stimuli and perceptual responses is even greater than indicated here.

For example, the perception of pitch change has been found to depend on the gradualness or suddenness of the corresponding change in frequency (Zwicker, Flottorp, and Stevens 1957). Two tones sounded together appear louder if they are separated by more than about 300 cents (the critical band) than if they are closer together (Roederer: 1973: 79–80). The pitch of a tone seems to shift when another pitch appears with it (Terhardt and Fastl 1971). Thus, factors of duration, register, and simultaneity play a large role in pitch perception.

The list of such complex relationships can easily be augmented. For instance, the identity of the octave interval has been found to change with the listener's distance from the source of the sound (Stumpf 1911; Mursell 1937: 83). Depending on whether the sounds enter through one or both ears, they appear to sound 'thinner' or 'fuller,' respectively, but not necessarily softer or louder. And so forth.

The difficulty of creating a model for transforming sounds into sensations can be well illustrated by the case of timbres and pitches. First, the timbre of a sound is supposed to be predictable from the structure of its spectrum. However, the spectra of the sounds produced by a given musical instrument have been found to vary considerably from one end to another of its range. From an acoustical analysis alone, one would conclude that several instruments produced the sounds, not a single source. Yet listeners can identify the tones of a violin or *rebab* with considerably more precision than acousticians with their graphs of the sounds (cf. Mursell 1937: 53). Moreover, even when two instruments are playing at the same pitch and with the same intensity, listeners can identify the two sources. But from the scientists' point of view the two instruments produce a single unanalysable wave. Nevertheless, the listener has less information to go on since the upper partials of tones fuse into 'smears' of sound (Erickson 1975, 9–12, 26–8). Indeed, the upper partials of an instrumental tone need not have as their frequencies simple multiples of the fundamental frequency: the timbre of a piano, for example, depends on a certain amount of inharmonicity between the fundamental and its overtones (Erickson 1975: 30), and gonglike tones can be synthesized by stretching the intervals between otherwise harmonically related partials (Slaymaker 1970).

It follows that pitch sensations are not a simple result of analysing harmonic tones into partials and abstracting the most slowly vibrating member of the set. Indeed, it has long been known that the pitch of a tone will remain the same even though its fundamental and lower partials have been removed. Even in acoustically harmonic tones, the pitches of the lower partials when 'heard out' are not perceived as being the same as the pitches of pure tones of the same frequency (Schouten 1940). Finally, second-order beating (pattern modulation) is perceived in mistuned octaves, fifths, etc., though there is no acoustical correlate (Roederer 1975: 37).

One reason why these phenomena appear anomalous is that the perception of pitch and timbre depends only partly on the acoustical data, themselves, and to a great extent on neural processes of a relatively high order, which are as yet not even dimly understood. This lack of understanding prevents one from predicting beyond a ballpark guess what precise sensation will result from a given stimulus. This lack of predictability is even greater if one takes into account the great grey area of individual differences.

To judge from their responses in experimental situations, people differ greatly in their perceptions of sound. Some are deaf, and some can hear. Among the latter, there are people with pathological conditions who, without any lesion of the inner ear, do not discriminate among or recognize pitches (Mursell 1937: 53). There are also some who seem to listen to music indefinitely, distinguishing among the volumes of tones (i.e., the products of pitch and loudness) without distinguishing individual pitches or intensities *per se* (Mursell 1937: 67; Vernon 1934–5). Even among relatively normal listeners there is considerable variation in pitch perception. The range of audible frequencies varies from person to person, and decreases substantially with an increase in age (Roederer 1973: 18). Similarly other psycho-acoustical measures, such as frequency resolution and the range of the critical band, differ among individuals (Roederer 1973: 22, 28; Lundin 1953: 18).

Some individual differences might be biological in nature; others seem to be based on personal experience. For example, success at recognizing intervals increases with experience, and assignments of pitch values to simultaneously sounded intervals 'change with experience (Farnsworth 1969: 36). (The latter author provides a broad survey of findings that relate perception to experience.) Finally, even for a given individual, perception seems to vary with the amount and type of attention directed towards the stimulus. Erickson provides an illuminating case in point involving whispered vowels that can be heard as either pitches or timbres depending on the focus of the listener's attention (1975: 31, also 28).

The guidance for interpretation that psychologists provide is admitted by them not to match the exact and unique predictions that classical physicists and other 'natural' scientists once claimed. To the question, 'How do we perceive sounds,' the psycho-acoustician can only offer answers that are approximate and probabilistic. Like quantum physics, psychology perturbs the system that it measures. Its measurements reflect not the system itself, but the 'system under observation.' Repeated measurements condition the responses of the subject. And ultimately, the subject is always able to exercise 'free will' in responding, thus posing a dilemma not even confronted in the 'softer' natural sciences (cf. Roederer 1973: 8–11). In short, the psychology of perception is not an exact science.

These observations have profound consequences for interpreting music. First, one can expect different listeners – and even the same listeners at different times – to interpret the raw data of music in different ways. For example, transcriptions will diverge in many instances. Second, one cannot hope for a translation of sounds into scores by mechanical means that will reflect the perceptions of all, even within a relevant culture. A transcription based on a melogram and a single algorithm will not necessarily agree with everyone's perception of the piece. Third, notions such as pitch and interval must remain undefined; they cannot be reduced to their ultimate causes.

How then is one, for example, to transcribe pieces? Universally acceptable transcriptions are impossible to achieve. Due to the practical problems of submitting large numbers of people to psychological tests and the possibility of variations in their attentiveness, transcriptions that would reflect the consensus of more than a few people under very special conditions are not possible either. The solution lies not in the pursuit of an ultimate transcription of perceptions, but in the attempt to achieve a transcription that reflects the best interpretation of the piece. As long as a transcription does not *contradict* the observables, it can be considered at least acceptable and might contribute to the best interpretation. For example, if a transcription claimed that one interval included another when the reverse was the case, it would be obviously unacceptable. If it claimed that two tones matched each other according to given criteria and also made the same claim with regard to pitches that did not satisfy the criteria, it would not be acceptable. If it does not contradict the observables, it is always acceptable. One can, for example, slice the pitch continuum into as many bands as one might wish, and come up with acceptable transcriptions. But one will have to live with the interpretive consequences of any such slicing. There will be many instances where one is not sure whether a given pitch is higher than another with respect to given band-widths even after recourse to a mechanical transcription and a body of psychological lore. However, by adjusting the bands, it will always be possible to arrive at a single qualified decision. Ultimately, then, transcription need be neither rigidly deterministic nor wantonly subjective, for it can always be interpretively valuable. Disagreements about transcriptions are, then, disagreements over questions of interpretive value.

One of the contributions of psychology to interpretation in general and transcription in particular is its provision of information on what *can* be heard rather than on what *must* be heard. This information, though it is 'soft,' can be applied at both extremes of the interpretative spectrum. For example, one is aware that certain experienced, unusually attentive, or possibly gifted listeners can perceive pitch differences that correspond to very slight acoustical variations. Thus, a practical upper limit of perceptibility can serve as a guide to interpretation. At the other extreme, psychological experiments demonstrate that for many listeners no difference is perceived between tones whose acoustical correlates are quite different. From this knowledge, practical lower limits can be established to guide the interpreter in describing, for example, pairs of pitches as the same members of a given band.

COMPATIBILITY OF PSYCHOLOGY AND THE THEORY ADVANCED HERE

It follows from all this that psychology cannot dictate interpretations of music, it can only suggest boundaries for interpretation. This does not mean, however, that its findings are unrelated to the approach advocated here. A number of questions answered by the theory presented here are answered in a parallel way by psychology. Among these are problems that recurrently confront the interpreter. For example, throughout the present study, I have identified the time of a tone with the moment of its attack. One could just as well have taken the moment of decay as the orienting point, since every tone has two extremes that are special by virtue of their non-adjacency with other moments of the tone, and there is no a priori reason why the beginning should be favoured over the ending. The reason for considering attacks oriental was simply that it enhanced the ensuing interpretation. Psychologists also favour attacks, but their reasons are different. Of all the parts of a tone, the attack has been shown to be the most important in identifying timbre (Erickson 1975: 61). For example, one can splice a piano attack onto a 'cello spectrum and decay, and listeners will report a piano timbre. The same does not hold if one splices the steady-state of a piano tone's spectrum or its termination to the attack or decay of a 'cello tone (cf. also Mursell 1937: 61).

In all of the pieces interpreted so far, intervals have been considered identical on the basis of logarithmic rather than arithmetic criteria. According to a logarithmic reading, the following pairs of intervals could be considered equal: $c–c^1$, $c^1–c^2$; $c–g$, $g–d^1$; $c–e$, $e–g\sharp$. According to an arithmetic scale, the following pairs might be interpreted as identical: $c–c^1$, $c^1–g^1$; $c–g$, $g–c^1$; $c–e$, $e–g$. As it turns out, the ear appears to be constructed in a manner favourable to logarithmic interpretations. In the basilar membrane, vibrations are translated into positions according to a logarithmic scale: the acoustical correlates of, for example, c and c^1 are mapped into positions that are about the same distance apart as those for c^1 and c^2, c^2 and c^3, c^3 and c^4, etc. (The same holds, of course, for c–g, g–d^1, d^1–a^1, a^1–e^1, etc., as well as for c–e, e–$g\sharp$, $g\sharp$–c^1, c^1–e^1, etc. (cf. Roederer 1973: 22).) Thus, it appears that logarithmic scaling is 'built into' the first stages of tonal perception. What sorts of further translations are made at higher levels of neural processing remain, however, to be discovered. All the same, the activity of the basilar membrane suggests that the concept of interval quality has a basis in aural structure, for the perceptual quality of an interval seems to correspond to a given distance between the places where its acoustical correlates are first processed.

That intervals correspond to specific perceptual qualities has been demonstrated time and again by psychologists (Farnsworth 1969: 33; Meyer 1962; Ward 1962). Also recognized is the fact that such a quality will be perceived even though the interval is changed somewhat (Farnsworth 1969: 33).

Though the calculations involved are similar, the account of intervals as qualities should not be confused with the approach that describes them in terms of ratios. From the perspective of the theory presented here, the postulation of ratios is uneconomical, since (a) it involves invoking rational numbers rather than integers, which are logically prior to ratios, and (b) it does not explain anything that is not accounted for by integers (cf. Rahn 1978d). From the point of view of psychology, the assumption that intervals are perceived as ratios should be avoided because quantitative judgments, such as 'x is twice y' or 'a is one-half b' appear not to be very easy to perform or very reliable (Roederer 1973: 10). Much more consistent are responses that involve judgments of identity (x is the same as y; a differs from b) or sequence (a is higher than b, x precedes y) (Roederer: 1973: 10). The present theory avoids this problem by defining operations on intervals in terms of identity and adjacency. For example, d is considered to bisect c–f because the extremes (c and $f\sharp$, or $g\sharp$ and f) of the identical adjacent intervals formed by sections of gamuts based on the interval between d and c or f (i.e., c–d, d–e, e–$f\sharp$, or $g\sharp$–b, b–d, d–f) are included within the extremes (c and $b\flat$, or g and f) of the sections of gamuts formed by c and f (i.e., c–f, f–$b\flat$ or g–c, c–f) but are not included by c–f (figure 9.1). In this way, judgments of bisection need not rest on quantitative grounds, rather they can be reduced to qualitative bases.

Psychologists recognize a certain margin within which acoustically different intervals still appear identical. Subjects report that intervals differing by 20 to 50 cents still 'sound the same' (Mursell 1937: 87f; Moran and Pratt 1926; Pratt

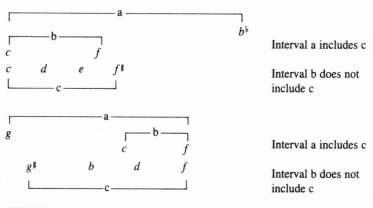

FIGURE 9.1

1931: 121). There is also much evidence that individual pitches are perceived as identical within a certain range. On the basilar membrane, it is not a single hair that is perturbed by a given frequency but a group of adjacent hairs known as a 'resonance region' (Roederer 1973: 20). From such a 'smear' of stimuli, a single pitch is perceived (Roederer 1973: 32). Similarly, a vibrato is heard as a single pitch (Farnsworth 1969: 34), and the same holds for bands of pink noise (Lundin 1953: 24). This sharpening of pitch perception allows for the standard practice of tuning the groups of three strings struck by a single hammer on a honky-tonk piano to different pitches a few cents apart. Even greater discrepancies are tolerated in the tuning of Indonesian gamelan instruments (Hood 1966; Rahn 1978b).

Of all the qualitative intervals that one can imagine, those corresponding to the octave and its multiples have been consistently chosen as the modular intervals for defining pitch classes in the present study. In psychophysics, the octave has a special status, for it defines the 'chroma' of a pitch (Roederer 1973: 144). Once again, the notion of chroma – like its analogue in the theory presented here, namely, pitch class – is qualitative, not quantitative. It is not the ratio 2 : 1 that defines the octave, since intervals can deviate considerably from 1200 cents and still be perceived as octaves, rather it is the quality of the interval band.

Throughout the examples discussed so far, absolute values have been neglected in favour of relative values. This is consistent with psychologists' findings that absolute pitch appears to be lost at an early age in most individuals (Farnsworth 1969: 50–3). As anyone who has speeded up or slowed down a recording will testify, timbre depends on absolute pitch, specifically, bands of pitches located at absolute regions (formants) of the spectrum (Roederer 1973: 137–8). In this sense, timbre, too, is absolute. It is not surprising that absolute pitch perception is closely linked with timbral recognition (Farnsworth 1969: 50–1; Riker 1946). Even so, investigators have been forced to allow a range of at least ten cents for subjects with so-called perfect pitch. Thus, it would be more appropriate from the point of view of the theory presented here to speak of absolute band perception.

The notions of adjacency and hierarchy that are central to the theory presented here are also reflected in psychological findings. From adjacency is derived the concept of extremity. According to the psychological principles of primacy and recency, the first and last events of a succession (i.e., the temporal extremes) tend to stand out, be remembered, etc. Although in the long run primacy and recency are equally effective, in the short run (i.e., immediately after the succession has been presented) last events tend to be favoured over first events. This would seem to be an instance of the specialness of relatively proximate events over more remote values. Accordingly, from the point of view of the theory presented here, the findings of primacy – recency research could be explained in terms of extremity and proximity effects.

Proximity of pitch and time also plays a role in the perception of pitch channelling. In pitch channelling, a single succession of pitches is perceived as a pair of simultaneous successions. Pitches that are too close together or linked by glissandos tend not to be separated into channels (Erickson 1975: 117–18). In order for a trill not to be perceived as a vibrato, the interval between its members must be wider than normal (Farnsworth 1969: 34). Thus it is not surprising that psychologists have invoked 'propinquity' – another word for 'proximity' – as a prerequisite for the perception of a melody as a unified entity (Lundin 1953: 77), and that stepwise progressions tend to be more frequent in music than wide leaps (e.g., Ortmann 1926).

Just as ethnomusicologists have considered pitches that appear frequently to be special, psychologists have invoked relative frequency as a reason why certain pitches stand out in a piece, and as a basis for melodic organization (Lundin 1953: 78). Ultimately, a more cogent explanation seems possible. For *ceteris paribus*, more frequent pitches will tend to occupy higher levels of the tonometric hierarchy. Accordingly, reports of their 'standing out' could be a result of listeners' interpreting such tones as oriental.

In psychology, the notion of hierarchy is most fully developed by members of the Gestalt school. Psychologists of music have invoked the Law of Prägnanz, which states that 'psychological organization will always be as good as prevailing conditions allow' (cf. Mursell 1937: 86; Koffka 1935: 110). Although the Law of Prägnanz as it has stood is too vague to be applied determinately, there is a way in which it might serve some useful purpose. The main problem is with the word *good*, which is never adequately defined by Gestaltists. However, if good organization in Gestalt psychology is equated with the 'best interpretation' in the theory presented here, some advance seems possible. The holistic view which Gestalt theory encourages is not only consistent with the hierarchical approach of the theory developed here, but is also corroborated by research into the organization of the brain. There it has been found that the right hemisphere, where spatial integrations and pictorial imaging normally take place, is also usually the seat of musical perception (Roederer 1973: 11). The intriguing fact here is that such holistic operations take place at higher levels of neural processing than are yet accessible to observation in any detail. Accordingly, one of the roles of the theory presented here can be understood as that of providing the basis for a metatheory for perception until more is known by neurologists.

CONCLUSIONS

In summary, one can assert that the psychology of music provides evidence for what some people can hear (i.e., interpret aurally) rather than what all people must hear. Thus, it serves as a useful guide – not a dictator – to the analyst. The findings of psychology represent gross tendencies among members of occidental culture and appear to correspond to the results of the best interpretations of both Western and non-Western pieces and repertoires with regard to the special statuses of the octave and the attack, the logarithmic transformation of frequencies into pitches and intervals, the intervallic processing of intervals, and the grouping of pitches and intervals into bands. Moreover, frequency, proximity, hierarchy, extremity, and relativity which are central notions in the psychology of music find determinate interpretations in the theory presented here and, thereby, special status in the analysis of pieces and repertoires. Accordingly, there need be little conflict between music theory and music psychology. That this should be so is not too surprising, if one remembers that music theoretical concepts precede psychological analysis. For example, one must have a concept of pitch before one can study pitch perception or pitch discrimination. That tendencies in the perception of Western subjects seem to correspond to tendencies inferred from the best analyses of pieces from diverse cultural backgrounds is, however, more startling and deserves further attention. But such a topic is outside the scope of the present study, lying as it does well beyond the borders of the theory presented here.

10

Cultural Correlates

Of the many definitions that might be advanced for culture, I will adopt the following: culture is behaviour shared by and transmitted among a group of people. In practice, one often leaps from an observation of shared units of behaviour to a conclusion that they have a common source in transmission. If doubt arises, however, one should be able to outline the frequently circuitous pathways of transmission in order to demonstrate that different manifestations of a given bit of behaviour do indeed belong to a single culture. Insisting that culture is essentially behaviour frees one from having to posit unobservable entities, such as thoughts or feelings. However, it does not forbid one from inferring constructs from behavioural observables, much as one infers scales from observable pitches. Generally, it would appear, indeed, that 'thoughts,' 'percepts,' etc., of the mentalists represent such inferred constructs, if they have any basis in reality at all.

Among the many aspects of culture that are of interest to the student of music, I will treat three: concepts, norms, and values. Concepts about music consist here of the verbal behaviour in terms of which music is described indigenously. Such concepts are of interest to the music theorist because they represent indigenous attempts at theorizing about music.

Musical norms for the present are considered to consist largely of non-verbal activities shared traditionally and connected in some way with the observables of music. Two broad categories are behaviour that is co-ordinated temporally with the observables, and behaviour that is merely associated with the observables. In the first category one groups the structures inferred from, for example, song texts and choreographies, especially when the resulting structures intersect coterminous musical structures. In the second category one can include the symbolism by which musical observables are linked to, or stand for, para-musical structures, in the sense, for instance that 'Happy Birthday' and carillon music symbolize particular occasions and institutions in the West, respectively.

Finally, values are embodied mostly in verbal behaviour of the forms: 'It is good that ...' or 'It is bad that ...' Such statements differ from conceptual behaviour (which can be represented by the forms 'It is true that ... ' or 'It is false that ...') for they involve predicates (e.g., good, bad) that cannot be checked. Nevertheless, one can check the veracity of the 'that ...' portion of such statements. And normative value statements can be dealt with if one checks the italicized portions of statements having the following form: '*It is true that x, y, and z say that* it is good *that* ... '

In order to show how the musical values that arise from an interpretation can be correlated with para-musical cultural phenomena, I will discuss concepts, norms, and values with regard to a single people, the Venda of northern Transvaal, in South Africa. In a series of articles (see especially 1965, 1969 a–c, 1970, 1971), John Blacking has provided a most comprehensive account of this people and their musical activities, and I will thus rely on his writings for the remainder of the present chapter.

MUSIC AND CULTURE AMONG THE VENDA

Concepts

The Venda have a term, *nyimbo* (Blacking 1965: 21), which corresponds in reference fairly closely to our generic term *piece* (of music). This Venda term designates pieces that are sung, performed instrumentally, or both. In this sense, it is rather similar to the medieval Western term *cantus* which designates both vocal and instrumental works. The term *nyimbo* also covers pieces that are recited metrically and its verbal form, *u imba* ('singing'), is contrasted in speech with the terms *u anetshela* ('narrating'), *u renda* ('reciting praises'), and *u amba* ('talking'). Furthermore, the term *lidza*, which designates instrumental perform-ance, is applied to a single tone blown on a stopped pipe or horn. Finally, the term *lungano* can refer to a complete *cante fable*, a song of similar structure to the latter and sung in similar circumstances, or a song in a *cante fable*.

To summarize, narration is in contrast with singing in the pair *u anatshela/u imba*, but they are grouped together under the term *ngano*. No single property unites pieces called *nyimbo*: they can involve instruments, vocal production, intervallic metre, and, by extension to *ngano*, recitation. What one confronts in these terms, then, is not a scientific paradigm of lexical types arranged by genus and species but a much looser ordering of the semantic domain. Purely vocal songs are associated with songs that are both sung and played, which in turn are associated with pieces that are performed purely instrumentally. Songs and pieces whose metre can be interpreted intervallically are associated with texts recited to an intervallic metre. On the other hand, a single tone that presumably cannot be interpreted metrically is associated with instrumental pieces that can. And finally, songs performed in *cantes fables* are associated with songs in a similar style that are performed under similar circumstances, and also with *cantes fables* as complete works. Thus, this slice of Venda terminology appears to be founded on a multi-dimensional continuum based on the relationship of resemblance rather than on a hierarchical arrangement based on the relationships of identity, diversity, and inclusion.

It should be clear that to point to any one term (e.g., *nyimbo*) as the Venda equivalent of our term *music* would be erroneous in such a situation. From the point of view of the theory presented here, Venda terminology treats certain observable sounds as though they were in contrast. From the point of view of orthodox English usage, the Venda do not distinguish between what are usually termed music and poetry. Thus, considerable confusion might arise if the Venda term *nyimbo* is interchanged with the English or music-theoretical term *music*. Indeed, this is not too surprising, for one does not expect to be able to match every term of one lexicon, be it from a natural language or a formal terminology, to every term from another. This situation of non-intersecting vocabularies should not constitute a problem for interpreting pieces of music, however. The only circumstance where difficulty would arise would be if one assumed *a priori* and mentalistically that the terms of a language matched the concepts (i.e., the mental contents) of their users and, furthermore, that these concepts in turn determined the observables.

The problem of matching indigenous terms and the observables of indigenous music becomes more vexed when the words involved appear to correlate with the terms of a metalanguage. For example, the Venda employ a number of metaphors for describing pitches. What English speakers metaphorically refer to as 'high' pitches they term 'small' or 'young'; what we call 'low' they describe as 'important' or 'senior' (Blacking 1965: 23). In other words, in place of the altitude terms in our natural language, they employ metaphors based on size, age, and status. Since young children are small and seem relatively low in social status in Venda society, the three types of metaphor appear to be handled consistently. Furthermore, it should be pointed out that any metaphor (including the English altitude terms) represents a conceit of some sort. All of the pitch terms here are isomorphic with the theoretical notion of pitch which embodies a linear continuum of discrete and adjacent values allowing for the relationship 'in a different direction from.' And this basic notion can be matched to other variables that can be similarly organized (e.g., altitude, size, age, and status). Since such natural language terms are invariably metaphorical, they represent one more remove from the observables: they constitute a natural metalanguage to the theoretical metalanguage by which pieces are interpreted.

A somewhat different situation is represented by the Venda term *mutavha*, which refers to sets of such things as dice, amulets, reed-pipes, and xylophone and hand-piano keys (Blacking 1965: 24). In each case, the set consists of similar entities that differ in appearance. One might go further and assert that in the case of sets of pipes and keys, the Venda 'conceive' of pitch as a digitized, not continuous, variable. However, one must distinguish here between an instrument and the observable sounds it produces: it is reed-pipes and keys that are digitized, not necessarily their sounds. That in fact it turns out that there is a good correlation between the interpreted sounds and their mechanical means of production is interesting to observe but of little consequence to a musical interpretation *per se*. The interest lies rather in the fact that inferred values in an interpretation are isomorphic with non-musical values, i.e., values lying outside the piece.

The latter point must be remembered when one comes to consider the names that the Venda apply to individual reed-pipes (Blacking 1965: 25–6). Each pipe has a name, and together seven adjacent members of each set produce a diatonic 7 from 12 by 7 (and 6) collection. Upper octaves are designated by the suffix *-na* ('little'). This is consistent with the size-pitch metaphor discussed above. Since each pitch of a scale is unique, the application of proper names is most appropriate and reflects a further incursion of inferred values in an interpretation into the lexical domain. Some of these terms have non-musical meanings as well (e.g., 'caller,' 'answerer,' 'raiser,' 'lifter,' 'head of cattle'). Whether these terms are semantically isomorphic with musical functions is not as yet clear. Blacking asserts that the tone produced by the pipe called 'lifter' should be described as a leading tone because it immediately precedes the tone produced by the orienting pipe *phala* in the national dance, and hence can be considered to be resolved by *phala*. However, one must wonder what musical function the tone produced by 'raiser' performs. And one must question Blacking's equation of the Venda term *phala* with the theoretical concept of 'tonic.' One cannot deny that *phala* is an oriental pipe, for musicians compare the *phala*s of different ensembles to determine whether they can play together 'in tune' (a notion to be discussed presently), and one can observe that the *phala*s of various ensembles within a tribe produce quite proximate pitches, but this does not have to lead one to propose that *phala* = tonic. For *phala* is the oriental pipe or key, not the oriental pitch which may or may not be produced by the instrument so designated. It orients the behaviour involved in tuning, not the values of an interpretation.

The Venda also have a number of terms referring to temporal aspects of the observables. For instance, they assert that the tempos of the genres *tshigombela* and *tshikona* 'go in different directions' (Blacking 1965: 22). This can be related to the notion of duration and by extension, tempo, as a linear continuum. Indeed the music-theoretical notion of 'in a different direction from' is here explicitly

♩. ♪. ♩. ♪. ♫ or ♩. ♪. ♩. ♪. ♩. ♪. ♫
or ♩. ♪. ♩. ♪. ♩. ♪. ♩. ♪. ♫ etc.

10.1

embodied in the expression. (The verb *go* might refer to the motor aspects of the associated dance steps: Blacking is not clear on this point.) The Venda employ an interesting metaphor to describe the prolonged tones that occur at the ends of pieces. These tones are said to be 'dragged' or 'pulled' (Blacking 1965: 22). Again, there is a clear isomorphism: length (also an English metaphor!) is matched to the theoretical notion of duration. And the physical aspect of dragging or pulling might reflect the physical effort involved in sustaining a vocal tone. Finally, with respect to temporal values, the Venda designate a group of drum beats by the term *tshilondo* (Blacking 1965: 25). Such drum beats take the forms shown in example 10.1 and appear at the beginning of a dance. A class of observables (a set of tones that establish a periodic succession which is interrupted at the end – by the eighth-note) is designated by a single term. As such, the indigenous term does not illuminate musical structure; rather, a music-theoretical interpretation of variants illuminates the meaning of the term.

With regard to the theoretical notion of loudness, the Venda employ the terms 'big' or 'visibly large' (Blacking 1965: 23). Again, there is an isomorphism with a linear continuum. More interestingly, the metaphor of size is employed not only for loudness but also for pitch, as has already been observed. Features of the observables that are interpretively distinct (i.e., relative pitch and loudness) are treated in the indigenous metaphor as though they were similar. If the analysis of indigenous concepts is not taken as a prerequisite for interpretation, however, this need cause no confusion – though it might, if one were to explicate one's interpretation to a Venda speaker. But the latter problem does not reside only between speech groups: in medieval European languages 'loud' and 'high' are both described by an altitude metaphor (cf. *altus, haut,* etc.). Indeed, as has been alluded to in the chapter on psychology (9), many Western speakers describe tones in terms of 'volume' rather than of its component determinants 'pitch' and 'loudness': this however, is a case of verbal behaviour joining together categories which are theoretically distinct. The collapsed term can be analysed into component values. And interestingly, these component and composite values are found to be highly correlated in psychological experiment.

The Venda also employ a number of terms that point to timbral referents. They refer to male and female voices as 'thick' and 'thin,' respectively (Blacking 1965: 23). Just what sort of variable this dualism is supposed to designate is unclear in the absence of sonographic analyses of voice quality norms among the Venda. It is possible that the designation might vary with the degree of concentration of formants but this cannot be stated with certainty at present. There is little doubt that the relevant variable would vary ordinally or at a lower level of measurement. Since timbres can be characterized ordinally or as simple qualities, nothing appears to be added to the interpretation by the Venda notion of timbral thickness. The quality of low and high tones is characterized by words for 'snoring' and 'closing the throat,' respectively. This, however, appears to be an instance where an effect is described in terms of its cause, as when we speak of 'head-tone' or 'falsetto.' Less explicable are the Venda descriptions of the sound of a little reed-pipe and an alto drum as being 'like a bush partridge' and 'like a martial eagle which cries out in a grove of tall trees.' Since Blacking has not pursued the significance of these similes further, one can only speculate on whether the isomorphism which allows for the metaphors is based on pitch, timbre, or loudness, and how the metaphors relate to other associations with such creatures.

Finally, one can consider a situation which broaches the topic of value, for a Venda singer in an exclamation of self-praise has sung that '[his] voice is like a barbed arrow ... [his] long yell is a barbed arrow' (Blacking 1969c: 225). In part, this appears to be a para-musical metaphor, for the singer in question makes his living (i.e., 'hunts for food') by means of his voice. Nevertheless, there would appear to be a spatial correlate for the duration and continuity of the tones of which he is so proud.

One can make a number of general observations about Venda musical terms. First, a single term or expression can refer to the observables themselves (e.g., pitches and durations), the immediate causes of the observables (e.g., instruments, vocal techniques, and performers), or to other para-musical phenomena (e.g., typical performance situations and the expressed functions of performance). When there is any direct connection with the observables and this connection has been or can be checked empirically, there appears to be an isomorphic relationship between the concepts of the theory presented here (e.g., pitch and duration) and the variables embodied in the metaphorical expressions used in natural language. Since the terms of the theory developed here form a metalanguage (i.e., they are 'beside the music'), the use of metaphorical terms takes one to yet a further remove from the observables. With regard to an interpretation, such metaphorical terms appear to be 'beside the point,' if you will. Nevertheless, they are not without interest. In the first place, they can function heuristically, that is, as part of a discovery procedure by which aspects of a piece or repertoire that might otherwise be overlooked would be investigated for possible structural significance. For example, the male-female dichotomy might turn out to be musically functional at some level or other – probably near the surface of a piece's inferred structure. In the second place, such terms provide a direct link between the observables and para-musical phenomena, as broadly defined as the culture as a whole, that forms the provenance of a piece or repertoire. For instance, the metaphors by which music is described are embedded in a semantic field that exists outside the observables themselves. Within such a semantic domain, they form relationships among themselves and with other terms and take on a structural life of their own. Accordingly, one can consider purely musical structures to be projected into the realm of meaning in the usual sense. Presently I shall consider how the observables can be linked to the realms of general behaviour (as opposed to merely verbal behaviour) and value. Before taking up such questions, however, an important point deserves mention.

If one reflects back on the types of isomorphisms found between verbal behaviour and the observables, one notices that the highest scale recognized is ordinal: the relationships expressed in Venda terms are those of identity, adjacency, and sequence. In other words, there appears to be no recognition of the notion of interval or relationships among intervals, be these in the pitch or time domains. A linguistic or cognitive determinist might assert then that intervallic relationships are not relevant to a discussion of Venda music. But such an approach would be self-stultifying. At best this approach would implicitly posit a dependence between the observables and the linguistic domain, a dependence that is hypothetical in the extreme. Quite another conclusion can be drawn, namely, that the intersection between natural language and the observables takes place at a relatively superficial level of structure, since intervallic relationships, which yield the most profound structural richness, are not embodied in language. A cursory reflection on the situation in other natural languages will reveal that this appears to be a general occurrence. From this it seems evident that one cannot afford to be bound to the concepts of a given culture's language in analysing that culture's music. In short, the direction is not from the concepts of natural language to interpretation of the observables, but the opposite: given a few music-theoretical concepts and a set of observables from a culture one can eventually explicate the meanings of the terms used in that culture to describe its music. In this sense, music theory is not a terminal discipline but rather initiates other musical studies, much as analytic philosophy and mathematics are prior to the propositions of other fields.

Norms
Turning from speech usage to other forms of normative behaviour, one finds much the same situation prevailing. Among the Venda, heptatonic instruments are tuned by comparing adjacent tones and the results checked by playing a piece

involving all the tones (Blacking 1965: 25). In this way indigenous practice is consistent with the approach of the theory presented here in emphasizing the relationship of adjacency and the overriding primacy of an holistic interpretation.

The types of behaviour that one expects to be most highly correlated with the observables are those that take place coterminously with them. Among the Venda, a considerable amount of normative motor activity is directly co-ordinated with music. For example, dance steps coincide with the beats of the tenor drum (Blacking 1970: 10), so that choreographies can be considered to articulate – that is, point up, emphasize, or match – duration contours that are musically marked by timbre: just as timbre cuts a 'path' through the observables, the dancers' steps tread the same path. A similar instance prevails in possession dances where the entranced dancer's choreography coincides with sixteen presentations of a basic rhythmic sequence, thereby weakly articulating a very high level of the metrical hierarchy (Blacking 1965: 42). In both these instances, motor activity is co-ordinated with units that are audible in the music itself. Much the same relationship holds in the case of normative behaviour associated with drumming. Here the hands and arms are kept in constant motion between the beats (Blacking 1965: 22–3) so that what are heard as time-intervals between discrete moments are gesturally articulated as continuous durations pointing up in an ingenuous way the intimate relationship between durations which can be defined in terms of their extremes and the intervals formed by such a pair of moments. In all these instances, purely musical structures can be considered to be supplemented by motor structures resulting in combined motor-musical structures. Significantly, however, the supplementary structures do not achieve the richness of their purely musical counterparts, if only because there appears to be no gestural analogue to pitch organization. The paths that dancers and drummers cut through a piece are merely analogues of timbral paths in music.

Music and behaviour are also interrelated in ways that do not yield specifically musical structures but rather serve to articulate social or cultural units. For example, self-delectative pieces, children's songs, boys' reed-pipe dances, and Christian church music are each marked by peculiarities of timbre and loudness which serve to distinguish them from other genres. Since each of these repertoires is unambiguously associated with a particular cultural unit or social group, timbre and dynamics can be considered to articulate social or cultural structure. Each of these cases is an instance of the broader phenomenon of generic behaviour observed in chapter 8.

A major difference between the genres cited here and those discussed in earlier chapters consists in the musical variables by which they are defined. Whereas the Venda genres have been defined in terms of identities and differences that lie at the surface of the musical structures, previous chapters have revealed that generic *definientes* can reach into the very bowels of hierarchic structure. Closer examination of Venda music might reveal similarly profound generic phenomena, and if this were so, the resulting interpretation would be highly desirable, because the notion of best interpretation encourages one not only to expand the range of data among which structural relationships can be posited but also to maximize the richness of relationships among the data selected for structuring. Here one must confront one of the most vexing problems that arise when musical structures are correlated with para-musical structures, namely, the relatively simplistic nature of non-musical relationships. For example, in the domains of semantic and social structure, one can at best posit the relationships of inclusion, status, and association. One can illustrate the relationship of inclusion by the relationship that obtains between the Venda as a whole and Venda women in particular; the latter are included in the former, and the relationship is necessarily irreflexive, antisymmetric, and transitive. If one asserts that older people have higher status than younger people, one is similarly invoking a relationship that is irreflexive, antisymmetric, and transitive. And if one associates 'abandoned' gestures with *matsige* drumming (Blacking 1965: 41), one is positing a relationship that is reflexive, symmetric, and intransitive. In this way, the primary relationships among social, behavioural, and semantic categories are isomorphic with certain basic relationships in musical structures, such as adjacency (cf. association) and sequence (cf. inclusion and status). But nowhere does there appear to be an analogue to the notion of interval and the corollary three-place relation of bi-section on which immensely rich structures of music are founded.

Values

In his discussion of Venda music, Blacking considers a number of values that he has discerned in connection with the culture's music. Values differ from norms and concepts. Whereas norms can be inferred empirically if unstated, and checked if verbalized, and concepts can be analysed for their isomorphism with music theoretical categories, statements of value are not verifiable since they represent purely emotive propositions. Nevertheless, many value statements have an empirical component which is subject to verification or falsification. Among the musical correlates of Venda values are loudness, tempo, and timbre. Female initiates are admonished to perform the vocal hocket piece called *khulo* 'through [their] noses' (Blacking 1969c: 223) and to 'play the drums nicely ... [not to] play them too fast' (Blacking 1969c: 223). By means of such statements one is drawn to consider the timbres of vocal performance and the band-widths of moments in a given genre. In this way, value statements can serve heuristically as potential indicators of generic phenomena.

To judge from Blacking's account, a high degree of loudness appears to be greatly valued by the Venda. Women initiates are urged: 'sing up, my children; join in the chorus so that everything may be good,' and they are scolded as follows: 'the chorus is just like an empty space: when I sing the solo, you respond half-heartedly' (Blacking 1969c: 222). A singing specialist brags: 'I sing loud like a donkey; my voice brays like a donkey' (Blacking 1969c: 225). A good singer is lauded because he 'nearly bursts his diaphragm,' and a performance using rattles is praised because the instruments are 'shaken so that they nearly break' (Blacking 1965: 23). In the latter two instances, the immediate causes of the relative loudness are praised, so that loud dynamics could be considered as a symbol of physical behaviour which is valued because of the inferred effort associated with it. The Venda also consider relative loudness as a symbol of the number of performers involved in a piece; such a great number in turn serves as a symbol of political support and ultimately prestige for the sponsor of the performance (Blacking 1965: 38). Accordingly, valued aspects of the observables can be highly correlated with social values. Such correlations can be elaborated in other ways. For example, social structures are correlated with various parts of a texture, as in the case of initiation songs where the master of initiation sings the solo parts, graduates sing the characteristic melodic line known as *bvumela*, senior and experienced novices play the drums, and junior and inexperienced novices sing the chorus parts (Blacking 1969c: 259). Here the purely musical aspect of the correlation would appear to be relatively uninteresting in that it involves only certain superficial aspects of texture. The effect of status values seems to lead an existence of its own outside the observables proper. Nevertheless, each component of the texture can be regarded as a symbol for the social status co-ordinated with it.

Finally, observable differences in a piece can symbolize status differences. Drummers whom the Venda consider less skilled strike the wooden ends of their drums between beats in such a way as to coincide with beats in other drum parts (Blacking 1969c: 256). The observable difference between skilled and unskilled performance consists then in a timbral excess, moments normally coinciding with a single timbre being performed with two.

CONCLUSIONS

In attempting to correlate music with cultural phenomena, the unwary can be tempted by a number of pitfalls. With regard to discourse, one must confront the problem of translating the terms of one language into those of another, whether two natural languages (e.g., English and Venda) are involved, or a natural and a formal language (e.g., the terms of the theory presented here). Clear distinctions must be made between the extensions of terms in different natural languages, and between the theoretical terms of a formal terminology and the metaphors of a natural language. One must also beware of the recurrent conceptual poverty of natural languages as represented by their general failure to account for intervallic relationships at any but the most superficial levels of theory-building. Furthermore, one is continually forced to distinguish between terms and behaviour that are associated with the observables themselves and those that are more directly related to the immediate causes of the observables or their more general context.

If such problems are avoided, one can go a long way towards correlating the observables with their immediate cultural context. At all points, one is interested in (a) establishing what isomorphisms, if any, can be found between the observables and the metalanguage used to describe them on the one hand, and para-phenomena on the other; (b) checking the referents of indigenous concepts and statements of value; (c) illuminating indigenous usage in terms of a metalanguage, and (d) examining the ways in which musical structures can be correlated with para-musical structures. In the case of (d), one can expect to find that co-ordinated supplementary structures (e.g., choreographies and performance gestures) articulate purely musical structures, and merely associated structures (e.g., status constructs and institutions) are symbolized by musical values.

It follows, then, that there need be no conflict between a purely musical study and a consideration of the immediate cultural context of a given set of observables. The key in such studies would appear to lie in recognizing that music theory is prior to musical interpretation, which, in turn, is prior to establishing correlations between music and culture. In this way, musical theorizing and interpretation are not terminal activities but rather first steps in any study that deals seriously with music.

PART V
REVIEW

11

Conclusions

Throughout the present study, I have had occasion to come to a number of conclusions concerning music theoretical discourse and its empirical applications. It seems unnecessary to rehearse in detail the conclusions of individual chapters here, as they can easily be referred to. Nevertheless, a brief accounting of some achievements of the preceding pages appears in order. What follows, then, is a brief summary of the implications of the theory as developed here. These are roughly divided into two groups, depending on whether they are music theoretical or ethnomusicological in import. The lists are highly selective, representing conclusions, approaches, or points of emphasis that cut across the organization of the present work.

For several conclusions, the individual implications are not wholly original; rather the emphasis that has been placed on them and the grouping of them together into a 'point of view' are novel. Certainly one could adumbrate much of the present study by referring to works by analytic philosophers and structuralists. Indeed, I am tempted to label the approach taken here as a sort of positivist structuralism, but it appears preferable to be labelled by one's critics rather than assume the burden of naming oneself, if only because single labels tend to give rise to distorted stereotypes and encourage critics to throw out the baby when something has been found wanting in the bath water.

IMPLICATIONS FOR MUSIC THEORY

Throughout the history of music theory, both East and West, a dualism has existed between rhythmic and tonal aspects of musical structure. For the most part, theorists have discussed pitch and time separately. Exceptions to this rule occur in certain parts of Common Practice theory, the formulations of recent twelve-tone theorists, and some recent work by Komar (1971) and Yeston (1976).

Apart from the latter studies, the co-ordination of rhythm and tonality in Common Practice theory has largely been restricted to isolated topics, such as non-harmonic tones, rather than adopted as a thoroughgoing approach. And in twelve-tone theory, one is concerned with order-determinate relationships which seem to have little relevance to the music considered in the present study.

In an era of inquiry when synthesizing previous dichotomies seems a highly fashionable endeavour, the attempt in this study to co-ordinate metrical and tonal values might be looked upon as merely another otiose exercise in collapsing existing barriers between long established categories. Nevertheless, there appear to be at least two good reasons for indulging in such a synthesis. First, the resulting tono-metric structures are much richer than would be so if pitch and time were considered separately. Indeed, it often appears that tonal and temporal structures cannot be handled satisfactorily in isolation from each other. When one speaks of rhythm, one can only mean the rhythm *of* a given non-temporal content. Similarly, a pitch value is a pitch *at* a given moment or during a given span. Pitch and rhythm are 'transitive' nouns: they must be completed by specifying the pitch 'of what' or the moment 'of what.'

The interconnection of pitches and moments can be extended to include timbres and loudnesses on the pitch side as well. The very intersection of the two broad domains (time and the content in time) is not only an empirical given in any set of observables but also an interpretive *desideratum*. One result is that one can construct such entities as 'resolutions.' These are not merely pitches or moments, but pitches at given moments, things that one might term *tones*.

A second reason for adopting a truly 'tono-metric' approach (as opposed to a pitch-plus-time approach) is that it makes good strategic sense. In general, pieces retain both their tonal and metrical identities on repetition, and up to a certain point such different performances are referred to by members of a given culture as though they were identical. *Etenraku* can be varied a certain amount and still be described as *Etenraku*. Failure to deal with pitches and times simultaneously would be self-stultifying, for it would prevent one from defining adequately a given cultural unit (e.g., a piece) corresponding to the observables. Though the latter goal is not strictly music-theoretical, it is not entirely vacuous. It would seem to be the responsibility of music theory to provide the basis for achieving such goals in much the same sense that mathematics is responsible for providing the rational numbers in terms of which one can solve empirical (i.e., extra-mathematical) problems of physics.

Traditionally, music theory has attempted to provide single readings of observables. True, a certain amount of ambiguity has been tolerated with regard to 'pivot chords' (as in the case where a *d*-minor triad can be read as ii in c-major or iv in *a*-minor) and other topics, but such concessions to ambiguity have not been comprehensive. The approach taken here has been quite different, treating ambiguity as interpretively desirable. According to a hierarchical interpretation, as many aspects as possible of a piece are considered multivalent. For example, the first beat of 4–4 might also be considered the first beat of a two-measure phrase and the first beat of the first half of a 4–4 measure. Such multivalence is relatively benign as far as traditional approaches are concerned, for it involves no apparent paradox. However, when one considers passages that can be interpreted in 6–8 or 3–4, or pieces that can be oriented around *c–g* or *e–b*, emotions are apt to run high. Although it would seem that anything goes in an interpretive approach that encourages multivalence, there need be no fear of analytic licence if one remembers that the type of ambiguity encouraged is in all cases determinate and valuable. It is ambiguity of the sort represented by puns (which have limited meanings) rather than by nonsense syllables (which might mean anything or nothing). Moreover, in pieces that can be read two ways, the competing interpretations are not just any old readings but the pair that tie for first place.

A third tendency in traditional theory has been to over-interpret the observables. A long-standing case of this sort has involved the recurrent fascination of theorists with numbers, especially rational numbers. However, since the relationships described here have been based on qualitative relationships such as identity and adjacency, ordinal relationships such as before, after, higher than, lower than, louder than, and softer than, and the minimally quantitative operation of bisection, numbers as such have played only a little role in the present interpretations. The problem that rational numbers pose the interpreter is that they involve the assumption of the operation of division which is not implied in lower types of quantities (e.g., integers and ordinal values), but no use can be made of this operation, since it does not give rise to preferable interpretations. As such, division represents a fifth wheel in an interpretation. This is not to deny that there might be a situation where employing rational numbers might enhance an analysis; rather it is to assert that in the music considered here, they are of no value, and one doubts strongly whether a piece might be found where they could be applied fruitfully.

IMPLICATIONS FOR ETHNOMUSICOLOGY

In the past few years, there have been two sad strains running through ethnomusicological discourse. These have been composed of what I would term a self-stultifying preoccupation with preliminaries and an unhealthy scepticism. With regard to preliminaries, one often has the impression that it is almost impossible to get started on an ethnomusicological study for fear that one's assumptions might not be impeccable. One also frequently finds that one's colleagues seem to be knocking their heads against walls in order to achieve methodological purity. Often the perfection which they seek seems to consist of an unattainable – and hence, self-stultifying – objectivity. At other times, ethnomusicologists appear to be trying to solve at a single swoop not only musical problems – which, as the preceding pages testify, are difficult enough to handle – but also non-musical problems.

The sources for what I have described as an unhealthy scepticism are to be found perhaps in the long tradition of debunking, which at times has appeared to be a major program of the social sciences in general and cultural anthropology in particular. In this tradition, assumptions are attacked and hypotheses are cast aside almost as soon as they have been proposed. Unfortunately, the adherents to this tradition – or better, anti-tradition – do not manifest any feeling of responsibility for replacing what has been debunked with something better.

According to the program advocated here, the problems of getting started and dealing with scepticism are lessened in a number of ways. First, assumptions – as embodied, for example, in one's undefined concepts – are reduced to a minimum. Second, only the most modest of goals – for instance, interpreting sounds and scores – are entertained at a given time, rather than juggling both music and its epiphenomena. And third, with one's assumptions and ambitions reduced, more emphasis is placed not on the first steps of a study, i.e., getting started but on the last steps, i.e., evaluating what has been accomplished. The proof of the pudding, after all, is in the eating. By constructing determinate calculi in terms of which interpretations can be evaluated – as has been done formally in the relatively simple case of metrical analysis (chapter 8; see also Rahn 1978d and 1981b) – one is encouraged to compare interpretations, and thus not only to debunk, but also to replace discarded readings with something demonstrably better. Since any interpretation can be evaluated, a way is open for retrieval of the good aspects of previously rejected hypotheses, so that the baby need not be thrown out with the bath water.

If there is an immediate future for the theory developed here, it would appear to lie largely in the area of developing further formal calculi in terms of which interpretations might be evaluated and compared. As the latter program is carried out, ethnomusicologists might no longer feel compelled to procrastinate over assumptions or cavil over findings; rather each might feel encouraged to enter the search for better interpretations.

SOME APPARENT UNIVERSALS

In the meantime, I would advance the following hypotheses, to be tested in the future. These are based on my own scattered interpretations of music from diverse cultures, and each should be prefaced by the phrase, 'In the best interpretation of a piece, one will find that.'

1 If modular intervals are invoked, one of these will correspond to the octave.
2 If the time of a tone is identified with a given moment, it will be the moment of attack.
3 If quantitative values are assigned to intervals of pitch and time, they will be of an interval scale or lower (i.e., ordinal or nominal).
4 If a referential construct for pitches or moments is invoked, it will be based on bisection.
5 If pitch intervals are compared, they will be compared according to a geometric progression and if time intervals are compared, they will be compared according to an arithmetic progression.

The ways in which these hypotheses might be falsified are as follows. If modular intervals are invoked, but positing an octave modulus detracts from the interpretation, statement 1 would be falsified. If a better interpretation resulted when one considered some other moment than the attack as the time of a tone, one would dismiss statement 2. If a rational or irrational scale of measurement yielded a more elegant analysis, one would decide against statement 3. If one's interpretation improved when a referential construct, based not on bisection but on some other relationship, was posited, one would reject statement 4. Finally, if another scale (e.g., an arithmetic progression for pitch or a geometric progression for time) resulted in a better analysis, statement 5 would be withdrawn.

Though it is highly tempting to end my account of the theory presented here with such a triumphant, though short, list of universals, the very approach advocated here argues against such a rhetorical tactic. Since, as I have emphasized, every interpretation is open to re-evaluation, it seems preferable to entertain objections that might be raised to the present work. Accordingly, the following chapter attempts to deal with criticisms that might be advanced against the position adopted here.

12

Some Possible Objections

As was pointed out in chapter 1, the perspective developed here is quite icon-oclastic. Since the basic implications of the point of view established here should be clear at this point, a consideration of possible reservations seems in order. (To have discussed such objections earlier would not have been fair to the theses developed in the book.) Accordingly, the present chapter is devoted to taking up such points from the perspective of the work as a whole. The first, and perhaps most contentious, issue to be treated concerns the theoretical status of minds in musical studies.

MINDS

If one accepts the theory developed here, is one required to reject the existence of minds? No, for the concept of mind does not appear in the theory itself (i.e., from chapter 4 onward), nor is any substitute proposed. Indeed, whether one believes in minds or not is irrelevant to applying the theory.

One way in which the notion of mind might be introduced into an interpretation consists of positing mental processes as inferred entities as opposed to observed entities. At first, this might seem parallel to the positing of inferred entities or hypothetical processes in other fields. For example, in the natural sciences, mass and gravity are posited although they are not directly observed. Rather their measurement depends on inferences based on their effects, as in the case where objects are weighed on the basis of spatial displacements in balances or scales. Accordingly, one might suppose that mental processes or entities, which also are not observed directly, could be inferred from their effects, as in the instance where thoughts and emotions are attributed to people on the basis of the words they utter, the gestures they make, the pieces they perform or hear, etc. However, there is an important difference between the two types of inference. In the case of physical properties and processes, there is a reliable, one-to-one correlation between the observed effects and the roles that the inferred values play in interpretation. For example, the mass of an object can be defined operationally, so that observations of other aspects of the object's behaviour accord with this measurement and the role that mass and other inferred properties and processes play in theoretical constructs. The same cannot be said of mental processes whose effects can be feigned or inadvertently masked. I would not deny that feigning and inadvertent masking might be subject to analysis eventually, but considerably more would have to be known about the physical aspects of mental processes before such an analysis could approach the falsifiability, operationality, replicability, and 'public-ness' which one requires of factual statements.

The way in which the notion of mind has been often employed – especially in musical studies – is not as 'high-minded' as this: mental properties and processes are typically dragged in ad hoc to explain away discrepancies between observation and theory or to account for relationships that are adequately handled in terms of observable entities and hypothetical entities immediately and reliably derivable therefrom. In this way, the mind has been the last – or all too frequently, the first – refuge of the lazy or the over-ambitious: a convenient *deus ex machina* to save the theoretical day or face.

THE THEORY PRESENTED HERE AS A THEORY

A second possible reservation to the theory presented here concerns its status as a theory. One must admit immediately that it has no pretensions to being a theory in the usual, scientific meaning of the word: it embodies no notion of causality, even in the broadest sense of the term. All the same it is not entirely abstract like mathematical theory, for it has observable content; pitches, moments, intervals, etc. As a theory, it occupies a middle ground between the two: it has empirical content which mathematics lacks (and science possesses), but lacks the deterministic formulations that much of science cultivates. This is not to say that causality could not be introduced into musical studies. Indeed, limited relationships of covariation can be observed in the descriptions of repertoires included in chapter 8. But one is still far from universal predictions, even in the broadest sense of the word. We are still at the point where no one can deny that anything can happen in a piece, whatever its context, although it must be recognized that certain things tend to happen in specific contexts. Nevertheless, the notion of universality is not without applicability.

Although universal deterministic patterns have not emerged, certain categories – the undefined concepts of chapters 5 and 6 – can be applied universally to arrive at the best interpretation. The latter notion represents the 'resistance' against which the universality of such categories as pitch, moment, etc., can be assessed. In this role, the best interpretation functions in an analogous way to causal universality in the physical sciences. If one discerned another set of categories that provided better interpretations, the concepts and relationships discussed in chapters 5 and 6 would have to be replaced as the universals of musical discourse, just as the discovery of discrepant data forces the scientist to revise previously accepted universal theories. Accordingly, the notion of the best interpretation is intimately tied to the status as a theory of the theory presented here.

CAUSALITY

One might also claim that acceptance of the theoretical approach developed here would hinder studies of the determinants of music. However, since the theory itself makes no statement either for or against causal statements, this would be a vain complaint. No one would like to discern the causes of musical observables more than I. All the same, I must admit that very little has been discovered in this regard. Nevertheless, I would go so far as to assert that the theory presented here encourages the discovery of causal connections, if only because of its topographical, descriptive nature. This is so, because in order to ask 'Why?' one must first have answered 'What?' And in this regard, the present theory provides the best framework I know for answering 'What?' If one wants to know what causes musical observables, one had best have a good notion of what there is to be caused.

THE BEST INTERPRETATION

The idea that there could be an interpretation that is best might seem rather forbidding. However, one should not view it as an absolute notion. I am not proposing that the best interpretations that I have advanced are the best for all time. Rather they represent interpretations that are better than others that have been offered thus far. I look forward to the prospect that even better interpretations might be offered, but these would have to be assessed in each case. The word *assessed* is important here: with the advent of the approach presented here, one can no longer merely assert that one interpretation is better than another. One must substantiate such a claim in terms of a calculus. As the discussion of Asaadua (cf. Rahn 1978d and 1981b) has shown, such calculi can be developed, and as pointed out above, the immediate future of the theory lies in the construction of additional calculi.

OTHER APPROACHES

Since the present approach encourages one to compare interpretations, something should be said about their status *vis-à-vis* the present theory. Does the acceptance of the theory mean that other approaches need to be rejected? Must one throw traditional music theories overboard if one accepts the principles of the theory developed here? No. As long as these theories satisfy the requirements for adequacy outlined in chapter 3, they can be translated into the terms of the theory presented here. In a sense, the present theory represents a 'theory of theories': inapplicable concepts from other theories are rejected and applicable concepts can be analysed in a simpler, more meaningful way.

BINARISM

One might also wonder why there is an overwhelming tendency to binarism in the analyses presented here. Does an acceptance of the categories of the theory and the critical precepts of a calculus force one to adopt a binaristic approach? Not necessarily. Even more elegant interpretations might result from another analytical perspective, though I have no idea what such an approach would be like. Binarism seems appropriate because in an hierarchical model it ensures the greatest number of values among different levels. If a single value on one level corresponds to two values on the next, and each of these correspond to two on the next level, and so forth, one can assign a miminim number of values (at each level) to a maximum number of levels leading to a maximum overall number of levels and values. This is the appeal of binarism. It encourages discovery of the best interpretation, which in turn forms a 'resistance' to the universality of the theory.

MUSICAL FACTS

Further, one might wonder about the factual status of analytic assertions made according to the approach advocated here. If one states that a certain piece is in A-major, in triple metre, or syncopated, etc., is one making a statement of fact? In orthodox usage, such statements are considered to be factual. But in this study, such statements have been arrived at only by invoking values such as simplicity, complexity, and richness. A positivist might balk at the proposal that an apparent statement of fact is the result of an evaluative process. Nevertheless, I would assert that non-trivial statements about musical structure are facts based on both facts and values. For example, one can only assert that a given piece is in triple metre on the basis of a proposed best interpretation. Accordingly, to the two recognized methods of arriving at factual statement, induction and deduction, I would add a third: evaluative inference. Whether the method is traditional or novel, it forms a 'resistance' to the arrival at facts. Anything does not necessarily 'go.' Though one is seldom required to do so, it might happen that one can only justify the characterization of even a given band of pitches or span of moments as a single unit on the basis of a best interpretation rather than purely objective criteria. In this way, even the most elementary facts on which an interpretation is based might be subject to evaluation. Indeed, a primary merit of interpreting music in this manner is that one must confront continually the fact that one's facts – especially the more interesting ones – are ultimately rooted in values.

ETHNOCENTRICITY

One could also object that the approach advocated here is ethnocentric. After all, the concepts in terms of which I have interpreted music of other cultures can be considered Western in the sense that they are the products of theorists, including myself, who are from the West rather than of theorists indigenous to the cultures that produced the music. However, there are a number of reasons why I feel this fact does not detract from the approach.

First, the concepts applied here are not representative of Western culture in contrast to other cultures. If they reflect any constituency at all, it is a small band of Western scholars – seemingly diminishing day by day in proportions and importance – rather than 'Western culture.' The latter construct, if conceived as anything approaching unity in this regard, can only be considered a fiction. (Similarly, the more fulsome theories produced in non-Western 'high' cultures (e.g., India, China, or Japan) are also unrepresentative of those cultures as wholes.)

Second, the basic concepts are not entirely peculiar to the West. Other cultures have concepts corresponding to pitch, interval, etc., though their systematic working-out of the implications of these concepts may leave something to be desired from a theoretical point of view.

Finally, I am sufficiently optimistic to believe that verbal communication between cultures is possible, and do not believe that only insiders can describe their own products adequately. If this were not so, there would be no ethnology, not to mention ethnomusicology. Where would studies of social phenomena be without concepts such as status, role, and norm? Whatever their correlates in other cultures, concepts such as these are Western in the same, restricted sense as are those that I have invoked. To deny such concepts admission to ethnological discourse would be to cut off one's nose to spite one's face. This even holds true for the interpretive values that I have cited throughout. To deny them admittance to cross-cultural discussion solely because of their Western origin would amount to the same thing as refusing to acknowledge the efficacy of the logical convention of non-contradiction in studying other cultures simply because this is a Western, albeit Aristotelian, notion.

THE TWELVE-SEMITONE SYSTEM

One might also object that I have a covert bias towards tonal systems based on the twelve-semitone gamut. Indeed, this particular gamut is quite fascinating to me if only because of the immense variety of tonal structures which it makes available and which are found throughout the world. All the same, I am fully cognizant of other possibilities than have been discussed here. Rahn 1977a describes equipentatonic, equiheptatonic, and other systems, and Rahn 1978b discusses the pélog, nine-tone system of Indonesia. There is still, unfortunately, a paucity of published materials about these systems generally accessible to Western readers, so accounts of pieces of these kinds have had to be foregone. Nevertheless, both of these studies are consistent with the approach advocated here and to a certain extent add further support to the present theory.

THE COMPREHENSIVENESS OF THE THEORY

Finally, one might wonder whether the approach developed here can be applied to all music. My main purpose in the present work has been to extend Western music theory to account for non-Western forms, and at the same time not preclude other types of music. From the demonstrated flexibility of the theory as evidenced in the preceding pages, it should not seem impossible to apply it advantageously to non-Western music in general. Recent indications are that modal music of the West might similarly yield to such an approach (Rahn 1978c, 1981b). Benjamin Boretz (1969–72) has shown how a similar approach can account for tonal music through Wagner. By adding the concept of order as embodied in the cardinal numbers from one to twelve, one can account for serial music as Boretz, again, has demonstrated (1969–72). And by extending this approach further, more atonal music can be interpreted as Allen Forte (1973) has shown.

Still there remain two types of music that seem recalcitrant. First, there are pieces based on chance principles or otherwise structurally opaque. Perhaps these works are immune to deep hierarchical interpretation. Maybe there are realms of organization based, for example, on timbral relationships only dimly anticipated as yet. At present one can only surmise. All the same, it seems best not to erect impenetrable barriers of a music-theoretical sort to such works at the outset.

A second category of problematic work is that which is conceived in terms of a highly elaborate pre-compositional scheme – the formulas of Schillinger, the transformations of Messiaen, and the prescriptions of Hindemith are ready examples. It is obviously easier – lazier? – to posit such precompositional systems, when they are known, as the bases for interpretation, rather than search out a potentially more elegant formulation which, furthermore, might link the works more directly with other music. But one should remember that the effort might be worthwhile. After all, a successful anagram is not simply an exercise in permutation, but also an exercise within a natural language. In other words, the significance of pre-compositionally recalcitrant pieces might not rest so much in their esoteric techniques as in their ability to be related to other works. All these are problems for the future. Suffice it to emphasize that with an approach that yields fruitful results for tonal, modal, serial, atonal, and non-Western music, one is well on the way to accounting for all music.

In sum, I feel that the theory described here gives rise to interpretations of non-Western pieces that are more than adequate. It clarifies traditional theoretical issues, provides the vocabulary in which psychological and cultural statements about music can be rendered meaningful, and uncovers apparent universals of music. Certainly improvements might be made on the present formulations, but that remains for the future. In the meantime, the theory and its applications, as outlined here, can stand.

Glossary

The following technical terms appear in chapters 5 to 9. Though I have tried to avoid neologizing and to employ terms consistently throughout, it still happens that words are used in the present work in different senses than the reader might be accustomed to. In each case, the headings (a) Traditional, (b) Metatheory, (c) Theory, and (d) Interpretation at the beginnings of definitions indicate whether the usage is drawn from (a) the traditional lexicons of music theory, ethnomusicology, psychology, or acoustics; (b) the theoretical discourse of allied fields, such as logic, mathematics, and statistics; (c) the theory developed in chapters 5 and 6; or (d) applications of the concepts of the theory to actual works (as in chapters 7 and 8), respectively.

accent (Interpretation) oriental moment in a metrical hierarchy, marked 0 in analyses; (Traditional) sign ($>$) indicating that a note (and therefore its corresponding tone) is relatively louder than surrounding notes.

adjacency (Theory) type of relationship between two parts of a piece which are next to each other. The relationship is primitive, or undefined, and is irreflexive, symmetric, and non-transitive. It can obtain between pitch, time, or loudness values.

adjacent (Theory) see **adjacency**. (Interpretation) two values can be adjacent in two ways, linearly or cyclically. A good image for cyclic adjacency consists of the numbers on a clock, where, for example, 4 is adjacent to 3 and 5, and 12 is adjacent to 11 and 1. A corresponding image for linear adjacency consists of the digits on a ruler, where 4 is again adjacent to 3 and 5, but 12 is only adjacent to 11 (i.e., not to 1). Beyond the foreground level, values can be considered adjacent with respect to different metrics or scales. E.g., c is adjacent to d with respect to the diatonic, 'white-note' collection, but not with respect to the twelve-semitone gamut, where it is adjacent to b and $c\sharp$.

after (Theory) type of precedence relationship. If B is after A, A is before B. The relationship is primitive, or undefined, and is irreflexive, antisymmetric, and transitive.

algorithm (Metatheory) formula for transforming one set of values into another.

altitude (Theory) type of sequential relationship pertaining to pitch, hence, irreflexive, antisymmetric, and transitive. The two subtypes it comprises are the opposites 'higher than' and 'lower than.'

ambitus (Traditional) interval between highest and lowest tones of a melody.

amplitude (Traditional) primary acoustical correlate of loudness; varies with the amount of energy in sound wave.

anacrusis (Traditional) first tone of a piece or section thereof which begins on a relatively unaccented portion of the measure and is followed by a relatively accented tone. (Interpretation) as a deviation from strict commetricity, an anacrusis is resolved afterwards but not before.

anticipation (Interpretation) event that occurs on a relatively unaccented part of the metrical hierarchy and is followed immediately by an event having the same content (e.g., the same pitch, chord) and occurring on a relatively accented moment.

antisymmetric (Metatheory) if A is related to B in a given way, but B is not related to A in the same way, the relationship between A and B is antisymmetric. The opposite type of relationship is called *symmetric*. An example of an antisymmetric relationship is 'before,' as in 'A is before B.'

appoggiatura (Interpretation) event having a non-oriental (1) value in terms of content (e.g., pitch) which occurs on an oriental moment of the metrical hierarchy. Appoggiaturas represent a complete reversal of the usual co-ordination of pitch and time values.

approximate bisection (Interpretation) type of bisection in which halves are unequal (e.g., the cases where 12 is bisected into 7 + 5, 7 into 3 + 4). Also called *intervallic* or *integral bisection*. The opposite type, where halves are equal, is termed *rational, simple, precise,* or *pure.*

arithmetic progression (Metatheory) series of numbers in which the difference between the nth and the $(n - 1)$th is the same as that between the $(n + 1)$th and nth. E.g., a, a + d, a + 2d, a + 3d, etc.; 1, 3, 5, 7, etc.; 1, 2, 3, 4, etc.; 9, 8, 7, 6, etc.

arpeggiation (Interpretation) consecutive presentation of pitches belonging to a single sonority or 'chord.'

articulate (Interpretation) if A articulates B, it is coterminous with, but is less complexly structured than B. Typically patterns of loudness and timbre articulate patterns of pitch and time. (Traditional) way in which tones are joined or separated in performance. E.g., if rests between tones are minimized the articulation is legato, as opposed to staccato.

atom (Metatheory) irreducible, unanalysable value of an event. (E.g., in music, the pitch or loudness of a tone.)

attack (Traditional) beginning of a tone, often marked by a sharp increase of loudness. (Interpretation) first moment of a pitch; time of a pitch.

auxiliary (Interpretation) non-oriental value (e.g., a pitch) occurring at a non-oriental moment of the metrical hierarchy and adjacent to oriental values at oriental moments. (Traditional) non-harmonic tone occurring in a relatively unaccented portion of the measure as compared with its resolutions, which consist of the next-higher or -lower scale degree.

background (Interpretation) lower levels of a hierarchy corresponding to greater spans of a piece; a virtual synonym is *deep structure*; opposites include *foreground, higher levels of a hierarchy*, and *surface.*

band (Interpretation) set of pitches which are linearly adjacent; corresponds to notion of pitch function (in Boretz's *Meta-Variations*), which is defined as a group of pitches which match each other but are not necessarily identical to each other.

band of intervals (Interpretation) group of intervals corresponding to two pitch bands. By extension, if intervals of $6/12$, $7/12$, and $8/12$ are functionally identical (as bisectors of $12/12$), they can be considered to constitute an interval band of $6–8/12$.

beating (Traditional) fluctuations in perceived loudness of two or more tones caused by the interference of one wave with the other.

before (Theory) type of precedence relationship. If A is before B, B is after A. The relationship is primitive, or undefined, and is irreflexive, antisymmetric, and transitive.

below (Theory) type of altitude relationship. If A is below B, B is above A. The relationship is primitive (or undefined), and is irreflexive, antisymmetric, and transitive.

between (Interpretation) if B is linearly adjacent to A and to C, B is between A and C. This is a special case of 'between-ness,' where in general, if X and Y are on opposite sides of Z, Z is between X and Y. E.g., in C-pentatonic, d is between c and e in the narrow sense and between a and g in the wider, cyclic sense.

beyond (Interpretation) if B is adjacent to A and C, A is beyond B and C. In general, if X, Y, and Z form a connected graph based on linear adjacency, such that X ≠ Y, X ≠ Z, and X is not between Y and Z (in the linear sense), X is beyond YZ. The notion of 'beyond-ness' is like 'between-ness' in that it does not apply to cyclic adjacency.

binary (Traditional) type of form consisting of two halves, of which the first ends on the dominant and the second on the tonic; duple (with regard to metre).

bisection (Interpretation) three-place relation. If B bisects AC, $2AC/3 \geqslant AB \geqslant AC/3$. By extension one can say that AB (or BC) bisects AC, or that the grid to which AB (or BC) belongs bisects the grid to which AC belongs. Furthermore, a given interval (e.g., the pitch interval c–$f\sharp$) can bisect another interval (e.g., $e\flat$–a) 'modularly' if one member of the first bisects the second, and the other (e.g., c) bisects the second's complement (e.g., a–$e\flat$). Bisection can be posited for pitch- and time-intervals, but not for loudness or timbre.

bisector (Interpretation) if B bisects AC, B is a bisector of AC. Similarly, if AB or BC bisects AC, AB or BC is a bisector of AC.

bivalent (Interpretation) having two values in an interpretation.

boundary (Intrepretation) value not found in a group of pieces.

chain of thirds (Interpretation) construct in heptatonic scales consisting of every other scale degree (e.g., a–c–e–g–b^1–d^1–f^1). Since such a construct cuts across the pitch class organization (e.g., a in the above example appears in one octave of the construct but not in the other), it confounds the modular basis of pitch organization, superimposing another ordering.

chromatic (Traditional) non-diatonic, i.e., a pitch that does not belong to the scale that is referential is considered chromatic.

class (Metatheory) group of entities that share at least one feature; the critical relationship is identity with respect to the feature which is shared. (Interpretation) a class of pieces constitute a repertoire; the members of a given pitch or moment class belong to the same modular gamut or pulsation.

coda (Traditional) literally, tail, final section of a piece, typically resembling other sections less than they resemble each other.

coextreme (Interpretation) if one extreme from each of two extents are coincident, and the other extreme of one coincides with a moment of the other the extents are coextreme.

collection (Interpretation) set, usually having special properties such as 'cyclic-ness'; the term is used especially with regard to scales.

commetric (Interpretation) if the presented moments in a passage are such that presented upbeats are preceded and followed by presentations of downbeats (at the same level of the metrical hierarchy), the passage is commetric; synonyms include *regular, four-square*; opposite terms are *contrametric* and *syncopated*.

commixture (Traditional) in medieval and Renaissance modal music, a modulation such that there is a change of referential dyad.

complement (Metatheory) if a set A is divided into two subsets B and C such that no members are shared by B and C, and B and C include among them all the members of A, then B and C are complements with respect to A. (Interpretation) if two extents are tangential to each other and coextensive with a third, they are complements with respect to the third. It follows that the intervals corresponding to the extremes of the extents are complements.

connected graph (Interpretation) set of entities, A, B, C, etc., such that A shares features with B, B with C, but A does not necessarily have anything in common with C. Such a group of entities constitutes a connected graph based on the relationship of resemblance. By analogy an extent can be considered a connected graph of points since adjacency and resemblance are isomorphic types relationships, being symmetric and non-transitive. Non-transitivity is the key feature of relationships which give rise to connected graphs.

construct (Metatheory) structure based on, or inferred from, presented data. Generally such constructs have special properties, such as symmetry, so that they form a primary source of elegance in an interpretation.

construction (Metatheory) synonym for **construct** (q.v.).

contiguous (Interpretation) if two extents are contiguous, they share no points and an extreme of one is adjacent to an extreme of the other.

contrametric (Interpretation) not **commetric** (q.v.); syncopated; noun form is contrametricity.

controlled extension (Interpretation) if two adjacent spans, A and B, are such that A bisects A + B and A is shorter than B, and if B consists of values in its first half that are repeated in its second half, B is an instance of controlled extension.

critical band (Traditional) series of frequencies within which two acoustically different frequencies are heard as one pitch.

cross rhythm (Interpretation) simultaneous presentation of different bisectors of a given modular time-interval, as in the following:

Cross rhythm depends on the non-coincidence of 1's (i.e., upbeats at a given level). Note that the following is not an instance of cross rythm because the resultants of both patterns, namely, a quarter-note pulsation, are identical:

cycle (Interpretation) set of point classes separated by the same size of interval, whether this is calculated strictly according to identity or more loosely according to approximate bisection; the notion is applicable to pitch and time values.

cyclic (Interpretation) type of structure in which all members of a set are adjacent to two others, i.e., there are no extremes, as would be the case in a linear structure.

deep (Interpretation) structures corresponding to lower levels of hierarchy or longer spans of piece. Synonyms are *background, global*; opposites are *surface, superficial, foreground, local*.

degree (Interpretation) member of a scale.

derived (Interpretation) selected from or transformed. A derived construct constitutes a subset of another construct which is considered the original, or it forms a transformation of the original.

diatonic (Interpretation) referring to a scale or belonging to a scale. (Traditional) white-note collection (*c, d, e, f, g, a, b*) or a transposition thereof.

different (Theory) principal relationship of diversity symbolized by the sign ≠. The relationship is irreflexive, symmetric, and non-transitive.

direction (Interpretation) if *A, B, C, D, E*, ... form a connected graph, *A* and *B* are in a different direction from *C* than *D* and *E* (i.e., *A* and *B*, and *D* and *E* are on opposite sides of *C*).

discrete (Interpretation) if two extents are discrete, none of the points of one coincides with any of the other.

dissonance (Interpretation) value in an interpretation that is unresolved at some level. (Traditional) interval that is not consonant (e.g., second, seventh, tritone in Common Practice theory). Lack of consonance can be equated with lack of correspondence to a referential construct.

diverse (Interpretation) same as **different** (q.v.).

dominant (Traditional) fifth degree above the tonic in a heptatonic scale. (Interpretation) pitch with the value I that bisects the interval between adjacent versions of the tonic.

dominant alternate (Interpretation) chromatic tone in pentatonic which belongs to one of the heptatonic scales of which the pentatonic is a subset and which lies beyond the pentatonic on the dominant side of the cycle of 7/12 and 8/12 intervals which is defined on the twelve-semitone gamut.

dotted (rhythm) (Traditional) rhythmic figure involving a dotted note (e.g., 𝅘𝅥𝅭. 𝅘𝅥𝅮). (Interpretation) set of presented moments such that one is resolved by its immediate successor but not by its immediate predecessor.

downbeat (Traditional) first beat of a measure. (Interpretation) oriental moment at a given level of a metrical hierarchy.

duration (Theory) time interval; pair of moments; span with extremes corresponding to a given time interval. Generally, presented time intervals are more important syntactically than their corresponding spans.

duration span (Interpretation) set or range of durations defined by a pair of spans, i.e., two clusters of moments. Cf. **interval band**

dyad (Interpretation) pair of pitches or pitch classes; term is usually used in reference to scales and modes.

equal temperament (Traditional) acoustical construct in which pitches are separated by 100 cents so that frequencies correspond to the geometric progression, a, $2^{1/12}a$, $2^{1/6}a$, $2^{1/4}a$, $2^{1/3}a$, $2^{5/12}a$, ...

equivalence (Theory) type of relationship between two entities that are the same, identical, etc. in some respect; typically applied to pitches or moments, and symbolized by ' = .' The relationship is primitive, or undefined, and reflexive, symmetric, and transitive.

extension (Traditional) process by which the length of a section is increased. Cf. **controlled extension**.

extent (Interpretation) span or band, or its point correlate, an interval of time or pitch, respectively.

extremes (Interpretation) members of a span or band that are adjacent only to one other member; term can only be applied to linear-connected graphs.

feminine cadence (Traditional) type of phrase ending in which the penultimate tone is accented and the final tone is unaccented. (Interpretation) presented moment at the end of a section that is resolved by the preceding presented moment but not by the immediately following moment.

finalis (Traditional) last tone of a melody in Gregorian-chant theory.

first (Interpretation) member of a span which is before all others; depends for meaning on notion of sequence.

five-cycle (Interpretation) cycle consisting of five members (e.g., pentatonic scale).

flat hierarchy (Interpretation) hierarchy in which there is only one level. Such a hierarchy can be referential but the notion of orientation is inapplicable to it. Examples include gamuts and pulsations.

fling, highland (Traditional) popular dance (and its accompanying music) current in eighteenth and nineteenth centuries.

foreground (Interpretation) local structures in a piece. Synonyms include surface, superficial levels; opposites include background, deep structures.

formant (Traditional) part of a tone's spectrum which is highly resonant.

frequency (Traditional) primary acoustical correlate of pitch, dependent on the rate of vibration of energy source.

frequency resolution (Traditional) selection by an auditor of fundamental frequency from a complex wave.

function (Interpretation) value which makes a difference at a given level of an interpretation; for example, two versions of what is functionally the same pitch (e.g., 254 and 257 cps as *c*) might not make a difference at the level of the gamut but at the level of nuance, as in the leading-tone effect.

functional (Interpretation) structural, expressible in terms of relationships.

functionalized (Interpretation) described in terms of a positive relationship.

fundamental frequency (Traditional) in a complex wave consisting of several harmonically related waves, the frequency of the lowest.

gamut (Interpretation) pitch correlate of pulsation; set of pitches separated by the same interval (e.g., *c*, *c♯*, *d*, *d♯*, *e*, *f*, *f♯*, *g*, *g♯*, *a*, *a♯*, *b*).

geometric progression (Metatheory) series of numbers in which the quotient of nth and $(n - 1)$th is the same as that of $(n + 1)$th and nth = (e.g., *a*, *ab*, *ab²*, *ab³*; 1, 2, 4, 8; 1, 3, 9, 27; 2, 6, 18, 54; 1, $2^{1/12}$, $2^{1/6}$, $2^{1/4}$).

genre repertoire corresponding to a cultural unit.

glissando (Traditional) quick and smooth change of pitch.

global (Interpretation) as opposed to local values, global values apply to relatively longer spans or ultimately to the piece as a whole.

grid (Interpretation) general term for pulsation or gamut.

half (intervallic) (Interpretation) quantity that is between two thirds and one third.

harmonics (Traditional) components of complex waves that vibrate faster than the fundamental frequency.

heptatonic (Interpretation; Traditional) scale or collection of pitches consisting of seven members.

hierarchy (Metatheory) construct consisting of values at various levels such that values at one level are related to values at another level according to a relationship which is antisymmetric and transitive and usually (though not always) irreflexive.

higher (level) (Interpretation) unless otherwise stated, more foreground (q.v.). Confusion arises because in Schenker diagrams background levels appear at the top and in transformational grammar diagrams deep functions (e.g., V and NP) appear at the top. Similarly, in other hierarchical diagrams (e.g., taxonomies) the more inclusive levels appear at the top. But the terms *superficial* and *surface* encourage one to turn these schemes upside down so that deep structures would appear appropriately at the bottom. Generally, the context should dispel any confusion that might arise in individual cases.

higher than (Theory) primitive, or undefined, relationship between pitches depending on the notion of sequence or absolute direction; opposite is *lower than*; both relationships are irreflexive, antisymmetric, and transitive; primary acoustical correlate is faster rate of vibration.

highest (Interpretation) higher than all others; see **higher than**.

homophonic (Traditional) texture in which melody is accompanied chordally.

hornpipe (Traditional) popular solo dance (and its accompanying music) current in eighteenth and nineteenth centuries.

imbricative (Interpretation) relationship between two extents such that one extreme of one is between the extremes of the other, and the other extreme is beyond them.

inclusive (Interpretation) relationship between extents such that both extremes of one span are between the extremes of the other.

integer (Metatheory) type of number that can be added or multiplied by itself or another of its type to yield yet another of its type. E.g., the numbers $-3, -2, -1, 0, +1, +2, +3$.

intensity (Theory) primitive, or undefined, sequential relationship between loudnesses. The two types of intensity relationship are *louder than* and *softer than*. Since these relationships depend on the notion of sequence, they are irreflexive, antisymmetric, and transitive; primary acoustical correlate is the amount of energy in a wave as reflected by the wave's amplitude.

interval (Traditional) pair of pitches; (Theory) pair of points (i.e., pitches or moments) that can be compared with another pair in terms of identity not of the pitches but of their intervallic qualities that constitute primitive, or undefined, values.

interval band (Interpretation) set of intervals defined by a pair of pitch bands (i.e., two clusters of pitches).

intervallic (scale of measurement) (Metatheory) pertaining to a scale of measurement according to which quantities are compared in terms of a unit. E.g., temperature readings are intervallic. The numbers used in an intervallic scale are always natural or whole numbers (e.g., $0, +1, +2, +3$) or integers (e.g., $-3, -2, -1, 0, +1, +2, +3$).

intonation (Traditional) if different pitches constituting a band function as the same pitch (e.g., 438, 440, and 442 cps functioning as *a*), the differences between them can be considered to be ones of intonation or nuance.

intransitive (Metatheory) pertaining to a type of relationship such that if A and B, and B and C, are so related, it follows that A and C are not so related; opposite relationship is transitive.

irreflexive (Metatheory) pertaining to a type of relationship that cannot obtain between a thing and itself; opposite is *reflexive*; e.g., different from, adjacent to, before.

just above (Interpretation) above, or higher than, and adjacent to.

just before (Interpretation) before, or preceding, and adjacent to.

larger than (Interpretation) relationship between extents that are coterminous or inclusively related. The extent having at least one extreme that is between the extremes of the other is smaller than the others, i.e., the other is larger than it.

last (Interpretation) sequential value that is ascribed to the member of a span which is after all other members.

leading tone (Traditional) seventh degree of the heptatonic scale, one degree below the tonic; often sharpened somewhat in performance, producing a nuance or intonation effect in accordance with its proximity to the tonic.

level (Metatheory) set of values in a hierarchy that bear a given relationship to immediately higher and lower sets.

linear (Interpretation) type of set in which all members are adjacent to two others except for two, the extremes, which are each adjacent to only one other member; opposite is **cyclic** (q.v.).

local (Interpretation) pertaining to relatively short spans; opposite is **global** (q.v.).

logarithmic progression (Metatheory) same as **geometric progression** (q.v.).

longer than (Interpretation) larger-than relationship between two spans (or corresponding durations or time intervals).

loudness (Theory) primitive, or undefined, value corresponding primarily to the acoustical correlate of amplitude.

lower than (Theory) opposite of **higher than** (q.v.).

lower auxiliary (Traditional) auxiliary tone that is lower than its resolutions.

maqam (Traditional) Arab tonal system based on a scale and forming the basis for a piece.

measure (Interpretation) unit of a metrical hierarchy based on the coincidence of pulsations and including at least one oriental moment. (Traditional) portion of score enclosed within bars.

melodic progression (Traditional) pair of pitches that are temporally adjacent.

member (Metatheory) entity belonging to a set; a primitive, or undefined, concept notated by the sign ϵ (e.g., $a_N \epsilon A$, read a_N is a member of the set A).

metric (Interpretation) pertaining to a hierarchy of pulsations. (Metatheory) pertaining to measurement or mensuration in general.

midway between (Interpretation) if B is midway between A and C, B bisects AC. Note that in Boretz's formulation B must bisect AC precisely (i.e., rationally, exactly, etc.) rather than approximately. However, at one point he does allow the pitch class e to be considered midway between pitch classes c and g, suggesting approximate bisection.

mode (Traditional) one of the ecclesiastical tonal systems of the Middle Ages and Renaissance (e.g., Dorian, Phrygian, Lydian). (Interpretation) scale with an oriental pitch or sonority.

modular interval (Interpretation) interval larger than a unit interval of a grid that forms a set of supergrids each of which forms a subset of the original grid: for pitch intervals a typical modulus is the octave. (Metatheory) a counting system (e.g., binary or decimal) is based on a modular interval (e.g., 2 or 10, respectively.)

modular pulsation (Interpretation) pulsation that forms a proper subset of unit pulsation.

modulation (Interpretation) change of oriental construct for pitches. (Traditional) change of key in the major-minor system.

modulus (Interpretation) interval or extent consisting of more than one unit intervals or extents.

moment (Theory) irreducible portion of time; a primitive, or undefined, notion.

monophonic (Traditional) pertaining to texture in which one tone is presented at a time (i.e., with no accompaniment, harmony, or counterpoint).

more accented (Interpretation) moment that is oriental for a lower (i.e., more background or deeper) level of a metrical hierarchy is considered more accented.

musical bow (Traditional) musical instrument consisting of a bow that is plucked or beaten with a stick and resonated orally or by means of an attached device (e.g., a gourd). Fundamental frequencies can be varied by stopping the bow string manually. By means of a resonator harmonics can be made audible.

neighbour tone (Traditional) non-harmonic tone that is adjacent in terms of scale degrees to its resolutions.

neighbour triad (Interpretation) see **neighbour tone**; triad consisting of neighbour tones (e.g., f–a–c vis-à-vis e–g–b).

nominal scale of measurement (Metatheory) qualitative basis of comparison; e.g., the difference between red and yellow is normally considered to be nominal since it is not established quantitatively.

non-harmonic tone (Traditional) tone that does not belong to sonority which is considered referential at the time; e.g., passing note, suspension, appoggiatura, échappé.

non-transitive (Metatheory) pertaining to a type of relationship such that if A and B, and B and C, are so related, it does not necessarily follow that A and C are so related; e.g., adjacent to, resembles.

normal distribution (Metatheory) distribution of frequencies of occurrence of a given variable quantified according to a rational (or often, an intervallic) scale of measurement. In a normal distribution, the mode (the most frequent value of the variable) is the same as the mean (the average value) and the median (the middlemost value). Other frequencies are distributed symmetrically about these.

octave (Traditional) interval corresponding to pitches having frequencies in the ratio of 2 : 1 (approximately).

opposite (Interpretation) if A, B, C, D, E, etc., form a linear connected graph, one can say that A and E are on opposite sides of B, C, and D (i.e., in different directions from B, C, and D).

ordinal scale of measurement (Metatheory) metric scheme according to which quantities are compared in terms of more and less without recourse to a unit.

oriental (Interpretation) pertaining to a construct that forms a proper subset of a referential construct. Generally, oriental constructs feature special properties; for example, the tonic can be the centre of a symmetrical voice-leading arrangement; typically, oriental values are co-ordinated with oriental values in other dimensions as in the case where the o's and 1's of pitch and time constructs are co-ordinated.

orientation (Interpretation) see **oriental**. Sometimes orientation arises from a basic asymmetry, as in the case where values are compared not in terms of being in a different direction from a given value but in terms of an absolute direction (e.g., higher than, lower than, before, or after).

original (Interpretation) set from which others are derived; there is no temporal (or historical) connotation to the term as applied here; the derived set is typically a subset or mapping (transformation) of the original.

oscillation (Interpretation) another term for a pendular process in which oriental and non-oriental values alternate.

ostinato pattern (Traditional) succession of tones that is repeated without interruption throughout a piece or part of a piece.

outside (Interpretation) another term for **beyond**. If A, B, C, D, E, etc. form a linear connected graph, A and B are outside the extents defined by C–D, C–E, or D–E.

parallelism (Traditional) relationship of identity between temporally analogous portions of complex spans, e.g., a passage with the form ABAC features parallelism in that the As appear at the beginnings of the two parts: AB/AC.

partial (Traditional) components of a complex wave including the fundamental frequency and harmonics.

partitioning (Metatheory) operation by which a set is divided into two or more subsets that have no members in common and that together include all the members of the original set. E.g., 1, 2, 3, 4, 5, 6, 7, 8 can be partitioned as follows, where parentheses surround subsets: (1, 2) (3) (4, 5, 6) (7, 8); (1, 3) (2, 4) (5, 7) (6, 8); (1, 2, 5) (3, 4, 6) (7, 8); etc.; but not (1, 2) (3, 4) (5, 6, 7) since 8 is missing, and not (1, 2) (2, 3, 4) (5, 6) (7, 8), since 2 appears in two of the subsets.

passing tone (Traditional) non-harmonic tone that is between, and adjacent to, its resolutions both temporally and in terms of scale degrees.

pendular process (Interpretation) succession of oriental and non-oriental values in alternation.

pentatonic (Traditional) scale of the following type: $c, d, e, g, a, c^1, d^1, e^1$, etc.

perfect fourth (Traditional) interval of three heptatonic scale degrees and five semitones.

periodic succession (Interpretation) **pulsation** (q.v.).

piece (Interpretation) set of observables among which relationships are posited.

pitch (Theory) irreducible, unanalysable value, of which the primary acoustical correlate is frequency; undefined concept. (Interpretation) frequently used as a synonym for **pitch band** or **pitch class** (q.v.).

pitch band (Interpretation) linear connected graph of adjacent pitches.

pitch class (Interpretation) set of pitches separated by a given interval (e.g., all the c's). The given interval is the modulus; the octave is a typical modulus.

pitch content (of a span) (Interpretation) set of all pitches within a given passage.

pitch space (Interpretation) set of all pitches. Each pitch can be considered to occupy a position in pitch space. The primary feature of pitch space is that all the pitches form a linear connected graph based on adjacency.

plain rhythms (Interpretation) rhythms that are four-square, completely commetric, i.e., resolved before and after.

point (Theory) general term for a pitch or moment. The validity of this category rests on the isomorphism of pitch and time relationships.

Poisson distribution (Metatheory) asymmetrical distribution of frequencies that approaches normal or binomial distribution when the probability of a given value is relatively small and the mean is equal to the product of the probability and the number of cases.

polyrhythm (Interpretation) simultaneous presentation of differently oriented metrical hierarchies [including such flat hierarchies as pulsations where each moment is considered oriental (o)]. As opposed to cross rhythms, polyrhythms are based on the non-coincidence of o's, not 1's.

position (Theory) irreducible, unanalysable value in time or pitch space, i.e., a point.

precedence (Theory) relationship of the before/after type. Precedence relationships are irreflexive, antisymmetric, and transitive, and are thus isomorphic with intensity and altitude relationships.

presented (Metatheory) actually observable in the data as opposed to constructed or inferred.

prime to (Metatheory) two integers are prime to one another if they do not share common factors (other than 1). E.g., 12 and 7 are prime to one another, but 12 and 8 are not since they share the common factors 2 and 4.

primitive (Metatheory) undefined. The meaning of primitive terms is taken to be self-evident, though in an interpretation they can be defined operationally.

process (Interpretation) construct in which the same content relationships hold between A and B, as between B and C, C and D, etc., where A, B, C, D, etc. form a linear connected graph of spans based on adjacency.

proper (Metatheory) pertaining to a subset that does not include all members of the set. Sets that are plural (e.g., $A = a, b, c$) have proper subsets (e.g., $a, b; a, c; b, c; a; b; c$).

proximity (Interpretation) nearness, two values are equally proximate to a third if they are adjacent to it and a given interval away from it.

pulsation (Interpretation) class of moments spaced equidistantly in time; by extension, the set of identically long spans defined by such a class.

pure tone (Traditional) sound produced by a sine wave.

rational scale of measurement (Metatheory) pertaining to a scale of measurement based on rational numbers; i.e., ratios. The set of rational numbers is defined by the operation of division that, if applied to two numbers, yields a third value which also belongs to the set (e.g., $3/2 \div 4/3 = 9/8$).

rational bisection (Interpretation) type of bisection in which halves are equal;

simple, precise, or pure bisection. Such an operation is only possible with integers that are even. E.g., 4 can be simply bisected into 2 + 2; 2 into 1 + 1, etc., but 7, 5, 3, etc., cannot be simply bisected.

referential construct (Interpretation) subset in terms of which other members of original set are described. E.g., in C-major, *c, d, e, f, g, a,* and *b* form a subset of the twelve-semitone gamut and non-members of the scale are described in terms of the referential set, as where $c\sharp$ is considered a raised version of *c*.

reflexive (Metatheory) pertaining to a relationship that holds between a thing and itself. E.g., identity is reflexive, since A = A is always true. Diversity is not because A ≠ A is not true.

register (Interpretation) two pitches belonging to the same pitch class but otherwise differing (e.g., *c* and *c¹*) are said to belong to different registers. In the example, the *c*'s can be considered registral variants of each other.

regular (Interpretation) pertaining to a rhythm that is completely commetric or four-square; a regular repertoire is a group of pieces in which quantitative values assigned to individual pieces are distributed in a way that approximates a normal or Poisson distribution.

release (Traditional) end or decay of a tone almost invariably marked by a decrease in loudness at the very end.

repertoire (Interpretation) musically unified set of pieces.

resonance region (Traditional) set of adjacent hairs on the basilar membrane corresponding to adjacent frequencies.

resultant (Interpretation) pulsation implied by two pulsations that are not completely coincident; the intervals of a resultant pulsation are always shorter than those of the presented pulsation. A resultant is a derived construct.

rondo (Traditional) in the most general sense, a form in which a given content (e.g., A) alternates with others (e.g., B and C) as in ABACA.

scale (Interpretation) referential construct for pitches; subset of a gamut having the following properties: (a) alternate members of the cycle of bisection are adjacent; (b) there is a determinate correlation between interval sizes expressed in terms of degrees and the gamut's unit interval; (c) bisectors of intervals between scale degrees are also bisectors in terms of the gamut.

scale of measurement (Metatheory) system for comparing quantities. Three such systems are ordinal, interval, and rational.

Scotch snap (Traditional) rhythmic figure of the following type: ♪♩. The second attacks of such figures are resolved before but not after:

second-order beating (Traditional) psychological effect similar to that produced by beating and consisting of a perception of fluctuations of loudness due to a perceived interference among the partials of simultaneous tones.

section (Interpretation) set of adjacent members of a cycle of bisection.

segment (Interpretation) part or passage of a piece.

sequence (Theory) type of relationship that is irreflexive, antisymmetric, and transitive, e.g., altitude, precedence, intensity.

set (Metatheory) group of entities, undefined concept represented by sign ϵ ('is a member of ').

same side of (Interpretation) in a linear connected graph such as A, B, C, D, E, etc., A, B, C, are on the same side of, or in the same direction from, D.

simple bisection (Interpretation) see **rational bisection**.

simultaneous (Interpretation) generally two spans are considered to be simultaneous if they are coextensive; they might also be considered simultaneous if they are coterminous, inclusive, imbricative, or tangential.

span (Interpretation) linear-connected graph of moments.

spectrum (Traditional) acoustical term designating the loudness pattern of a set of harmonics.

stress (Traditional) loudness accent.

strophe (Traditional) passage of music that is repeated to different words.

structure (Metatheory) set of relationships.

sub-scale (Interpretation) section of a **scale** (q.v.) which has all the properties of a scale except cyclic bisection.

superficial (Interpretation) pertaining to the surface, foreground, or local structures.

symmetric (Metatheory) type of relationship between two entities, such as A and B, that is valid not only between the first and second but vice versa as well. E.g., if A is adjacent to B, B is adjacent to A. Opposite type of relationship is antisymmetric.

syncopated (Interpretation) contrametric, not commetric; deviating from an oriental metrical organization in that one or both of the immediately adjacent presented moments to a given moment is not resolved.

syntactical (Interpretation) pertaining to the co-ordination of relationships in two domains, e.g., pitch and time.

systemic unit (Interpretation) set of pieces for which a single system provides the best interpretations. In the extreme situation, an individual piece in all its uniqueness defines a systemic unit; all-music forms a systemic unit in terms of the system of the theory presented here.

tangential (Interpretation) pertaining to two extents that share only one point.

taqsim (Traditional) improvisatory Arab work frequently forming a prelude to a set piece.

timbre (Traditional) quality or 'colour' of a tone as opposed to its pitch and loudness; acoustical correlates include frequency and amplitude of component waves as these vary in time.

time (Theory) moment; e.g., the time of a pitch is usually identified with the moment of its attack.

time-interval (Theory) duration, pair of moments.

tonal (Traditional) pertaining to pitch relationships; pertaining to major-minor system; derived notions include tonal organization, tonal system, tonality.

tone (Traditional) sound corresponding to a note in a score; every tone has an attack, spectrum, and decay.

tonic (Interpretation) orienting pitch of a **mode** (q.v.).

tonic sonority (Interpretation) orienting set of intervals; e.g., in modal seven-tone music, a dyad such as *d–a*; in major-minor music, a triad such as *c–e–g*.

transitive (Metatheory) pertaining to a relationship, which, if it holds between A and B, and B and C, necessarily holds between A and C. The relationship 'before' is transitive, for if A is before B, and B is before C, it follows that A is before C.

tremolo (Traditional) type of performance practice in which loudness fluctuates within a tone.

triad (Interpretation) set of three pitch classes or pitches; term is used particularly with reference to scales; generally the middle member bisects the others (as in *c–e–g*).

trill (Traditional) ornament consisting of rapid alternation between two adjacent pitches or scale degrees.

undefined (Metatheory) see **primitive**.

unit span (Interpretation) shortest span in a pulsation.

upper neighbour (Interpretation) neighbour-tone that is higher than its resolutions.

vibrato (Traditional) type of performance practice in which the pitch of a tone fluctuates.

voice (Interpretation) set of pitch classes that form a subset of a scale and consist of adjacent degrees; membership is determined by a symmetrical construct.

within (Interpretation) between, as between two points that define a linear extent.

References

Adriaansz, Willem. 1973. *The Kumiuta and Danmono Traditions of Japanese Koto Music*. Berkeley and Los Angeles: University of California Press

Armstrong, Robert P. 1963. 'Notes on a Java Year,' *Tri-Quarterly* (Northwestern University), 5, 3–11

Asch, Michael I. 1975. 'Social Context and the Musical Analysis of Slavey Drum Dance Songs,' *Ethnomusicology*, 19 (2), 245–57

Becker, Judith 1969. 'The Anatomy of a Mode,' *Ethnomusicology*, 13 (2), 267–79

Besmer, Fremont E. 1970. 'An Hausa Song from Katsina,' *Ethnomusicology*, 14 (3), 418–38

Blacking, John. 1959. 'Problems of Pitch, Pattern and Harmony in the Ocarina Music of the Venda,' *African Music*, 2 (2), 15–23

– 1965. 'The Role of Music in the Culture of the Venda of the Northern Transvaal,' in Mieczyslaw Kolinski (ed.), *Studies in Ethnomusicology*, New York: Oak Publications 2, 20–53

– 1969a. 'Songs, Dances, Mimes and Symbolism of Venda, Girls' Initiation Schools, Part I: *Vhusha,' African Studies*, 28 (1), 3–35

– 1969b. 'Songs, Dances, Mimes and Symbolism of Venda, Girls' Initiation Schools, Part III: *Domba,' African Studies*, 28 (3), 149–99

– 1969c. 'Songs, Dances, Mimes and Symbolism of Venda Girls' Initiation Schools, Part IV: The Great *Domba* Song,' *African Studies*, 28 (4), 215–66

– 1970. 'Tonal Organization in the Music of Two Venda Initiation Schools,' *Ethnomusicology*, 14 (1), 1–56

– 1971. 'Deep and Surface Structures in Venda Music,' *Yearbook of the International Folk Music Council*, 3, 91–108

Boilès, Charles L. 1967. 'Tepehua Thought-Song: A Case of Semantic Signalling,' *Ethnomusicology*, 11 (3), 267–92

– 1973. 'Les Chants Instrumentaux des Tepehuas,' *Musique en jeu*, 12, 81–99

Bonny, Helen L. and Savary, Louis M. 1973. *Music and Your Mind: Listening with a New Consciousness*. New York: Harper and Row

Boretz, Benjamin. 1969. 'Meta-Variations: Studies in the Foundations of Musical Thought' (I), *Perspectives of New Music* 8 (1), Fall-Winter, 1–74

– 1970a. 'Sketch of a Musical System (Meta-Variations, Part II),' *Perspectives of New Music,* 8 (2), Spring-Summer, 49–111

– 1970b. 'The Construction of Musical Syntax (I),' [Meta-Variations, Part IIIa] *Perspectives of New Music,* 9 (1), Fall-Winter, 23–42

– 1970c. 'Meta-Variations: Studies in the Foundations of Musical Thought: Group Variations I,' PH D Dissertation, Princeton University

– 1971. 'Musical Syntax (II),' [Meta-Variations, Part IIIb] *Perspectives of New Music* 10 (1), Fall-Winter, 232–70

– 1972. 'Meta-Variations, Part IV: Analytic Fallout (I),' *Perspectives of New Music,* 11 (1), Fall-Winter, 146–223

Bronowski, Jacob. 1962. *Science and Human Values*. New York: Harper and Row

Cassidy, Harold Gomes. 1962. *The Sciences and the Arts: A New Alliance*. New York: Harper and Row

Cazden, Norman. 1971a. 'A Simplified Mode Classification for Traditional Anglo-American Song Tunes,' in *Yearbook of the International Folk Music Council,* 3, 45–78

– 1971b. Review of *Folk Songs from Newfoundland* by Maud Karpeles, in *Yearbook of the International Folk Music Council,* 3, 165–67

Chenoweth, Vida. 1974. *Melodic Perception and Analysis: A Manual on Ethnic Melody,* 2d. ed. Papua New Guinea: Summer Institute of Linguistics

Cooke, Peter R. 1971. 'Ludaya – A Transverse Flute from Eastern Uganda,' in *Yearbook of the International Folk Music Council,* 3, 79–90

Crossley-Holland, Peter. 1971. 'A Cante-Fable from Sillé-le-Guillaume (France),' *Ethnomusicology,* 15 (1), 1–37

Densmore, Frances. 1918. *Teton Sioux Music*. Washington: Bureau of American Ethnology, Bulletin 61

Dirac, Paul A.M. 1963. 'The Evolution of the Physicist's Picture of Nature,' *Scientific American,* 208 (5, May), 45–53

Divenyi, Pierre L. 1971. 'The Rhythmic Perception of Micro-Melodies: Detectability by Human Observers of a Time Increment between Sinusoidal Pulses of Two Different Successive Frequencies,' *Experimental Research in the Psychology of Music,* 7, 41–130

England, Nicholas M. 1965. 'The Text of *Du*: A Postscript to the Symposium,' *Ethnomusicology,* 9 (2), 149–52

Erdeley, Stephen and Chipman, Robert A. 1972. 'Strip-Chart Recording of Narrow

Band Frequency Analysis in Aid of Ethnomusicological Data,' in *Yearbook of the International Folk Music Council*, 4, 119–36

Erickson, Robert. 1975. *Sound Structure in Music*. Berkeley: University of California Press

Farnsworth, Paul R. 1969. *The Social Psychology of Music*, 2d. ed. Ames, Iowa: Iowa State University Press

Feld, Steven. 1974. 'Linguistics and Ethnomusicology,' *Ethnomusicology*, 18 (2), 197–217

Forte, Allen. 1973. *The Structure of Atonal Music*. New Haven: Yale University Press

Garfias, Robert. 1964. 'Symposium on Transcription and Analysis: Transcription I,' *Ethnomusicology*, 8 (3), 233–40

Goodman, Nelson. 1966. *The Structure of Appearance*, 2d ed. New York: Bobbs-Merrill, 1966

Harding, Frank (comp. and arr.). 1891/1932. *Harding's Original Collection of Jigs and Reels: 200 Jigs, Reels and Country Dances for Piano, Violin, Flute or Mandolin*. New York: Paull-Pioneer Music Corp.,© 1891, transferred to Paull-Pioneer, 1932

Hardy, Godfrey Harold. 1940. *A Mathematician's Apology*. Cambridge: Cambridge University Press

Herndon, Marcia. 1971. 'The Cherokee Ballgame Cycle: An Ethnomusicologist's View,' *Ethnomusicology*, 15 (3), 339–52

– 1974a. 'Analysis: The Herding of Sacred Cows?' *Ethnomusicology*, 18 (2), 219–62

– 1974b. Review of *Melodic Perception and Analysis*, by Vida Chenoweth, *Ethnomusicology*, 18 (2), 303–4

Herzog, George. 1946. 'Comparative Musicology,' *The Music Journal*, 4 (6, Nov.–Dec.), 11 and 42–4

Hood, Mantle. 1966. 'Sléndro and Pélog Redefined,' *Selected Reports*, 1 (1), 28–48

Jairazbhoy, Nazir A. 1972. 'Factors Underlying Important Notes in North Indian Music,' *Ethnomusicology*, 16 (1), 63–81

Jeffrey, Charles. 1973. *Biological Nomenclature*. London: E. Arnold

Kaeppler, Adrienne L. 1971. 'Aesthetics of Tongan Dance,' *Ethnomusicology*, 15 (2), 175–85

Kauffman, Robert. 1972. 'Shona Urban Music and the Problem of Acculturation,' in *Yearbook of the International Folk Music Council*, 4, 47–56

Kaufmann, Walter. 1968. *The Ragas of North India* (Asian Studies Research Institute, Oriental Series, 1). Bloomington: Indiana University Press

Kebede, Ashenafi. 1970. Review of *Ethiopian Music*, by Powne, *Ethnomusicology*, 14 (3), 501–4

Koestler, Arthur. 1964. *The Act of Creation*. London: Hutchinson

Köhler, Wolfgang. 1947. *Gestalt Psychology with an Introduction to New Concepts in Modern Psychology*. New York: Liveright

Koffka, Kurt. 1935. *Principles of Gestalt Psychology*. New York: Harcourt, Brace & Co.

Kolinski, Mieczyslaw. 1959. 'The Evaluation of Tempo,' *Ethnomusicology* 3 (1), 45–57

– 1964. 'Symposium on Transcription and Analysis: Transcription II,' *Ethnomusicology* 8 (3), 241–51

– 1967. 'Recent Trends in Ethnomusicology,' *Ethnomusicology*, 11 (1), 1–24

– 1970. Review of *Ethnomusicology of the Flathead Indians*, by Merriam, *Ethnomusicology* 14 (1), 77–99

– 1972. 'An Apache Rabbit Dance Song Cycle as Sung by the Iroquois,' *Ethnomusicology*, 16 (3), 415–64

– 1973. 'A Cross-Cultural Approach to Metro-Rhythmic Patterns,' *Ethnomusicology*, 17 (3), 494–506

Komar, Arthur, J. 1971. *Theory of Suspensions: A Study of Metrical and Pitch Relations in Tonal Music*. Princeton: Princeton University Press

List, George. 1964. 'Symposium on Transcription and Analysis: Transcription III,' *Ethnomusicology*, 8(3), 252–65

– 1971. 'On the Non-universality of Musical Perspectives,' *Ethnomusicology*, 15 (3), 399–402

– 1974. 'The Reliability of Transcription,' *Ethnomusicology*, 18 (3), 353–77

Lundin, Robert William. 1953. *An Objective Psychology of Music*. New York: Ronald Press

McDermott, Vincent and Sumarsam. 1975. 'Central Javanese Music: The Patet of *Laras Sléndro* and the *Gendèr Barung*,' *Ethnomusicology*, 19 (2), 233–44

Merriam, Alan P. 1964. *The Anthropology of Music*. Evanston: Northwestern University Press

– 1967. *Ethnomusicology of the Flathead Indians* (Viking Fund Publications in Anthropology, 44). Chicago: Aldine

– 1969. 'Ethnomusicology Revisited,' *Ethnomusicology*, 13 (2), 213–29

Meyer, Leonard B. 1956. *Emotion and Meaning in Music*. Chicago: University of Chicago Press

– 1973. *Explaining Music: Essays and Explorations*. Berkeley, Los Angeles, London: University of California Press

Meyer, Max F. 1962. 'New Illusions of Pitch,' *American Journal of Psychology*, 75, 323–4

Moran, Helen and Pratt, Carrol C. 1926. 'Variability of Judgement on Musical Intervals,' *Journal of Experimental Psychology*, 9, 492–500

Mursell, James Lockhart. 1937. *The Psychology of Music*. New York: W.W. Norton & Co.

Nattiez, Jean-Jacques. 1973. 'Analyse musicale et sémiologie: Le Structuralisme de
Lévi-Strauss,' *Musique en jeu*, 12, 59–79
Nattiez, Jean-Jacques and Hirbour-Paquette, Louise. 1973. 'Analyse musicale et
sémiologie: À propos du Prélude de Pelléas,' *Musique en jeu*, 10, 42–69
Naud, Gilles. 1975. 'Aperçus d'une analyse sémiologique de *Nomos Alpha*,' *Musique
en jeu*, 17, 63–72
Nettl, Bruno. 1964. *Theory and Method in Ethnomusicology*. London: Free Press of
Glencoe
– 1974. 'Aspects of Form in the Instrumental Performance of the Persian Āvāz,'
Ethnomusicology, 18(3), 405–14
Nettl, Bruno and Riddle, Ronald. 1973. '*Taqsim Nahawand*: A Study of Sixteen
Performances by Jihad Racy,' in *Yearbook of the International Folk Music Council*,
5, 11–50
Nketia, J.H. Kwabena (ed.) 1963. *Folk Songs of Ghana*. Legon: University of Ghana
Olsen, Paul Rovsing. 1972. 'Acculturation in the Eskimo Songs of the Greenlanders,'
in *Yearbook of the International Folk Music Council*, 4, 32–7
Orlando, Francesco. 1975. 'Propositions pour une sémantique du Leitmotiv dans
l'Anneau Nibelungen,' *Musique en jeu*, 17, 73–86
Ornstein, Robert Evan. 1969. *On the Experience of Time* (Penguin Science of Human
Behaviour). Harmondsworth: Penguin Books
Ortmann, O. 1926. 'On the Melodic Relativity of Tones,' *Psychological Monographs*,
35, 1–47
Pantaleoni, Hewitt. 1972. Review of *Folk Song Style and Culture*, by Lomax,
Yearbook of the International Folk Music Council, 4, 158–61
Parsons, Talcott. 1951. *The Social System*. New York: The Free Press
Peek, Philip. 1970. Review of *Codification of African Music and Textbook Project*, by
Tracy, Hugh T. et al., *Ethnomusicology*, 14 (3), 504–7
Petrović, Radmila. 1970. 'Some Aspects of Formal Expression in Serbian Folk
Songs,' in *Yearbook of the International Folk Music Council*, 2, 63–76
Piaget, Jean. 1978. *Behaviour and Evolution* (translated by Donald Nicholson-Smith).
New York: Pantheon
Poincaré, Henri. 1946. *The Foundation of Science: Science and Hypothesis, The Value
of Science, Science and Method* (Science and Education, 1). Lancaster, Pa: Science
Press
Pratt, Carrol C. 1931/1968. *The Meaning of Music*. New York and London: McGraw-
Hill Book Co. (repr. New York: Johnson Reprint, 1968)
Provine, Robert C., Jr. 1974. 'The Treatise on Ceremonial Music (1430) in The
Annals of the Korean King Sejong,' *Ethnomusicology*, 18 (1), 1–29
Rahn, Jay. 1976a. 'Text Underlay in Gagnon's Collection of French Canadian Folk
Songs,' *Canadian Folk Music Journal*, 4, 3–14

- 1976b. 'Text-Tune Relationships in the *Hora Lunga* Versions collected by Bartók,' *Yearbook of the International Folk Music Council*, 8, 89–96
- 1977a. 'Some Recurrent Features of Scales,' *In Theory Only*, 2 (11–12), 43–52
- 1977b. 'Text Underlay in French Monophonic Song, ca. 1500,' *Current Musicology*, 24, 63–79
- 1978a. 'Melodic and Textual Types in French Monophonic Song, ca. 1500,' PH D Dissertation, Columbia University
- 1978b. 'Javanese Pélog Tunings Reconsidered,' paper read at annual meeting of Niagara Chapter of Society for Ethnomusicology, Kent State University, Kent, Ohio, 1978; in *Yearbook of the International Folk Music Council*, 10, 69–82
- 1978c. 'Constructs for Modality, 1300–1550,' *Canadian Association of University Schools of Music Journal*, 8 (2), 5–39
- 1978d. 'Evaluating Metrical Interpretations,' paper read at annual meeting of Society for Ethnomusicology, University of Texas, Austin, Fall 1977, in *Perspectives of New Music*, 16, 2, 35–49
- 1981a. 'Structure and Frequency in South Indian Mēlas,' in *Proceedings of the St. Thyagaraja Festival, Cleveland, 1978–81* (ed. T. Temple Tuttle), 109–28
- 1981b. 'Ockeghem's Three-Section Motet *Salve Regina*: Problems in Co-ordinating Pitch and Time Constructs,' *Music Theory Spectrum*, 3, 117–31
- 1981c. 'Stereotyped Forms in English-Canadian Children's Songs: Historical and Pedagogical Aspects,' *Canadian Folk Music Journal*, 9, 43–53
- 1982a. 'Simple Forms in Universal Perspective,' in *Cross-cultural Perspectives in Music: Essays in Honour of Mieczyslaw Kolinski*, edited by Robert Falck and Timothy Rice, 38–49. Toronto: University of Toronto Press
- 1982b. 'Where Is the Melody?' *In Theory Only*, 6 (6), 3–19

Rhodes, Willard. 1964. 'Symposium on Transcription and Analysis: Transcription IV,' *Ethnomusicology*, 8 (3), 265–72

Riker, B.L. 1946. 'The Ability to Judge Pitch,' *Journal of Experimental Psychology*, 36, 331–46

Roederer, Juan G. 1973. *Introduction to the Physics and Psychophysics of Music*. London: English Universities Press; New York: Springer-Verlag

Sanger, Penelope and Sorrell, Neil. 1975. 'Music in Umeda Village, New Guinea,' *Ethnomusicology,* 19 (1), 67–89

Schouten, J.F. 1940. 'The Residue: A New Component in Subjective Sound Analysis' in *Proceedings, Koninklijke Nederlandsche Akademie van Wetenschappen*, 43 (3), 356–65

Seeger, Charles. 1941. 'Music and Culture,' in *Proceedings of the Music Teachers' National Association for 1940*, 64, 112–22

- 1958. 'Prescriptive and Descriptive Music Writing,' *Musical Quarterly*, 44, 184–95

- 1960. 'On the Moods of a Music-Logic,' *Journal of the American Musicological Society*, 13, 224–61
- 1968. 'Factorial Analysis of the Song as an Aproach to the Formation of a Unitary Field Theory,' *Journal of the International Folk Music Council*, 20, 33–9
- 1969. 'On the Formational Apparatus of the Music Compositional Process,' *Ethnomusicology*, 13 (2), 230–47
- 1971. 'Reflections upon a Given Topic: Music in Universal Perspective,' *Ethnomusicology*, 15 (3), 385–98
Slaymaker, F.H. 1970. 'Chords from Tones Having Stretched Partials,' *Journal of the Acoustical Society of America*, 47 (6), 169–71
Snow, Sir Charles Percy. 1964. *The Two Cultures and a Second Look*, 2d. ed. Cambridge: Cambridge University Press
Spector, Johanna. 1970. 'Classical '*Ud* Music in Egypt with Special Reference to *Maqamat*.' *Ethnomusicology*, 14 (2), 243–57
Stern, Theodore and Stern, Theodore A. 1971. 'I Pluck My Harp: Musical Acculturation among the Karen of Western Thailand,' *Ethnomusicology*, 15 (2), 186–219
Stumpf, Carl. 1911. 'Konsonanz und Konkordanz,' *Zeitschrift für Psychologie*, 58, 321–55
Terhardt, E. and Fastl H. 1971. 'Zum Einfluss von Stortonen und Storgerauschen auf die Tonhöhe von Sinnstonen,' *Acustica*, 25, 53–61
Touma, Habib Hassan. 1971. 'The *Maqam* Phenomenon: An Improvisation Technique in the Music of the Middle East,' *Ethnomusicology*, 15 (1), 38–48
Vernon, P.E. 1934–5. 'Auditory Perception I: The Gestalt Approach,' *British Journal of Psychology*, General Section, 25 (2), 123–39
Wade, Bonnie. 1973. 'Chīz in Khyāl: The Traditional Composition in the Improvised Performance.' *Ethnomusicology*, 17 (3), 443–59
- 1975. Review of *The* Kumiuta *and* Danmono *Traditions of Japanese Koto Music* by Adriaansz, in *Ethnomusicology*, 19 (1), 137–40
Ward, W. Dixon. 1962. 'On the Perception of the Frequency Ratio 55:32,' *Journal of the Acoustical Society of America*, 34 (5), 679
Yeston, Maury. 1976. *The Stratification of Musical Rhythm*. New Haven: Yale University Press
Zuckerkandl, Victor. 1956. *Sound and Symbol*, translated by Willard R. Trask. New York: Pantheon Books
Zwicker, Eberhard; Flottorp, Gordon; and Stevens, S.S. 1957. 'Critical Bandwidth in Loudness Summation,' *Journal of the Acoustical Society of America*, 29 (5), 548–57

Index

This index contains page references for people, places, and things mentioned in the main body of the work. For definitions of specific terms, the reader should consult the glossary.

quarter tones 123

range of applicability, as a criterion 7
rational scale of measurement. *See* Scales of measurement
recency. *See* Primacy effects
recursion, illustrations of 120–5
reference, distinguished from orientation 77–83, 150–1
referential meaning in music. *See* Communication
register, illustrated 123
regularity, statistical: in a repertoire 129–30; in Confucian songs 163–5
relationships: richness of 37–9; distinguished from values 39; compared with values 50–1; types of 213, 214–15
repeatability, as a criterion of interpretations 45
repertoire: defined 5, 129–30; distinguished from piece 91–2; distinguished from cultural unit (genre) 129, 191; related to piece 129–30
resemblance, as a relationship between pieces 162, 191
resolution: and orientation 80–1; illustrated 119–24, 148–50, 166
resultant pulsation 64–6
Rhodes, Willard, transcription and interpretation of Hukwe bow song by 104–13
rhythmic cycles, parallel to pitch cycles 73–4
richness in an interpretation 51; and bisection 71; distinctions enhance 96; *see also* Aesthetic values, Beauty, Elegance
Riddle, Ronald 95, transcription and interpretation of *taqsim* in *maqam* Nahawand by 116, 125–6

Sanger, Penelope 8–9, 16
scale, musical 32; as subset of gamut, 71; properties of 72–4, 80, 145–6
scales of measurement: in music theory 64, 197–8, 223; in social science 197; universal significance of 225
Schenker, Heinrich 5
Schillinger, Joseph, pre-compositional theory of 232
Schoenberg, Arnold 5
sciences 3–4, 29, 37; compared with humanities 43–5, 55; aesthetic criteria in 45–9; compared with mathematics and music theory 227–8
Scotch snap, and syncopation 138
Seeger, Charles 6, 7, 10, 11, 13, 14, 21, 53
self-delectative music 12
self-sufficiency, as a criterion for interpretations 23–4
semiotics 197
sequence, as a relationship 57
serial music. *See* Twelve-tone music, Atonal music
set: as undefined concept 52–3; used to define band 57–8
set theory 52–3
sharpening. *See* Flattening and sharpening, Intonation
simplicity in an interpretation 50–1; compared with simplistic-ness 51
Snow, Sir Charles Percy 43
sociology of music 13
Sorrell, Neil 8–9, 16
span, defined 57
Spector, Johanna 9
staccato, compared with legato 60
statistics, in comparison of repertoires 186; *see also* Regularity